P9-DMJ-929

The Transition to Parenthood

The Transition to Parenthood

How a First Child Changes a Marriage

Why Some Couples Grow Closer and Others Apart

BASED ON A LANDMARK STUDY

Jay Belsky, Ph.D., and John Kelly

Published by
Delacorte Press
Bantam Doubleday Dell Publishing Group, Inc.
1540 Broadway
New York, New York 10036

Library of Congress Cataloging in Publication Data
Belsky, Jay, 1952–
The transition to parenthood : how a first child changes a marriage : why some couples grow closer and others apart : based on a landmark study / Jay Belsky, and John Kelly.
P. cm.
Includes bibliographical references.
ISBN 0-385-30616-4
1. Parenthood. 2. Marriage. 3. Interpersonal relations. I. Kelly, John, 1945– II. Title.
HQ755.8.B45 1994
306.87—dc20 93-14625 CIP

Manufactured in the United States of America
Published simultaneously in Canada

February 1994
10 9 8 7 6 5 4 3 2 1

RRH

Contents

Preface

Had someone informed me when I first enrolled in graduate school in 1974 to study human development that twenty years later I would be the author of a volume on marriage, I most certainly would not have believed it. After all, when I decided to pursue postgraduate training, my interests lay in children, especially young children, and their parents, particularly their mothers. But as I became more interested in the role of the father and the broader topic of child development in the family, there was no getting away from the fact that I could not avoid studying in some detail the marital relationship. And so began, in the early 1980s, what has become known as the Penn State Child and Family Development Project, a research effort designed to illuminate a variety of issues pertaining to marriage, parenting, and child development.

When John Kelly approached me in 1989 about doing a popular book about my research, the idea appealed to me. A book-length treatment of our research findings pertaining to the effect of the child on the marital relationship provided the opportunity to share with many families the discoveries we had made about how marriages change when the first child arrives and factors that account for why some couples cope with the transition to parenthood more successfully than do others. Moreover it provided an opportunity to move beyond the narrow confines of scientific scholarship to share in a more literary manner the conclusions I had drawn from our extensive investigation of hundreds of families bearing and rearing a first child and from my reading of the scientific literature on this topic and marital relations more generally. Not only could I disseminate scientific results, but such a book afforded the opportunity to share the ways families experienced the transition to parenthood, particularly with regard to its effect upon the marital relationship.

In order to achieve this goal, John Kelly and I decided that the best way to approach the material I had available from my research was to tell the story of three particular couples whose transition experiences exemplified those families whom they were selected to represent—couples whose marriages had declined, improved, or generally showed no change in quality from pregnancy through three years postpartum. Because it was our goal to tell the story of these three prototypical couples in a way that would highlight the factors and processes that contributed to the effect of the transition to parenthood on their marital relationships, it was necessary to exercise some literary license in the book we have produced. The fact that the work reported in this book was undertaken in a series of small, interrelated towns in central Pennsylvania where people knew each other and thus might be easily identifiable in a volume such as this required that we take numerous steps to protect the privacy and confidentiality of the three couples who are the principal focus of the book. Thus not only did we use fictitious names throughout the volume but identifying details of the lives and families discussed also had to be altered at times. Moreover, because of the structure of the book—highlighting both a factor affecting marital change across the transition to parenthood and a particular couple in chapters Three through Eight—there were times when information not immediately available to us had to be obtained via other means. Sometimes this necessitated relying not simply on information we had gathered during the course of the study proper but on follow-up interviews we carried out in the summer of 1991 with some couples seven to eight years after their first child was born. At other times it required culling from the experiences of other families we had studied and modifying them to fit our purposes for the families under consideration. In exercising such literary license, we have endeavored to preserve the character of the families described and, above all else, to portray accurately the transition-to-parenthood process.

It goes without saying that this volume could not have been produced without the help of many. First and foremost my appreciation goes to the hundreds of families who participated in our research. It is my fervent hope that the ultimate benefit of their extensive cooperation in the scientific enterprise will take the form of many other parents and parents-to-be learning from their experience. That, fundamentally, is why this book was written.

Appreciation also needs to be extended to the too-numerous-to-mention undergraduate and graduate research assistants from Penn State University who played critical roles in the research process. Without their help in recruiting families, visiting them at home and seeing them in the laboratory, and discussing with me what we were observing and learning, it would not be possible for a single scientist, working with a professional writer, to share the results of research based on hundreds of families and many times that number of home observations, interviews, and laboratory assessments. My thanks must also be extended to colleagues at Penn State and at other universities carrying out related research whose intellectual companionship over the years also contributed in innumerable ways, many of which I am sure I am not fully aware, to the ultimate success of the Penn State Child and Family Development Project. Finally, thanks need to be extended to the National Science Foundation, the March of Dimes

Foundation, the National Institute of Child Health and Human Development, and the National Institute of Mental Health, without whose grant support much of this research would not have been undertaken.

Jay Belsky
May 1993

PART ONE

THE TRANSITION TO PARENTHOOD

1

What's Happening to Us?

Almost every evening that summer before Will's birth, Carol Norris would slip out onto the patio behind the kitchen with an iced tea and curl up in one of the new green-and-white deck chairs she and Tom had bought at the Kmart over in State College. Most nights Carol would bring a magazine along, but usually she would find herself too preoccupied to read. She'd begin thumbing through its pages, then suddenly the words and images would blur and she would find herself thinking instead about the new life growing inside her.

Usually around seven Tom would join her, and the two of them would sit talking quietly in the gathering twilight. With the baby's birth only a few months away, the Norrises had a hundred practical things to decide. But after discussing which bassinet to buy, which day-care arrangements to inspect, and what colors to paint the baby's room, Tom and Carol would find themselves once again returning to their favorite topic of patio conversation—the future.

On those long-ago summer nights the future seemed to spread out before the Norrises like a magic carpet. They knew that the next few years would be filled with new worries, new work, and new financial pressures, but they were even more sure of the new joys and gratifications that lay ahead of them. There would be a new sense of closeness in their marriage. They would gain a new sense of "us," and at the heart of this new "us" would be a new child to shape and mold, to celebrate and love.

But after the birth of their baby, Will, something happened to the Norrises, something troubling and unexpected. Instead of growing closer together, Tom and Carol found themselves drifting apart. Each of them constructed a myth to explain this surprising development. Carol blamed Tom's selfishness. "Do you know how we spend our mornings now?" she said to me during our last interview. "I come into the kitchen with Will, make breakfast, and clean up. Tom gets the portable TV, goes into the bathroom, and locks the door behind him."

Tom's myth centered on Carol's sullen anger and nagging. "What does she expect of me?" he said one night while the two of us were standing in the Norrises' driveway. "I make a good living, I help out around the house, I try to be a good father. Why is Carol always at me? Doesn't she realize she's driving me away?"

Underneath the mutual finger pointing and accusations, however, both Norrises were truly confused by the changes that had occurred in their marriage. Will was everything they had hoped their new baby would be, and they still loved each other, didn't they? Yet undeniably parenthood had changed something fundamental between them. Increasingly the relationship that had once warmed and nurtured them, had shielded them from the world and all its tribulations, felt empty and lifeless. And what made this change all the more troubling was that neither Tom nor Carol understood what was behind it.

Many of the three million other couples who become new parents each year find themselves riding the same roller coaster of elation, despair, and bafflement. Like the Norrises they approach parenthood full of high hopes and soaring dreams, and like Tom and Carol, six months or a year after the child's birth they, too, find themselves wondering, "What's happening to us?"

The goal of this book is to answer that question, to put a name on the faceless something that leaves so many new parents feeling disillusioned with each other and with their marriage. Much of the material in the book, including the stories of the Norrises and the other couples you will meet later, are drawn from the files of the Penn State Child and Family Development Project, the largest and most extensive study ever conducted of the transition to parenthood, the period that runs from the third trimester of pregnancy to the child's third birthday. It is a time of profound and swift change in a marriage. It produces new worries, new challenges, new stresses and tensions, and new and often distressing feelings about one's spouse and one's marriage.

The Penn State Child and Family Development Project was designed to provide the first truly comprehensive look at this period. And its data provide a fresh and in many ways surprising answer to the question What's happening to us? If you consult the current literature on the transition, you will find it describes the new stresses the baby creates as the chief cause of marital estrangement and unhappiness among new parents. According to this view, the more stresses a child creates, the more likely his parents' marriage is to suffer; the fewer stresses he creates, the less likely the marriage is to be visited by that faceless something.

The data in the Penn State Child and Family Development Project, however, suggest that what happens to a marriage after the baby's arrival has its starting point not in stresses but in the transition's natural and normal tendency to polarize new parents. This polarization occurs in happy as well as unhappy marriages and, as we shall see later, has its roots in differences in the couple's biology, socialization, personal experiences, and family background. Whether a marriage improves or declines is largely dependent on the ability to reach across these differences, and we found that the ability to do so is determined by a set of six specific personal and marital capacities every man and woman brings to the transition. Simply put, couples who know or learn how to make these capacities work for them usually see their marriages grow stronger, richer, warmer—become everything they hoped the marriage would be. Conversely parents who don't learn how to make these capacities work for them often become as unhappy and alienated as Tom and Carol Norris.

Other important Project findings include:

- *Why one out of every two marriages now goes into decline after the baby's arrival*
- *Why when a marriage sours, it sours first and most dramatically for a woman*
- *Why the more attached a new mother is to the notion of work as a career, the more vulnerable she is to a drop in marital satisfaction*
- *Why, contrary to popular belief, conflict can be beneficial to new parents*
- *Why, despite more than a decade of egalitarian rhetoric, most men still expect their wives to do most of the housework and most of the baby work too*
- *Why marital satisfaction influences one's ability to be a good and sensitive parent*
- *And finally, why the discoveries a husband and wife make about each other during the transition often have a lasting effect on their marriage*

While the Penn State Child and Family Development Project was designed as an academic study, we knew from the outset that its findings would be of more than academic interest. Despite the near ubiquity of the transition experience (90 percent of all couples who can have children do so), most husbands and wives enter this period not knowing what to expect or how to evaluate the changes they encounter. For example, many new parents are troubled by the way sex changes after the baby's arrival and even more by the way communication does. All of a sudden there seems to be so little to say, and what is said, however innocent, often seems to lead to an argument. Why do these changes occur? Are they permanent or passing? And do they only occur in troubled marriages or in good ones as well?

The Transition to Parenthood represents a desire to bring the insights derived from the Project's findings on these and dozens of other important transition issues to a wider audience. In the pages that follow, you will not find anything that qualifies as how-to or self-help advice in the traditional sense of these terms. But as you watch our Project couples grapple with the challenges of the transition, I believe you will learn a great deal that can be of value to you and your spouse as you yourselves grapple with them.

HOW THE PROJECT ORIGINATED

If the Penn State Child and Family Development Project can be said to have a specific starting point in time, it was the summer of 1977 in the living room of Norman and Sarah Berkow. Norm and the Berkow's fifteen-month-old, Seth, were participating in a study on fathering I was doing as part of my Ph.D. thesis at Cornell. Because a major component of the study was in-home visits, periodically I would drive up to the Berkows' big old white Victorian on State Street in Cortland, New York, and spend an hour observing Norm and Seth. During these visits I began to notice something interesting: Whenever Sarah joined her husband and son, two things happened. Norm's parenting automatically became more sensitive; unconsciously he would begin reading Seth's cues and signals more accurately. The other change was in Seth. Whenever his mother appeared, he lit up like a 1,000-watt light bulb. *He's just happy to see her*, I thought at first. But as I watched Seth more closely, I realized that he was not responding to Sarah per se but rather to her and Norm's good-natured banter. Somehow his fifteen-month-old antennae were sensitive enough to pick up the quality of his parents' interactions, and because those interactions were uniformly positive, they made Seth purr with delight.

In 1977 the then-current developmental literature had very little to say about the phenomenon I was observing in the Berkows' living room. But as my study progressed and as I encountered more mothers and fathers in more and more living rooms across Cortland, I encountered the same two phenomena again and again. When a woman entered the room, the quality of her husband's parenting changed—usually for the better in good marriages and for the worse in troubled ones. And when the man and woman began talking, the quality of their interaction affected the child's behavior—for the better when the interaction was positive and for the worse when it was negative.

Was the parents' marriage a critical but overlooked developmental influence on even a very young child? I wondered.

In 1980 after joining the faculty at Penn State University as an assistant professor of Human Development, a personal experience made me start thinking about this question in a new way. Around that time I and many of my friends and colleagues were starting families. And as I was later to discover, our experiences as new parents were common to the point of generic. We all felt overtired, overstressed, and overworked. But what was perhaps most instructive was how many of us felt that the baby's arrival, though he was dearly loved, made our marriages less happy, less fulfilling. Many fathers I knew seemed to feel neglected and ignored, and every mother I knew, disillusioned and disappointed. "I thought I had married Alan Alda," a woman friend said to me one day, "but it turns out I've ended up with Fred Flintstone."

Many of the new mothers in my circle also felt isolated and alienated by a lack of husbandly understanding, a lack of sensitivity to what they were going through. At a party one evening in the fall of 1980 another woman friend, who was then on maternity leave, wondered out loud to me about this male insensitivity. "What is it with you men?" she said. "Why can't you understand that when a woman has a baby hanging on her half the day, she doesn't feel like having a man hanging on her half the night?"

As I listened to such complaints and as I thought about the observations I had made during my fatherhood study, two thoughts occurred to me: (a) If a child's development is affected by the quality of his parents' marriage, the marital disruptions of the transition period might create difficulties for millions of children; and (b) if we could get a better idea of why marriages change in this period and why those changes are so often negative, perhaps we could devise intervention programs for new families.

During a visit to the National Institute of Child Health and Human Development (NICHHD) in the spring of 1981, I mentioned these thoughts to officials there and proposed what ultimately became the Penn State Child and Family Development Project. After some discussion NICHHD officials and I agreed that to be of real benefit to new parents, my proposed study would have to answer four questions:

1. What characteristics make the transition such a tumultuous time in a marriage?
2. Is a decline in marital quality an inevitable part of the new-parent experience, or can marriages change in other ways as well?
3. If marriages do change in a number of ways, what factor or factors determine the direction of change?
4. And finally how does an individual's marital satisfaction influence the ability to parent?

Institute officials and I also agreed that if my proposed study was to answer these questions in a definitive way, I would have to do what no one had ever done before: follow a large number of couples through the entire transition cycle, monitoring them at various intervals for emotional, psychological, and attitudinal changes. Because such a study would demand a sizable investment of time and energy from participants, my staff at Penn State and I were full of trepidations when we began putting up recruiting posters in obstetricians' offices and Lamaze centers throughout central Pennsylvania in the winter of 1982. Would many couples be willing to make the investment of time we were asking? The answer turned out to be a resounding yes.

Prospective parents, it turned out, were as eager to learn about the transition as we were. Almost everyone we screened seemed to know someone whose marriage had begun to falter after the birth of their first child. We heard stories of friends who had had affairs, gotten divorced, or stopped sleeping with their spouses during the transition. Many of our couples said they hoped their participation in the Project would make this period easier for the new parents who followed them.

In the summer of 1982 we launched the Project with an initial pilot group of 50 couples; a second group of 75 was added in the spring of 1983, and a third group of 125 in early 1984. Most couples were followed from pregnancy to the new child's third birthday. But because most of the critical marital changes that occur during the transition occur between the baby's birth and his first birthday, we concentrated the bulk of our attention and effort on this period. In terms of actual visits this meant that we first saw our families during the third trimester of pregnancy for what we called an intake interview. These visits were used to assess each individual couple's marital strengths and weaknesses as they approached the transition's starting gate. Then we revisited them again for in-home observations at one, three, and nine months postpartum.

Typically these observations lasted two and a half to three hours, and during this time we collected several kinds of data. In order to determine how the husband and wife were faring as new parents, we spent an hour during each observation simply watching them interact with the baby. How sensitive to his cues and signals were they? Who played with him and who watched television? How did the couple behave toward each other in his presence? Usually the remainder of the observation was devoted to collecting other information we believed might have a subtle but important influence on a marriage during the transition years. We asked participants about their division of labor. Who did what with the baby and around the house? And how did each feel about this division? If both parents were employed or if the mothers worked outside the home—as was the case for nearly 50 percent of our couples—we also asked how they allocated career sacrifices. Were they shared equally, or was one partner making more sacrifices than the other? How did each spouse feel about this arrangement? We also asked participants about their relationships with family and friends. Was the baby changing them? And if so, how did the couple feel about these changes?

At the end of each observation we left a Marital Quality Questionnaire with our couples. It contained questions about division of labor and social support, but its main purpose was to track changes in a couple's feelings about each other. We knew there were a lot of things our husbands and wives would not say in front of each other, so we used the questionnaire (each participant received his or her own) to collect this information. It contained questions such as Does your partner gratify you sexually? Does he or she shy away or turn down your sexual advances? How often does your partner say "I love you"? Do you feel he or she praises you enough? Does he or she share important experiences with you? Does your partner dominate conversations or criticize you frequently? Does he or she do things to deliberately annoy you (such as smoke in your presence or leave the lights on)?

After filling out the questionnaires participants returned them to our offices at Penn State via mail, where they were scored in terms of the four indexes we used to rate marital satisfaction: feelings of love toward spouse, feelings of ambivalence toward spouse, changes in communication, and incidence of conflict.

At the end of the baby's first year and then again at the end of his third year we brought each Project family—husband, wife, and child—into our laboratories at Penn State for a series of videotaped interactions. These were used to assess how a couple's marital satisfaction was influencing their parenting.

WINNERS AND LOSERS IN THE TRANSITION TO PARENTHOOD

The Project produced a number of major surprises, and one of the most important of them centered on the reason why the transition is such a tumultuous—often divisive—period in a marriage. Like Tom and Carol Norris, most couples approach parenthood imagining the new baby will bring them closer together, giving them a new and deeper sense of "us." In time this often occurs. But *initially* a child has the opposite effect. He tends to push his mother and father apart by revealing the hidden and half-hidden differences in their relationship.

Many of the gaps that develop in a marriage after the baby's arrival have their roots in biology and socialization. Nature and nurture have conspired to make men and women feel, think, and perceive in very different ways. And as we shall see in the next chapter, few experiences in life highlight these fundamental male-female differences as sharply as the birth of a child. Even couples who think of themselves as like-minded often find their priorities and needs diverging dramatically when they become parents. Differences in family background and personality also contribute to transition-time marital gaps. No matter how much they love each other, no two people share the same values or feelings or have the same perspective on life, and few things highlight these personal differences as pointedly as the birth of a child.

Of course such differences are present in a marriage long before the child arrives. But as we watched our husbands and wives move from pregnancy to parenthood, we made a second important observation: A new child deprives a couple of many of the mechanisms they once used to manage differences. For example, in our homes where division of labor was a major source of contention, often, prebaby, a part-time housekeeper was used to finesse disagreements about who did what. Similarly, in homes where there was a big difference about whose work was more important—the husband's or the wife's—or where there were major value differences between the couple, these issues were finessed by the even simpler expedient of avoiding discussions about work and values. *But once the baby arrived,* we saw many of these management tools vanish. Now if there were disagreements about who did what around the house, they had to be confronted because there was no money for a part-time cleaning lady. And if there were differences about work, they had to be dealt with because someone was going to have to put his or her career on the New Parent track in order to take care of the child. Now if there were differences about values, they also had to be faced because there was a new life to shape and mold.

Another major surprise to emerge from the Project involved the way marriages alter during the transition. At the start of our study the then-current research held that there was only one major form of marital change among new parents—decline. But our data indicated that a marriage can change in one of four ways, and in each case the direction of change is determined by the couple's ability to overcome the polarizing effects of the transition.

Severe Decliners

Judging from our data, 12 to 13 percent of all new parents become so divided by differences that they begin to lose faith in each other and in their marriage. If these couples do not fall out of love, they come perilously close. On all four of the indexes we used to assess marital change, our Severe Decliners suffered dramatic negative alterations.

	FEELINGS OF LOVE TOWARD SPOUSE	FEELINGS OF AMBIVALENCE	CONFLICT	COMMUNICATION
Women	fell 34%	rose 160%	rose 60%	fell 31%
Men	fell 28%	rose 77%	rose 60%	fell 33%

Moderate Decliners

The 38 percent of our couples who fell into this category managed to avoid a dramatic marital tailspin during the transition. But at its end these couples were more polarized than they had been at its start.

	FEELINGS OF LOVE TOWARD SPOUSE	FEELINGS OF AMBIVALENCE	CONFLICT	COMMUNICATION
Women	fell 10%	rose 98%	rose 31%	fell 15%
Men	fell 10%	rose 64%	rose 37%	fell 15%

No Change

The 30 percent of our couples in this category conducted a holding action. They overcame enough of their differences to prevent a marital decline, but not enough to gain a new sense of closeness.

	FEELINGS OF LOVE TOWARD SPOUSE	FEELINGS OF AMBIVALENCE	CONFLICT	COMMUNICATION
Women	fell 1%	0	rose 1%	rose 2%
Men	fell 2%	fell 1%	rose 1.5%	rose 2%

Improvers

The discovery of this group came as a big surprise. Were some couples really able to defy the long-acknowledged odds and fall more deeply in love after the birth of a child? Our data indicated yes. For 19 percent of our couples the process of overcoming transition-time marital gaps and divisions brought them closer together.

	FEELINGS OF LOVE TOWARD SPOUSE	FEELINGS OF AMBIVALENCE	CONFLICT	COMMUNICATION
Women	rose 16%	fell 31%	fell 15%	rose 20%
Men	rose 13%	fell 33%	fell 24%	rose 17%

Another major Project finding involved the factors that determine how and in what direction marriages change. And this discovery really was not much of a surprise to us. At the start of the Project we hypothesized that a couple's ability to overcome transition-time divisions and disagreements would be determined by six personal and interpersonal capacities that they brought to parenthood. We called these six capacities the six transition domains and we envisioned them as bridge builders. We imagined that our couples who scored high on them would have enough resources available to throw bridges across their differences, while couples who scored low would remain stuck in their own individual poles of the marriage.

How we identified the domains was via a form of backward logic. We began by asking ourselves what characteristics would be most important in facilitating a husband's and wife's smooth passage through the transition. We concluded that six characteristics in particular would be very important to such a passage. They were the ability to:

- *Surrender individual goals and needs and work together as a team*
- *Resolve differences about division of labor and work in a mutually satisfactory manner*
- *Handle stresses in a way that does not overstress a partner or a marriage*
- *Fight constructively and maintain a pool of common interests despite diverging priorities*
- *Realize that however good a marriage becomes postbaby, it will not be good in the same way it was prebaby*
- *Maintain the ability to communicate in a way that continues to nurture the marriage*

Next we looked at each characteristic individually and asked ourselves what resource in the individual or in the marriage would determine how a couple scored on it. In some cases the answer to this question turned out to be fairly obvious. For example, the ability to surrender personal goals and work together as a team would require a husband and wife to merge their two individual selves into a larger "us," and in order to handle all the new differences that arise during the transition, it would require some skill at conflict management. In other cases the answers did not seem so clear. For instance we suspected that gender ideology, or the individual's beliefs about how men and women ought to behave, might have an important influence on a couple's ability to resolve chore and career differences amicably, but we were not sure. Our review of these six characteristics produced the six resources that then became our six transition domains. They were Self (or the couple's ability to merge their individual selves into a large Us), Gender Ideology, Emotionality (a marker of personality that governs vulnerability to stress), Expectations (how did the husband and wife think the baby would affect their marriage?), Communication (could they keep talking?), and Conflict Management.

When we analyzed our data in the late 1980s, it bore out our hypothesis about the importance of these six domains. Taken together, these factors determine who wins and who loses in the transition to parenthood. Our couples who scored high on four or more of them usually ended up in our Improvers column. After the baby's arrival their marriages grew deeper, richer, more meaningful. Our couples who scored high on three or low on three ended up in our No Change column. Our husbands and wives who scored low on four or more of them ended up in one of our two Decliner columns. These couples usually saw their marriages visited by that faceless something.

This is a social scientist's explanation of why some marriages decline and others improve during the transition. If you asked the Project participants themselves why they thought their marriages got better or worse, they would give you a different, more personal answer. Even couples in Improver marriages would say that they were surprised by how many differences surfaced after the baby's birth and at how much time they spent disagreeing about them. But these Improvers would also say that as they watched the way their partners responded to those differences, important discoveries about that partner began to be made. A story one Project wife told me one afternoon provides a case in point.

I don't think anyone would choose this woman's husband as a poster child for male sensitivity. An auto mechanic, he is a big, burly man with a tattoo on his right forearm and a wary relationship with the spoken word. But a few days prior to my visit he'd surprised and touched his wife with an act of unexpected understanding. The couple was lying in bed about to make love when their three-month-old began whimpering in the other room. "Stay," the husband pleaded. "Kevin will fall back to sleep by himself." When the woman said no, she couldn't, her husband snarled, "For Christ's sake." Returning to the bedroom a few minutes later, the woman expected to encounter a very ugly scene. What she encountered instead was a guilty and very apologetic husband. As she explained to me, "Carl said he was sorry for being so nasty and promised he'd be more understanding in the future."

Suddenly the woman smiled.

"If I've learned anything in the last few months," she told me, "it's that in the end and usually in spite of himself, Carl's good intentions always break through."

Couples who see their marriages decline also make important discoveries about each other. But the discoveries they make are more disturbing and disillusioning. The wife discovers that her husband is unwilling to curtail his gym schedule or Saturday afternoon fishing to make more time for his new family. Or the husband discovers that his wife is too preoccupied with the baby, too caught up in the romance of new motherhood, to make any time in her life or heart for him.

On a personal level the story of what happens to a marriage during the transition is really the story of the discoveries a couple makes about each other as they try to resolve its divisions and polarizations. When these efforts reveal heretofore unrecognized capacities for self-sacrifice, understanding, empathy, and compassion in a marriage, usually the husband and wife grow closer together. But when they reveal heretofore unrecognized capacities for selfishness and stubbornness for "having it my way," usually by the end of the transition the couple feels like the disillusioned husband and wife in the John Updike short story "Too Far to Go."

In the story's concluding scene, Updike's couple is lying in a Caribbean hotel room at the end of what has proven to be a disastrous vacation. Each knows that their marriage hangs in the balance, and each also knows that some act of reconciliation, some gesture of understanding and compassion is urgently needed now. If there is to be any hope of saving their marriage, someone will have to try to reach across the four feet that separate their twin beds. As the minutes pass by, a great sadness begins to fill the room. Lying there in the stillness, Updike's couple makes a terrible discovery: There is now so little love, so little caring left between them that for both even the four short feet that separate their beds is now too far to go.

Our study's last major finding centered on parenting and it confirmed an observation I had first made a decade earlier in the living room of Norm and Sarah Berkow. Marital satisfaction does influence parental competence. The hows and whys of this relationship are complex, as we shall see in Chapter Twelve, but broadly speaking, we found that the more a marriage satisfies an individual's needs and desires, the less likely the individual is to insert those needs and desires inappropriately into the parent-child relationship. The positive side of this principle can be seen in the sensitivity our Improver couples displayed in videotaped interactions with their children. Unencumbered with distractions and preoccupations, Improver husbands and wives were attentive to their youngsters' cues and signals. Unencumbered by personal agendas, they were willing to let their boys and girls set the pace in interactions, which is what a child must do if he or she is to benefit from them.

The negative side of this principle can be seen in the videotapes we made of Tom and Carol Norris with son Will at the thirty-six-month point. Our data suggest that sometimes when a man feels his point of view is ignored in the marital relationship, he will attempt to impose that point of view on a more powerless figure, the child. Tom did this several times while he and Will were before our cameras. One of the tasks we assigned a parent and child in these periods of observed interactions was building a tower out of four blocks. Like most of the other three-year-olds in our study group, Will could, I am sure, have completed this task on his own. But his father had no intention of letting him attempt it alone. During the several minutes it took Will to get the blocks piled on top of one another, Tom constantly criticized, instructed, and obstructed. In fairness to him I should point out that his behavior was well intentioned. But the portrait that emerged from the videotape was of an interfering, overcontrolling parent, and both of these qualities have been associated with insecurity in a child.

We found that women in unhappy marriages also bring a personal agenda to the parent-child relationship. They often seek from it the closeness lacking in the husband-wife relationship. And very often this agenda manifests itself in a kind of maternal hypersensitivity. On an act-by-act basis everything Carol Norris did with Will while they were before our cameras was exactly right. When Will almost knocked over his block tower, Carol steadied it. When Will almost pushed the clown puzzle I had given him off the table, Carol caught it just before it went flying over the edge. However, when all of her individual acts of sensitivity were added up, a more disturbing portrait emerged. One of the ways a child develops the sense of mastery that one day will give him the confidence to begin moving away from a parent is by making mistakes and learning from them. By constantly saving Will from the consequences of his errors, unconsciously Carol was undermining the learning process that would allow Will to push away from her, somewhere down the road.

During the Project we also made one other important discovery.

While it does not directly touch on the six transition domains or the ways they influence marital satisfaction and parenting, it deserves mention here because it plays an important if supporting role in the story this book tells.

WHY THE TRANSITION IS HARDER FOR TODAY'S PARENTS

Though we did not set out to examine social influences, as we watched our participants grapple with the challenges of new parenthood, it became clear to us that the larger society is also an important player in a couple's transition experiences. Husbands and wives are rarely aware of it as a felt presence, but it is always there just beyond the front door, influencing the things they say, feel, and think about each other, the marriage, and the baby. It determines the kinds of things they do and do not fight about, the amount of support that is available to them when they run into trouble, and how much each partner will sacrifice—how far each will go for the sake of the other and for the sake of the marriage.

As the Project progressed, it also became clear to us that recent changes in the larger society have made the transition more challenging for today's parents in several ways. One is by depriving them of a single universally accepted set of behavioral rules. I do not think many of us who grew up in a 1950s family would be eager to adopt its traditional values and tenets wholesale. But for new parents of that generation the near universal acceptance of traditional values did have one important advantage: Couples entering the transition knew what to expect of each other. The man would function as the family's breadwinner, the woman as its nurturer and homemaker.

Today traditionalism competes with several more equality-minded views of male and female behavior. To varying degrees these views, which arose out of the feminist movement, hold that men and women should share, not divide, work responsibilities. And while in the long run I suspect that their growing popularity will lead to a new kind of family—one in which responsibilities are alloted according to talent, desire, and need, not outdated notions of masculinity and femininity—in the short run their emergence has had a less happy effect. More often than not today's new parents enter the transition not knowing what to expect of each other. And often once the baby arrives, they find their expectations so far apart, they spend a great deal of time fighting about issues earlier generations of new parents never gave a second thought to, such as who diapers the baby, who feeds and bathes him, who does the dishes and the laundry, who works and who does not, and if both partners work, who puts his career on the New Parent track during the baby's early years?

The Project's life span also paralleled the rise of another societal change. Making ends meet has always been difficult for new parents, but during the 1980s this difficulty became acute. There was a decline in real wages. Between 1973 and 1990 the average income of male high school graduates in the nineteen- to thirty-four-year-old age group—the group that contributes the largest number of new fathers—fell 19 percent, while the income of similarly aged male college graduates barely kept pace with inflation. At the same time the federal government's support of new families began dramatically to wane. In the early 1950s the $600 tax deduction allowed for a child represented 36 percent of the average worker's annual pay. In the 1980s that deduction had climbed to $1,200 but because of inflation it now represented only 12 percent of the average worker's pay.

On the whole the 1980s were relatively prosperous ones for central Pennsylvanians. But many of our families were also touched by the deeper economic trends at work in the larger society. As the Project progressed, the percentage of employed mothers in our study population increased dramatically—from 38 percent to almost 50 percent. And while this group included a number of women who returned to work out of desire, it also included a number who returned to work out of need. Sociologist Christopher Lasch once described the family as "a haven in a heartless world." But as economic pressures mounted, many of our families could find no refuge from this heartless world. Money concerns intruded at every turn, becoming as much a part of the transition as three A.M. feedings and breast pumps and causing a great deal of displacement. At the heart of many of the complaints we heard about marriages, spouses, and babies was the new parent's concern that there would not be enough money available to meet the next mortgage or car payment or to pay for a new stroller or crib.

As I watched our couples cope with financial concerns and with all the other challenges of the transition, I found myself deeply moved. The quiet dignity and courage of our new fathers and mothers—especially our employed mothers—was inspiring to behold. But as I watched them, I also found myself deeply troubled by how little public acknowledgment, how little public support and gratitude they and other new parents receive for their selflessness and devotion.

In its better moods our society now treats the family with benign neglect; in its darker moods, as a source of parody. None of our participants complained about the lack of public support for their family building, but it affected them—in many cases by making the routine sacrifices of the transition that much harder. It is difficult to sacrifice oneself when the larger society says the overriding purpose in life is devotion to self, not devotion to others. And in a few cases it made those sacrifices too far to go. The rising divorce rate, falling school scores, widespread drug use—all ills that plague the American family today—are complex and have many sources. But I think one major source is that our society no longer honors what I witnessed every day of the Project—the quiet heroism of everyday parenting.

It is my hope that in some small way this book will help change that attitude.

2

The His and Hers Transition

Most popular magazine articles about the transition to parenthood contain a singular peculiarity: They describe the struggles, problems, and tumult of this period as something "we" endure, as if new mothers and fathers are exposed in equal measure to its stresses and chaos. But as anyone who is already a parent knows, the reality is different. Men and women experience the transition to parenthood in such dramatically dissimilar ways that within a very short period of time "we" becomes "me."

I was reminded of this fact dozens of times throughout our study, most memorably during a conversation with a couple who was then nine months into parenthood. As the husband proceeded to paint a glowing picture of life with baby, his wife, who was sitting next to him on the sofa, began fidgeting with annoyance. Yes, the man conceded, the bills did pile up faster these days, and yes, sometimes the baby's crying became irritating. But chores and sleep were not the big problems he had expected them to be. "Overall," he said, "things are turning out surprisingly well." At that point his wife, who was now practically vibrating with annoyance, exploded. "Your transition may be going surprisingly well," she snapped, "but believe me, mine isn't!"

Behind this common husband-wife perceptual gap lay some profound differences in biology, upbringing, and perhaps even evolutionary programming. To state the obvious, men and women are very different. And once the baby arrives, these differences usually produce such widely different priorities, needs, and perspectives that in most marriages, not one but two transitions develop, a His and a Hers.

The two transitions are united by a common set of gratifications. Men and women alike report that parenthood makes them feel better about themselves, their parents, and the larger world. Men and women alike also find the baby irresistible. Also uniting the two transitions is a common set of concerns. In nearly equal degrees new mothers and fathers worry about all of the new work and financial pressures the baby creates and about how parenthood will affect their relationship with each other as well as their work.

What begins to divide the two transitions is each parent's different biological relationship to the new child. While men and women become parents at the same time, they don't become parents in the same way. Most of the profound changes that occur during the transition, especially in its early phase, happen to the woman—and that makes her transition much more tumultuous than her husband's. Some of this tumult is good; indeed, some of it approaches ecstasy. "Women have babies all the time," said one Project mother, "but when you have one of your own, you feel like no one has ever done it before. You think, 'I have created life.' " The love affair with her new creation adds to the new mother's ecstasy. One recent study found that love at first sight is experienced by two thirds of all new mothers.* Another study found that the only two people who hold their gaze longer than

* The one-third of mothers who do not form an instant attachment to the baby do eventually form a strong attachment. It just takes them a little longer to fall in love.

a pair of lovers are a mother and her new child. Even women who are determined not to be swept off their feet by the baby often are. I remember one Project mother, a successful attorney, who had approached parenthood with some ambivalence, telling me later, "I never dreamed I could love anyone like this."

Some of the tumult, however, is bad. In the weeks and months immediately following the baby's birth, many women suffer from chronic fatigue and exhaustion. Several recent studies suggest that new mothers may also suffer from anxiety, depression, and low self-esteem. To some extent these two phenomena are related. Fatigue and physical weakness create a vulnerability to sharp and unpredictable mood swings. But a great deal of the new mother's emotional upheaval arises from her unique relationship to the baby. For example, many women find their feelings toward the child so powerful that they start to become all-consuming. The woman cannot think of anything but the baby, and sometimes she finds it hard to remove herself from his presence. Doubts about parental competence also stalk many new mothers. Having brought this wonderful new child into the world, the woman wonders whether she is capable of giving him the love and understanding he needs.

Worries about self are another common feature of the mother's transition. A University of Minnesota study indicates that when a new mother is not worrying about her exhaustion, parental competence, or emotional volatility, she is worrying about the physical changes the baby has produced in her. "Loss of figure" and "general unhappiness about appearance" were two of the top five transition complaints of women in a University of Minnesota study. Reflecting this sentiment was the remark of one of our Project mothers, who said to me one day with more than a hint of ruefulness in her voice, "I look like a potato."

The father's transition is not free of upheaval and tumult either. There is some evidence that new fathers worry even more than new mothers about work and money. And to varying degrees, new fathers also worry about fatigue, intrusive in-laws, chores, and what their wives are enduring. On occasion new fathers even suffer from physical discomfort. While we did not encounter any cases of sympathetic pregnancy, two University of California investigators, Carolyn Pape Cowan and Philip Cowan, reported that several men in their transition study gained weight and complained of vague aches and pains in the months prior to the birth of the new child.

On the whole, though, life in His transition is more even-keeled. Paternal love is slower to take flight. In a recent survey 70 percent of new fathers reported that it took them weeks and months, not hours, to form a strong attachment to the baby. And that love is also easier to control. According to Milton Kolchuck of the University of Massachusetts, new fathers spend an average of ten to fifteen minutes per day in play with a new son or daughter. There are also fewer lows in His transition. While a new mother's stress levels continue to rise throughout the first year after the baby's birth, we found that the new father's stress leveled off after the first month. But there are fewer highs too. In another recent survey, only 1 percent of new fathers described the baby's first step as a "big thrill," compared with 17 percent of new mothers. Another common feature of His transition seems to be guilt. When investigators asked a group of new fathers, "Should child care be shared equally?" 74 percent said yes. But when asked, "Do you share child care equally with your wife?" only 13 percent replied yes.

OUR TRANSITION

The different characteristics of the His and Hers transitions give new mothers and fathers different priorities and needs. Bearing and caring for a child absorbs tremendous amounts of maternal energy; working full-time on top of it, as over 50 percent of new mothers currently do, absorbs still more. So one chief priority of Her transition is a reasonably equitable division of labor. The new mother wants a husband who will relieve her fatigue by taking an active role with home and baby—to be her partner, not just a helper. Spousal understanding and empathy are also important to her. The new mother wants a husband who understands her profound attachment to the baby well enough to know why she may sometimes neglect him emotionally and physically to be with that baby. Just as important, the new mother also wants a spouse who understands how powerful and hard to control her feelings toward the baby are and who helps her to regain her emotional balance.

Another priority of the mother's transition is emotional involvement. The new mother wants to feel that in his own way her husband is as involved in the transition and in their new family as she is. Translated into day-to-day terms, this means that she wants a spouse who will sit and listen when she wants to talk about her doubts, anxieties, and frustration; who will play with and care for the baby instead of returning him to her in ten minutes; and who will check the refrigerator to see if the family needs anything *before* he goes to the store. To repeat, what she fundamentally desires is a partner, not a helper.

The principal priority of His transition is work. Most men are brought up to believe that ensuring a family's financial security is a husband's primary responsibility. And even in this relatively egalitarian age this belief continues to exercise a powerful tug on new fathers; some begin to work longer hours or take a second job after the baby's arrival. Absent the physical and emotional upheaval of the mother's transition, however, most of the father's other priorities remain, in modified form, what they were in prebaby days. While he recognizes that the workload has increased dramatically and that the baby has become the chief priority in the marriage, a new father continues to want some affection and attention for himself, a reasonably active social life, and some freedom to pursue his hobbies and sports and to see his friends.

The chief hallmark of couples who transform the His and Hers transition into the Our transition is the ability to reconcile the conflicting priorities of their individual transitions. The husband does this by recognizing that his wife's need for physical and emotional support far outweighs any needs he may have and by surrendering some of his autonomy and stepping deeper into the marriage to provide her with that help and support. The wife does it by recognizing that her husband's wish for some attention and affection also represents a legitimate desire and by learning how to control her feelings about the baby so that she can meet him at least halfway on these desires. She also does it by recognizing that he will see the support he offers differently than she does and by meeting him halfway on this issue by giving him some of the gratitude he expects for his commitment to her and their new family.

Typically in homes where the two transitions become one, the major new-parent concerns such as Who does what? How do we spend our money? How often do we go out? and Who makes the career sacrifices for the baby? are solved in a mutually satisfactory manner. But the hundreds of small acts of self-sacrifice, consideration, and understanding that are necessary to produce these agreements also give such homes another characteristic: mutual empathy. The husband and wife become so attuned to each other that when differences do arise, they respond as Laurie Cowte did when husband Tom complained of being sexually ignored. Laurie, who had had a baby three months earlier, had legitimate reason to turn Tom's complaint aside. But she knew it was his way of saying, "I feel emotionally ignored." So she decided to put aside her fatigue and do something that would make Tom feel very attended to. A few nights later, when he stepped out of the shower, Tom found a naked Laurie standing in the bathroom waiting for him.

Traditionally two roadblocks have been thought to hinder a couple's journey to the Our transition. As we have seen and will see in greater detail later in this chapter, differences in upbringing do give men and women contrasting ideas of what it means to be a parent, and differences in biology contribute to a different relationship and feelings toward the baby. But if the findings of Dr. Jane Lancaster, a University of New Mexico anthropologist, are accurate, couples may also face a third obstacle on the road to the Our transition.

In a recent paper Dr. Lancaster argues that one other reason new parents often do not see eye to eye on chores, money, and work is that evolution has programmed men and women to prioritize parenting in different ways. The origin of this programming lies in each sex's reproductive abilities. Dr. Lancaster believes that a woman is "wired" to pull a man into the family because her limited reproductive capacity —she can only produce so many eggs per month and so many children during her fertile years—means that each child represents an enormous biological investment to her. Hence, the woman is programmed to protect her child in any way she can, most notably by getting as much help and support from her mate as she can.

According to Dr. Lancaster, the reason men often resist the woman's demand to settle in is that their reproductive capacities have produced quite a different kind of evolutionary programming. A man can continue reproducing well into his seventies and emits millions of sperm in a single ejaculation. Therefore he is "wired" to regulate his biological investment in any single child because that child represents only one of hundreds of potential offspring.* It is important to emphasize

* Some data from the recent mate-selection research tends to support Dr. Lancaster's theory. For men in all cultures the top priority in a mate is physical attractiveness, and while women may blame this preference on male shallowness, Dr. David Buss of the University of Michigan thinks the deeper impulse behind it is male reproductive needs. In order to spread his nearly inexhaustible seed, a man needs a fertile woman. And since for Ancient Man the two most reliable and ubiquitous markers of female fertility were youth (for obvious reasons) and physical attractiveness (because it indicates good health), Dr. Buss argues that over time evolution has programmed men to prefer young, pretty women. The qualities women prize in a mate also fit their reproductive needs. The high priority they put on wealth and status in a mate (and this preference also occurs in all cultures), reflects the female's need to secure resources to protect her large biological investment in the baby. The relatively low priority women put on male beauty points to the fact that a man of almost any age can get a woman pregnant.

that Dr. Lancaster's view does not mean that a man cannot form a strong attachment to any one single child or that when a woman complains of not getting enough help, it is because she is under the influence of some obscure, atavistic impulse and not because she is not getting enough help. But if Dr. Lancaster is right, then the disagreements today's parents have about money, chores, and careers may simply be the latest manifestation of an ongoing argument between the sexes that stretches back a million years to the African savanna, where the first human parents arose.

WHAT DIVIDES US

New parents disagree about many things, but when they fight, they usually fight about one of five things: division of labor, money, work, their relationship (who is responsible for the hole that has opened up in it), and social life (are we getting out enough). These five issues are so big, important, and all-pervasive, they might be said to constitute the raw material of marital change during the transition. Quite simply, couples who manage to resolve these issues in a mutually satisfactory way generally become happier with their marriages, whereas those who do not become unhappier. In order to understand how these five issues operate in a couple's relationship, it will help to know more about the issues themselves and how biology, upbringing, and perhaps evolution have conspired to make men and women see them so differently.

Chores and Division of Labor

On the whole, husbands and wives agree that this is the major stress of the transition. They also agree that while they expected the baby to create a lot more work, that expectation did not prepare them for what they actually encountered. One of our Project mothers compared the difference to "watching a tornado on TV and having one actually blow the roof off your house."

Some recent figures explain why the reality of a baby's impact is so much greater than the expectation. Typically nonbaby tasks, such as dishwashing, increase from once or twice a day to four times, laundry from one load a week to four or five, shopping from one expedition per week to three, meal preparation from twice a day to four times, and household cleaning from once a week to usually once a day. Nursing chores add further to the workload. On average a baby needs to be diapered six or seven times and bathed two or three times per day, soothed two or three times per night and often as many as five times per day. His helplessness also transforms once-simple tasks into complex, time-consuming ones. "These days," said one new father, not bothering to hide his exasperation, "going out for ice cream is like planning a moon shot. First I have to check Alex to see if he's wet. Then I have to wrestle him into his clothes, then into the stroller. Next I have to pack an extra diaper in case he wets himself and a bottle in case he starts acting up."

Compared with his 1960s counterpart, a man like this father is notably more involved in baby and household chores. Studies show that, on average, thirty years ago a man devoted eleven hours per week to home and baby, while today he devotes fifteen or sixteen hours. But this three- to four-hour increase has not significantly alleviated the new mother's burden. Even in a home where a woman works full-time, we found that her contributions to child care, such as diapering, feeding, and bathing, often exceed her husband's by nearly 300 percent. Or to put it another way, for every three diapers he changes, she changes eight. The new mother's contribution to household chores also increases during the transition, usually by about 20 percent.

One of the major changes that has occurred within Her transition over the past fifteen years is the way women themselves view this division of labor. What was acceptable for earlier generations of new mothers is not acceptable for new mothers of this generation. A combination of factors, including maternal employment, feminism, and egalitarianism, has made today's woman expect and feel entitled to a significant amount of help from a man. By the same token, men have not been untouched by the winds of change either. Men today want to be more involved with home and child, and they also realize that their wives shoulder burdens their own mothers never dreamed of shouldering.

Yet despite these changes, when men and women sit down to discuss who does what, they usually end up sounding like a Project couple I interviewed several years ago:

> Husband (with some self-congratulation): "My dad is always telling me and my brother he never changed a diaper in his life. I change them all the time, and I think I'm a better parent and a better husband for it."
>
> Wife (after husband left the room): "David knows his father never helped his mother, and since he gives me a little help, he thinks he's Mother Teresa. The truth is, I do about eighty percent of everything. You know what really burns me up though? The way David acts when his parents visit. Usually he does a little more then, and of course they think he's wonderful. 'Wow,' his dad keeps saying, 'I never did any of that stuff.' Ohhh, when I hear that, I'd like to take the pair of them . . ."

Why do so many new mothers feel that they don't get the help and support they need? Part of the answer lies in several aspects of His transition that make a man perceive his contribution to home and baby differently than his wife. One is that a man uses a different yardstick to measure his contribution to the division of labor. A wife measures what a husband does against what she does. And because what a man does looks small when measured by this yardstick, the woman often ends up as unhappy and disgruntled as the Project wife above. The man, on the other hand, usually measures his contribution to chores against what his father did. And because by that yardstick his fifteen to sixteen hours per week represent a 30 to 40 percent increase over what his father did, he often ends up feeling as good about himself and his contribution to the division of labor as the Project father above.

Frequently the man's perception of who does what is also influenced by the fact that, at least temporarily, he becomes the family's sole breadwinner. And because this is a role he has been taught to equate with parenting, fulfilling it not only makes a new father feel like he is already satisfying his parental obligation, it also makes the 20 percent he does at home seem like 200 percent to him. How can his wife not appreciate his contribution? The nature of transition chores can also shape a man's perception of the division-of-labor issue. Because his wife is usually more skilled at baby chores, the man sometimes concludes that his help is really not needed. The new father who hops on this train of thought usually gets off at the same station as the Project husband who said to me, "I expected to do more, I really did. But then I started thinking. Since Brenda's breast-feeding Jenny, Brenda should get up with Jenny. Then, pretty soon, 'getting up with Jenny is Brenda's job' became 'Jenny is Brenda's job.' "

It is only a suspicion of mine but on an unconscious level the man's evolutionary programming may also influence his contribution to the division of labor. When today's new father says "I can't stay and help;

you know Dan and I always play racquetball on Saturday morning," he may simply be displaying the most up-to-date manifestation of that ancient male impulse—limiting one's investment in the baby.

Sometimes aspects of Her transition can also contribute to an unequal division of labor. For example the yardstick a new mother uses to measure a husband's contribution to chores can produce such maternal disgruntlement and withholding that the man does even less because he does not get the gratitude he feels he is entitled to for surpassing his father's. In addition a woman's significant biological investment in the child can make her so critical of her husband's parenting that, without intending to, she drives him away.

I witnessed a dramatic example of this phenomenon at a neighborhood picnic last year. I was talking to another father—a man I'll call Jake—when a scream erupted from a nearby meadow. While we were talking, Jake's two-year-old, Bobby, had wandered off, fallen, and cut his forehead. As Jake comforted him, wife Nora, who had been off getting hot dogs with their older son, appeared. Grabbing Bobby out of Jake's arms, she asked, "What happened?" in a voice full of upset and reproach. Jake told her, then added defensively, "It's only a scratch." Nora, however, was unmollified. "I'm taking Bobby to the nurse," she announced, and proceeded to march off. "Wait," Jake said, running after her, "I'll come with you." "No," said Nora, spinning around. "You stay here. You've already done your work for the day."

As he watched his wife and sons disappear over a hill, I could see Jake struggling with himself. He knew Nora's sharpness was a product of her concern for Bobby, not a personal attack on him. She had simply "lost it" for a moment. Still, the sharpness hurt, and in the end that hurt won out. "Next time let her take the both of them to get a hot dog," Jake said. "I've had it."

Men who find themselves continually criticized for their inadequate diapering, bathing, and dressing skills often end up feeling similarly conflicted. On one level they know that their wives do not really mean to be hurtfully critical; on another level, like Jake, they feel humiliated and often conclude that the best (and safest) policy to adopt vis-à-vis child-care chores is a hands-off policy.

Money Worries

Income among Project couples averaged $25,000 per annum (or about $30,000 in current dollars). This is about the national average for new parents, and it explains why finances are also a major transition issue. Twenty-five thousand dollars does not go very far, particularly when, in addition to covering ongoing expenses such as mortgage and car payments, it has to cover the new expenses created by the baby, who despite his small size can be a formidable consumer. For example, the packages of Pampers or Huggies he goes through every three or four days cost $9.50 to $12.50; the Osh-Kosh jeans and shoes he outgrows every few months cost $20 and $30 if he is one year old and $30 and $40 if he is two. On average his new winter coat costs up to $50; his new stroller anywhere from $80 to $250. Depending on where he lives, his visits to the pediatrician can cost between $25 and $75. If his mother continues to work, child-care costs can run as high as $20,000 per year in some cities.

Most of the disagreements new mothers and fathers have about these expenses arise from another difference between members of the His and Hers transition: Parenting changes men's and women's self-perceptions in very different ways. When a couple joined the Project, one of the first things we asked them to do was play what we called the Penny Game. We gave the husband and wife fifteen pennies each and asked them to allot their money to three roles: spouse, worker, and parent, depending upon how closely they identified with these roles. At the start of the transition, women allotted almost as many pennies as men to the worker role—which is to say that mothers-to-be were almost as likely as fathers-to-be to identify themselves as workers. But after the baby's birth a divergence developed. Women (including working women) began allotting more and more of their pennies to the parenting role, men relatively more to the worker role.

The different forms of economic logic that new mothers and fathers develop arise from this divergence in self-perception. Many a man's thinking about money issues is dominated by his worker impulse to conserve and enhance financial resources. A new father frequently works longer hours to increase income and begins cutting back on his own consumption. Now he shuts off the lights when he leaves a room and brings a sandwich to work instead of eating lunch out. Many a woman's economic logic is often shaped by her close identification with the parenting role. New mothers also turn out lights and "brown-bag it" to save money. However, because a mother sees herself first and foremost as a nurturer, the woman's chief concern becomes the baby's well-being. And this often produces economic choices that put her in conflict with her conservation-minded husband.

Exhibit A of this phenomenon was Project wife Betty van der Hovel's decision to have the living-room windows babyproofed with sliding metal guards two weeks after son Luke's birth. Because husband Ted felt the windows would not pose a hazard until Luke was two or three years old, Betty's decision baffled and annoyed him. "Now on top of everything else I have to find a hundred and fifty dollars to pay for those goddamn guards," he told me one day. "Why couldn't Betty have waited?" But Betty felt that Ted had missed the point entirely. The issue was not money, it was their son's safety. And how could he possibly put economic considerations ahead of that? "Sometimes, you can be such a jerk," I overheard her tell Ted one afternoon during a conversation about the window guards.

Exhibit B of this phenomenon is a disagreement I witnessed one evening at the home of Project couple Tom and Maggie Davis. I was sitting in the kitchen with Tom when Maggie arrived home with a bagful of new baby clothes. "Look at these, Tom," she said, pulling a smock, hat, and booties out of the bag in rapid succession. "Won't Alexis look adorable in them?"

In a transition where conservation is an overriding priority, expensive baby clothes make as little economic sense as sliding metal guards, so Tom reacted to this fashion show the way Ted van der Hovel had to the guards. "Jesus, Maggie, how many times do we have to go through this?" he said. "We just bought a house, we're not making much money, we can't afford to keep buying baby clothes. How many dresses does Alexis need, anyway? She doesn't look in a mirror."

Maggie groaned as if to say, "You don't get it, do you?" And from the perspective of Her transition, Tom had not gotten it. Often for women new baby clothes represent a sensible economic choice because they advance another of the new mother's priorities: social presentation. This is the name given to her desire to present her baby —her creation—to the larger world of family and friends for admiration and praise. And since a thirty-dollar Osh-Kosh outfit and a forty-dollar pair of shoes will make her new creation look even more irresistible to that larger world, frequently the new mother believes them to be a sound investment.

One interesting sidelight of the employed-mother revolution is that it may have enhanced the incidence of clothes and toy buying for baby. When men were providing most of the family's income, a mother often had to curb her buying impulse if a husband said, "Enough," because it was money he earned that she was spending. But now that many new mothers have independent sources of income, they feel (within limits of course) that they have a right to spend their money as they choose.

Relationship Difficulties

It is harder to draw a statistical profile of marital estrangement and drift, but several numbers suggest why it is also an important transition issue. One comes from a recent *Parenting* magazine survey that found that new mothers and fathers are twice as likely to kiss the baby as they are each other. A recent University of Michigan study found that the incidence of sexual intercourse drops 30 to 40 percent in the first year after the baby's arrival.

Fatigue, of course, is partly responsible for these changes, and so is the baby, who attracts attention and affection his parents used to direct at each other. But the principal reason new parents touch less frequently is that they feel less connected, less in tune with each other. It is not accidental that one of the most enduring pieces of transition folklore—one that has been passed down from one generation of new parents to the next—is the story of the couple who, on their first night out alone, run out of things to say within five minutes. The sense of drift, estrangement, and loneliness that produces such tongue-tiedness is as much a feature of the transition in most marriages as are money worries and division-of-labor concerns. But once again, differences in upbringing and biology often make men and women blame these problems on very different things.

For men the chief culprit is maternal preoccupation with the baby. While most new fathers expect the baby to become the main priority in the family, many are stunned at how little wifely attention or affection is left over for them. Our Project fathers complained that after the baby's arrival much less interest was shown in their work, hobbies, concerns, or sexual desires. One Project husband described a recent sexual encounter with his wife this way: "Last Sunday, while Ellen and I were lying in bed, I reached over and touched her. She'd been half asleep, but as soon as I put my hand on her breast, she bolted upright, pulled a sheet over her and said, 'Don't. Not now. That's for

Jonathan.' Believe me, if I ever had any doubts about her priorities, that incident cleared them up in a hurry."

Often adding to the man's sense of estrangement is the coterie of advisers that surrounds the new mother. While men know why this happens, these figures—who include mothers, sisters, aunts, and other female relatives and friends—possess nurturing skills a man often does not. Their sudden importance in a wife's life often makes a husband feel shunted aside and unimportant. A University of Minnesota study found that while in-laws were not among the top five transition complaints of new mothers, they were the number-one complaint of new fathers, many of whom singled out mothers-in-law and sisters-in-law as sources of alienation and estrangement. "Sometimes I wonder if anyone remembers I'm still here," a Project father said to me one day.

When women talk about transition-time loneliness and estrangement, their chief culprit is what I call male self-focus. Because of upbringing and perhaps biology as well, a man's emotional energy and attention all too frequently tend to flow inward toward his own concerns and needs. Shared experiences which pull a man outside of himself and force him to concentrate on his partner's needs can sometimes disrupt this flow. But because none of the transition's major events absolutely require male participation—a man does not have to be in the delivery room if he does not want to be, for example—often the new father's focus remains relatively undisrupted. As before the baby's arrival, he continues to be preoccupied with his own wants and needs.

An example of how this self-focus can contribute to maternal estrangement and disaffection is a story a Project wife told me about a visit to her husband's parents six weeks after her child's birth. "I'd had a cesarean," the woman said, "so Norman carried Natasha into the house. But he was so concerned about getting to the TV set and the football game that the minute he got through the door, he practically threw her on the floor. He didn't take her out of her baby seat or unwrap her blanket; he didn't ask me what I wanted. He didn't do anything except vanish. Sometimes I wonder whether he realizes the two of us even exist."

An encounter another Project wife had with male self-focus left her feeling even more estranged and alienated. One night about three months after daughter Sarah's birth, mother Jill was standing in front of the bedroom mirror in her bra and panties when she happened to catch a glimpse of husband, Michael, examining her from the opposite side of the bedroom. The look on his face so horrified her that Jill rushed to the closet for a bathrobe. When she told one of our female observers about this incident, Jill said it confirmed what she had already begun to suspect about Michael: He was so wrapped up in what he wanted—"a perfect little beauty queen of a wife"—he had no understanding of or sympathy for what she was going through.

The association men make between work and parenting also contributes to maternal loneliness and estrangement. Just at the point when a new mother wants her husband home by her side, this association will often make the husband pull himself out of the family and immerse himself more deeply in his work. "I know Ralph means well," one of our wives told me, "but I don't understand why he only equates parenting with money. It's important, but right now having him here is a lot more important to me than the few extra dollars his overtime brings in."

Career and Work

At the Project's start in 1982, 30 percent of our wives were employed in the baby's first year, and most held traditionally female jobs. They were beauticians, nurses, teachers, and clerks. Most also worked for a traditionally female reason: Their families could not get by without their paychecks. At the Project's conclusion in 1988, maternal employment stood at 45 percent, and now our employed mothers included more professional women, such as accountants, lawyers, and office managers. An increasing number of our women also looked upon their work, whatever they did, as a career or as the steppingstone to one. Our data closely mirror national trends, which show that between 1970 and 1990 the number of employed mothers with young children almost doubled, from 30 percent to 53 percent.

This change in maternal employment has fueled another equally momentous change. For reasons of both ideology and need, over the past decade more and more employed mothers have come to embrace the notion of egalitarian role sharing. While today's employed mother expects parity or near parity on division of labor, her adherence to this ideal often leads her to expect something much deeper—marital parity. She expects her partner to share emotional responsibility for their child and family and to share in career sacrifices if they have to be made. Not every woman who goes to work embraces egalitarianism, of course, but enough do to have created another potent source of divisiveness between members of the His and Hers transitions.

Some men share their wives' egalitarianism. During the Project, we encountered a number of committed male egalitarians, and interestingly the ones most steadfast in their commitment to this ideal tended to be alike. (We will take a closer look at them in Chapter Seven.) For the most part they were low-key, usually nonideological (i.e., they did not have any special intellectual commitment to either egalitarianism or feminism), extremely secure, and often domestically skilled. Also noteworthy, they were all deeply in love with their wives. However, these husbands represented the exception. The norm among Project husbands—and I strongly suspect among husbands in general—is a man in transition. This individual also loves his wife and wants to support her, especially when she holds a paying job. But because he has a lingering allegiance to certain aspects of the traditional male role, he is often psychologically and emotionally unprepared to be the full partner his wife wants and expects.

Take chores. The woman's desire for parity or near parity on the division-of-labor issue frequently causes conflict because it bumps into the transitional man's belief that while a husband should contribute, a wife should remain first among equals in the nursery, kitchen, and laundry room. The working mother's belief that emotional responsibility for child and home should be shared also frequently causes conflict. Unlike his father or grandfather, a transitional man will bathe and diaper the baby. But like them he believes, or at least acts as if he believes, that chores that involve assuming emotional responsibility for home and child, such as scheduling pediatrician's visits, overseeing child-care arrangements, and making out shopping lists, are a woman's work—whether she has a job outside the home or not.

Career conflicts are also common between this man and his wife because his view of himself as the family's principal breadwinner (whatever the reality of the situation) produces an expectation that career sacrifices are also his wife's job. One area where this expectation caused a great many problems for Project mothers was when they had to work late. Usually if a man's desk was clear at five, he would agree to pick up the baby at the sitter or child-care center. However, if it wasn't—even if there wasn't anything terribly pressing on it—he would generally say, "No, I can't. I have to work too. You'll just have to make other arrangements."

Social Isolation

The weeks immediately following the baby's birth are a whirlwind of social activity. But sometime around the end of the first month the congratulatory calls and visits begin to taper off, and that is when the stress of social isolation really starts to make itself felt. Among Project participants, recreational activities in the form of visits to movies, restaurants, and friends' homes declined by 40 percent during the first year of the transition. And several findings from the *Parenting* magazine study suggest that their experience is the rule, not the exception. More than half the survey respondents reported that they did not go out at all during the first six months after the baby's birth unless a relative was able to sit. Even after the first year more than 81 percent had yet to spend a weekend alone, and 91 percent to take a vacation of five or more days alone.

On the whole, new mothers tend to suffer more from isolation than fathers, and new stay-at-home mothers suffer most of all. Said one such mother, "Sometimes it gets so bad, I find myself actually dreading Kate's naps. But when she's up, I spend most of my time wishing I had another adult here to talk to." Work protects men from this kind of desperate isolation. But the lack of date nights, parties, vacations, and extracurricular activities such as Saturday afternoon raquetball takes its toll on them too. In conversations we found men and women equally likely to complain about feeling isolated and cut off. But we also found that like the other major transition stresses, this one is perceived very differently by the two sexes.

Men generally take the position of Mike Evans, one of our Project husbands, who felt that the principal reason for his and wife Phoebe's isolation was what he called Phoebe's obsession with the baby. "She won't leave him alone," Mike complained one day. "I know mothers are supposed to be devoted to their babies, but Phoebe's gone way overboard. Every time David hiccups, she makes a federal case out of it. She won't eat unless he's on her lap or leave him if she thinks the slightest thing is wrong. Last week, an hour before we were supposed to go to the movies, Phoebe marched into the living room and announced that she'd just canceled the sitter. She thought David was coming down with a cold and didn't want to leave him. I went ballistic. We've been out exactly three times in the last eight months."

When I talked to Phoebe Evans a few days later, she was still feeling vaguely guilty about this incident. "I know sometimes I overfocus on David," she admitted, "but it's taken me a while to recognize that and also to recognize that it won't change unless I make an effort to change it." But like most women Phoebe also felt that a major factor in the Evans's isolation was her husband's attitude. "Mike's always telling me, 'Come on. Let's go out, let's go out,' and I want to, but I say no because I'm too exhausted. And that's Mike's fault. He barely lifts a finger to help me."

WHAT UNITES US

"One day, when Michela was four months old, I had an incredible experience with her. She'd been crying and I was trying to soothe her, but nothing worked. So finally, out of desperation, I began singing 'Row, Row, Row Your Boat' very softly. All of a sudden the tears stopped, her eyes got shiny and as big as nickels, and her little mouth formed into a perfect 'O.' She was straining every ounce to focus on me. No one had ever looked at me that intently before—as if I were the sun, moon, and stars all wrapped up in one. It made me so happy, I took Michela's little hand in mine and began waltzing her round and round the kitchen."

This story from a Project mother indicates what is wrong with the portrait of the transition I've painted over the last fifteen-odd pages—it leaves out all the good parts. If becoming a parent were an endless conflict about money, chores, work, the relationship, and social activity, babies would be a lot rarer than they are. But of course it is not an endless conflict. Along with the tumult, the exhaustion, the loneliness, and hurt feelings there are also moments of sublime happiness, moments when the new parent literally begins dancing with joy. And for the most part what sets new parents to dancing is the same. Among Project husbands and wives there was as much agreement about the transition's gratifications as there was about its stresses. But just as men and women perceive the stresses differently, often they also perceive its gratifications differently.

Take what everyone agrees is the transition's most exquisite gratification: the baby himself. Often when new mothers talk about why he is so wonderful, they speak the language of love. They say the baby has introduced them to a new dimension of this feeling, one they did not know—had not dreamed—existed before. Project mothers tried to explain the uniqueness of this love in many different ways. Some attempted to delineate its parameters in words, and often the words they chose were ones people use when they are trying to describe a profound spiritual awakening. Women talked about being seized by an "all-embracing," "all-encompassing" love. Other mothers employed metaphors to describe the specialness of what they felt. Said one Project woman, "Tilly's opened a door in me I didn't even know was there." Still others described the transforming effect of their new feelings. "The love that flows through Adam's eyes when I hold him makes me tingle," said one mother, while another compared her baby's smile to a "magic wand" that "chases my blues away." We also had a fair amount of new mothers who believed that human language had not yet invented words powerful enough to describe what they felt. "I love Cynthia more than words can say," declared one mother when I asked her to describe how she felt about her new baby.

While new fathers are also set to dancing by the baby, they usually dance more slowly and for different reasons. We had a few men who were as swept away by love as any new mother. Representative of this group was the man who said, "I can't fully express the feelings of love I have for Michael. He's a magnificent blessing. He's increased the love I receive and the love I give." But most new fathers are swept away by the baby for more traditional male reasons. Many look upon him as a terrific new playmate. A number of Project fathers echoed the sentiment of the man who described his new son as being "more fun than TV." Even more men seem to see the baby as a wonderful new cement that strengthens their feelings toward wife and family. "I feel much more deeply committed to my marriage now," said one new father.

While men and women used different verbal styles to describe their feelings about baby, when they talked about him, I noticed that they both used the same facial expression: They smiled.

Changes in feeling about oneself ranks as the second major transition gratification. At one point or another almost all of our mothers and fathers reported that parenthood had made them feel more mature, more grown-up. But these words meant different things to men and to women. Usually when a man used them, he meant that he felt more responsible about his work. Sometimes this would lead him to devote more hours to it; other times, to begin looking at it in a new way. Instead of seeing it simply as a source of revenue, now the new father would begin to look at his job as part of a larger life plan. As the child grew, the family's income needs would increase; did his job offer an opportunity for advancement? And even more important, his family would need a secure source of income. Did his present job provide that security?

New mothers also equated maturity with responsibility. But when a woman talked about responsibility, usually she meant the responsibility of shaping and molding a new life. Many women reported that motherhood made them behave more sensibly. "I used to be a real speed demon," said one woman. "But not anymore. Since Amy's birth, I don't think I've gone more than forty-five miles per hour. My husband can't believe it. But now that she's a part of my life, I don't feel I can afford to take risks anymore." Other women reported that their new sense of responsibility had awakened them to larger concerns. "I never paid much attention to environmental issues," one of our mothers told me one day. "I figured I don't live in Brazil, so why should I worry about the rain forest, and I'm not an Eskimo, so why should I worry about the whales? But Eddie's changed that. These things are a part of the world he's going to live in, and I want to make sure that when he's grown-up, they're still there for him to enjoy."

The new sense of family that the baby creates ranks as a third major transition gratification for most new parents. And interestingly it is one that mothers and fathers experience in the same way. When we asked Project participants why the baby enhanced their sense of family, men were as likely as women to cite the same reasons. One was that the new child had given the husband and wife what they had not had before: a biological connection. One Project father spoke for many of our study participants when he said, "Since the baby, I feel a lot closer to my wife emotionally and spiritually because she's not just my partner anymore. She's the mother of my child." The need to pull together to meet the demands of the transition can also enhance a couple's sense of being part of the same unit. "Suddenly you realize if you're going to survive this thing intact," said one woman, "the two of you are going to have to learn to work together in a new way, and that creates a tremendous sense of unity." The remark of another Project participant hints at a third reason why the baby often enhances a couple's sense of family: "When I was a little girl," she said, "we used to spend every summer on the Jersey shore. Since Jane's birth Everett and I have spent a lot of time talking about the traditions we want to create for our new family."

In interviews Project participants singled out one other aspect of the transition as being particularly gratifying: It brought them closer to their own parents. Sometimes this bond arose from empathy. Now that they were parents themselves, participants said they had a better appreciation of what their parents had given them and what they had gone through to give it. Said one man, "Being a dad myself, I realize what a good job my parents did with me and how much I owe them." A Project mother added, "It took me twenty-eight years, but I'm finally beginning to understand all the sacrifices my mom and dad made for me."

Other times the new bond with one's own parents was generational. Suddenly the mother and father felt linked in a great family chain that stretched back into some unknown past and now forward into the baby's future. Being part of this chain evoked powerful feelings in a new parent. A particularly dramatic case in point was the Project father who ended a five-year dispute with his father after his daughter's birth. The two men had not spoken since having a falling-out over the family business. "I felt my father had behaved very pigheadedly," the man said, "and I was angry at him. But after Natalie's birth I felt it was time to put our dispute aside. We're all part of the same family, and it would be silly to allow a business disagreement to continue disrupting the family. So I gulped hard and called him."

One of the things that became clear early in the Project is that couples who are able to focus their attention on what unites them and produces mutual joy usually end up at the end of the transition with a better, happier marriage. I think the reasons for this are fairly self-evident. The transition gives a couple dozens of new and potentially much deeper points of connection. There is the baby and the new biological link he creates between husband and wife; there is the new sense of unity, of family they experience as they join together to nurture him; and there is also the enormous satisfaction of knowing that you and your partner are growing together and growing in the same direction. However, in order to take advantage of these new points of connection, a couple first must learn how to deal with the new differences and divisions the transition also creates. Mutual delight in the baby won't do much for marital satisfaction if his parents spend 90 percent of their time fighting about who diapers, bathes, and clothes him.

This observation brings me back to the six transition domains I described earlier. A couple's Expectations, Gender Ideology, Self, Communication, Emotionality, and Conflict Management pretty much determine how successful or unsuccessful they are in settling differences about division of labor, money, work, relationship, and social activities. The experiences of the three Project couples you will meet in the next chapter are designed to illustrate how. As you follow them through the rest of the book, you will see why these factors help two of the couples resolve their differences and hinder one. I think what you learn from them will teach you not only something about the domains but perhaps something important about your own marriage as well.

PART TWO

AT THE STARTING GATE: THE COUPLES

As I watched her pass along the walk under my office window I found myself wondering who was this young woman with the brisk, purposeful walk? On college campuses people normally amble, yet she moved so hurriedly, as if she did not have a moment to waste. At the elm under my window she turned right, into my building. A few seconds later I heard the sound of muffled voices in the reception area, then of my office door opening. When I looked up, the woman was standing behind my secretary, who announced that a Sue Akers would like to see me.

Over the next few years I was to learn a great deal about Sue and her husband, Ron. But on the evening I drove out to the Akerses' home to conduct their intake interview, I knew only what Sue had told me during her visit a week earlier. She was an office manager at a local insurance agency, she had had a miscarriage a year and a half earlier, was pregnant again, learned of the Project from friends, and wanted to enroll. The purpose of the intake, or first, interview was to fill in this sketchy picture and assess the Akerses' current standing on six domains that determine a couple's ability to bridge the chasms and divides of the His and Hers transition.

The immediate purpose of this section of the book,

which takes the form of intake interviews with the Akerses and two other Project couples, the Renselears and the Carlsons, is to illustrate how we performed this assessment. The larger purpose of this section is to show how the past shapes a couple's transition experience, because the six domains are inherent in a relationship long before the baby arrives. At the conclusion of these interviews I think you will be as uncertain about the Akerses', Renselears', and Carlsons' prospects as I was when I interviewed them. But as we follow them through the transition itself, it should become increasingly apparent why, given the strengths and weaknesses each couple brought to the starting gate, one sees their marriage improve, another sees theirs decline, and the third stays the same in terms of marital satisfaction.

3

Ron and Sue Akers: Big Dreams, Small Dreams

Like several of our other Project couples, the Akerses met on a blind date. One day in 1976 a classmate of Ron's gave him Sue's telephone number and suggested he call her. Ron put the number in his wallet and promptly forgot about it until the following week when he was buying a notepad at the campus bookstore. Taking a bill out of his wallet, the piece of paper his friend had written Sue's number on fell out. Ron picked it up, finished paying for the notepad, then on impulse on the way out stopped at a phone booth in the store foyer and called Sue.

Seven years later the first date that followed his call remained vivid to both Akerses. Ron could still remember what Sue wore (a tight blue dress) and the movie they saw (*Jaws*). Sue remembered the rain shower that greeted them as they left the theater and how touched she was when Ron took off his sports coat and put it around her shoulders. For both Akerses, though, the most vivid memory of that distant April evening was the instant physical attraction they felt for each other.

From his phone voice Sue pictured Ron as short and dark ("Don't ask me why," she said later). But the boy who arrived at her dorm was nearly six foot three, lean and muscular, with reddish-blond hair and pleasant, uncomplicated good looks. Ron's first reaction to Sue, who has an intelligent, pretty face, blond hair, and a personality as emphatic as an exclamation mark, was more elemental. "Watching her come down the stairs in that dress, I thought, 'Mmmmmm, this is for me.' "

"I could tell he was smitten right away," Sue said, recalling that first date. "And I liked him. I thought he was very cute and refreshingly stable. I mean, this was the seventies, and Ron was the first boy I'd met in ages who wasn't into drugs. I was shocked when he asked me to marry him a month later, though. I said, 'Whoa, hold your horses, mister. We barely know each other. Don't even mention marriage again until we've been together at least a year.' "

At the time I conducted the Akerses' intake interview in the spring of 1983, Ron and Sue had been married for four years and were living in one of the new housing developments that had recently begun springing up around Penn State. Their home, a three-bedroom Cape Cod, sat on a small knoll above the development's main drive and, unlike the houses around it, was neatly landscaped. A row of shrubs bordered by brightly colored flowers ran across the front of the house, and on either side of the walk leading up to the front door stood two newly planted young trees. In this still freshly plowed, unfinished neighborhood, the effect was like coming upon a light in the window. Inside, the hall, decorated with family photographs, gave way to a living room with colonial-style furniture, mostly in muted plaids, and then a stairway that led down to a wood-paneled recreation room, where I conducted the interview.

Barely four months old, the Akerses' house and the development it was a part of were the latest manifestations of the economic upswing that had begun rippling through central Pennsylvania several years earlier. The first thing I learned about the Akerses was that they were riding the crest of this boomlet. Sensing a change in the air, in 1981

Ron and Sue had invested their two-thousand-dollar life savings in a plot of land off Route 322; two years later a commercial-property developer paid them nearly three times that amount for the plot. The condominium in University Park purchased with the profits from that sale had also turned out to be a financial bonanza for Ron and Sue. In addition to increasing 40 percent in value in eighteen months, it provided the Akerses with a steady source of rental income.

The source of all this unexpected financial information was Ron, whose eagerness to describe the family's financial holdings surprised me. Money and sex were not subjects our couples were normally eager to talk about during intake interviews. Even more surprising was Ron's openness in describing Sue as the author of the Akerses' financial coups. Even when the man in the family was not the family's chief financial decision maker—and in many cases he was not—he would present himself that way. Ron had done the opposite; he had almost gone out of his way to emphasize his opposition, first to the land and then to the condominium. "Both times I told Sue she was crazy," he said, "and both times she turned out to be right and me wrong." I was intrigued by this forthrightness, but before exploring it I first wanted to know more about the author of the Akerses' financial success, who looked crisp and pert that night in a blue-and-white pinafore smock and red espadrilles.

Over the course of the Akerses' involvement in the Project, I was to come to think of Sue as possessing two distinct sides. The first one I encountered the night of the intake interview was the domestic Sue, whose hopes and dreams were indistinguishable from any of the hundreds of other young women my staff and I interviewed during our study. This Sue was a relatively traditional figure, who said she valued home and family above all else and who, like many of our other mothers-to-be, also said she expected the new baby to enrich and enhance her marriage. "Ron and I know we'll have to give up a little of us for the baby. But on the deeper level I'm sure she—or he—will bring us closer together."

When Sue began talking about her background, however, another, more unconventional figure emerged. This young woman was bold, ambitious, strong-willed, and despite her earlier paean to traditional values, an egalitarian who early on had resolved not to become a traditional housewife like her mother. "Mom's fondest dream for me was to become a homemaker like her," Sue said. "But I told her, 'No way, José,' I wasn't going to spend the rest of my life getting up at six every morning so I could wait hand and foot on a man all day the way she did. She says now she only did it because Dad worked so hard. But he's been retired for three years, and she still acts like his slave."

This Sue was also a rebel who refused to submit when her farmer father made paying her tuition contingent on living at home and commuting to college. Nearly ten years later the memory of this paternal ultimatum still made her bristle. "I was absolutely furious when Dad told me that. I thought, 'I'll show them.' So I got a job, and as soon as I had enough money saved to pay my own room and board and tuition, I moved out." Sue said this act produced the one defiant act in her mother's marriage. "Mom told Dad he'd help me or she'd go on strike; no tuition for me, no cooking and housecleaning for him." But by the time her mother brought her father around, Sue was not in the mood for compromise. "The day Mom called and told me Dad agreed to pay my tuition, I told her no thanks. I was tired of being under Dad's thumb and hers. I'd pay my own way."

Sue stopped and frowned. This was not an episode she was particularly proud of, she said. "I was so young and full of myself, I couldn't see that Mom was moving heaven and earth to help me. Believe me, for her to stand up to Dad like that . . ." Sue stopped to think of some improbable event that she might compare her mother's defiance to, but nothing she could think of seemed improbable enough. "We've both changed a lot since then. I'm a little older and less headstrong, and Mom's more accepting. I think at some point she realized if we were going to have a relationship, she'd have to accept me for who I am, and gradually she has. We're very close now. When the baby's born, she's going to be my nanny and housekeeper."

Ron Akers was more low-key and stolid than his wife. He spoke in a slow, methodical voice and considered each of my questions with great deliberateness. His other notable qualities included a sly sense of humor, which he seemed to direct mostly at himself, and a sweetness that was winning and understated. He was also quite good-looking, in the style of the clean-cut, athletic young men you see in the Michelob and Budweiser commercials.

When I asked him about his background, he said he had grown up on a farm. But as he talked about his youth, it became apparent that, unlike Sue, Ron was a traditional child of his time and place, which was rural Pennsylvania in the late 1960s and early 1970s. Growing up, he said, he had been very close to his parents, three sisters, and brother. He was active in scouting and 4-H. His youthful hobbies suggested a risk-taking streak underneath his easygoing exterior. In college he raced dirt bikes and had been an avid skydiver until Sue insisted he give up both pastimes. After graduating from Penn State with a degree in horticulture, Ron joined a landscaping firm in Oak Hall, a small hamlet a few miles south of University Park, where he was now an assistant manager.

One biographical detail we paid particular attention to during these intake interviews was the couple's handling of a past relationship crisis. The transition is more than a rite of passage in a marriage; it is, as I think Chapter Two makes eminently clear, also a major challenge. In order to get through the transition and all the divisions and challenges it creates, a couple must be able to surrender individual priorities, needs, and perspectives and join forces. The ability to do this is mediated by a transition domain we called Self because it is made up of three related aspects of self: security, autonomy, and affiliation. Our principal means for scoring a couple on this domain was a series of questions appended in the Marital Quality Questionnaire we left at the end of the intake interview. But in order to get a preliminary sense of the participants' standing on it, often during the interview itself we asked them to tell us about a past crisis. We believed this could reveal something about their capacity for the qualities the Self domain mediates, such as self-sacrifice, empathy, and cooperation.

For the Akerses, the major crisis in their marriage had been Sue's miscarriage. And as such crises do, this one erupted out of the blue. One day getting up from her desk at work, Sue felt a sudden wrenching sensation as if something deep inside her had torn. The next thing she remembered, she was lying on the floor looking up at her supervisor, who was telling his alarmed-looking secretary to call an ambulance. Sue said the months following this incident were the bleakest of her life. "I kept asking myself, 'What's wrong with me?' I'd always thought of myself as a very capable person. Now all of a sudden here I was unable to do what every other woman in the world could do."

For Sue the low point of this period was a visit she and Ron made to a well-known Pittsburgh obstetrician. She had already consulted three other specialists, each of whom offered a different diagnosis. Now this man, who ran a series of chromosome tests on her, believed he had finally found the problem: Sue was infertile.* When she and Ron left his building, Sue remembers, it was raining. "We got in the car and just sat there for a while watching the rain run down the windshield, then we both began to cry." Sue stopped and took a sip of her coffee, the brisk, self-confident air gone. Suddenly she looked small and vulnerable. Ron placed his hand on hers.

* Sue's "infertility" was subsequently diagnosed as endometriosis, an easily remedied defect of the uterine wall.

"An experience like that either drives you apart or brings you closer together," Ron said. "It brought us closer together."

Sue nodded.

I scored the Self variable as a potential plus for the Akerses.

Then I reached into my briefcase, pulled out two rectangular-shaped jewelry boxes, and placed them on the coffee table between my chair and the sofa were Ron and Sue were sitting. Inside each box were fifteen pennies, divided equally into three containers marked Friendship, Partnership, and Romance. I told the Akerses I'd like them to play what we called the Penny Game. This version of the game was different from the one described in Chapter Two. It was used to gain insight into a couple's standing on another important transition domain: Expectations. How did the husband and wife expect the baby to change their marriage and their lives?

The idea that expectations might play an important role in the marital satisfaction of new parents first occurred to me during a conversation with a friend who had separated from his wife midway through the transition to parenthood. Like most recently divorced individuals, he was full of theories about why his marriage had failed; also like most such individuals, his theories all centered around his wife and her failings. However, as I listened to him, it occurred to me that the real source of his marriage's collapse had not been his wife but rather his own unrealistic expectations about what the transition would bring.

A baby can and often does add a new element of harmony and closeness to a marriage, and can and often does give parents a new sense of purpose. But a baby rarely produces these changes quickly, painlessly, or cheaply. It occurred to me as I listened to my friend that people like him who idealize the baby and the effect he will have would be much more vulnerable to the kind of violated expectations that can produce disillusionment with a spouse, a marriage, and even parenthood. This thought led me to form a hypothesis, which our data subsequently confirmed. Individuals who enter the transition with fewer idealistic (or what we usually referred to as romantic) expectations ("The baby will change my life and marriage") and fewer exaggerated ones ("He will change them tomorrow") are more likely to emerge from the transition happier about their marriages and their spouses than individuals who enter the starting gate wearing rose-colored glasses.

Over the course of the Project we developed three tools for measuring expectations. The first two were relatively direct and straightforward. We asked our couples to answer open-ended questions about their expectations and to fill out multiple-choice questionnaires. The Penny Game was designed to tap into expectations in a more subtle way. We used it to assess the "transition-readiness" of a husband's and wife's expectations as they entered the starting gate. Typically individuals who scored high on the Friendship and Partnership components of the game were less vulnerable to marital disillusionment because they tended to be pragmatists who took one day at a time, while individuals who scored high on the Romance component were very vulnerable because they tended to idealize both the baby and parenthood. Our players were not told any of this, however.

When I introduced the Penny Game during the intake interview, I would tell the husband and wife that we wanted to get an idea of how they viewed their relationship as they approached the transition. In order to help us do that, I asked them to remove the fifteen pennies from their boxes and to distribute them into the three containers in a way that they thought best reflected the relative weight they currently attached to the Friendship, Partnership, and Romance components of the relationship. If they saw their marriage primarily as a partnership of two people living under the same roof, working together to make life easier than it would on one's own, most of their pennies should go into the Partnership container. If they saw it primarily as a friendship of two people who shared mutual interests and confided in each other, their spending should reflect that attitude. If they saw their relationship as a romance between two people very physically attracted to each other, they should distribute the pennies accordingly.

Normally participants accepted my explanation at face value. Sue did not. After Ron finished inspecting the pennies in their boxes, she asked how much time they would have to play the game.

"Take as much time as you like," I said, "but it isn't a test. There aren't any right or wrong answers."

Sue said she understood that. "But the game must have something to do with the baby and marriage. You wouldn't be asking us to play if it didn't. True?"

"True," I admitted.

"So some of these roles must be better for new parents than others, true?"

I considered this for a minute, then said, "True."

"So in a way there are right and wrong answers."

"That depends on how you look at it," I replied.

I thought this answer sounded a little limp, and so did Ron, who, I noticed, was enjoying this exchange immensely.

Our participants' average scores on the Penny Game were a six for Friendship, a four for Partnership, and a five for Romance. An ideal score—that is, one that reflected very transition-worthy expectations—was a seven for Friendship, a five for Partnership, and a three for Romance. Ron's and Sue's scores, were a six, six, and three, respectively. I listed the Expectations domain as a potential plus for the Akerses.

Another transition domain we tried to get a feel for during the intake interview was a couple's Gender Ideology. This might be defined as one's belief about how men and women ought to behave. Does the individual see work solely or primarily as a masculine role and homemaking and parenting as solely or primarily a feminine role? Or does the individual see these as roles men and women can play interchangeably and equally well? The answers to these questions, which are often shaped by childhood experiences, become very important during the transition because they determine what kind of a partner (or helper) a wife expects to ask for and what kind of help or contribution a husband feels obligated to make. A shared ideology usually made this domain a plus for a couple because it meant the wife's requests for support and the husband's sense of appropriate involvement would dovetail, minimizing their vulnerability to division-of-labor and work conflicts. Disparate ideologies made it a negative because this generally meant there would be such a gap between what the wife wanted the husband to contribute and what the husband was actually willing to give that the couple would spend the better part of the transition fighting about who does what and who makes which career sacrifices.

Our principal tools for collecting information on the Gender Ideology were the Who Does What and Work sections of the Marital Quality Questionnaire. However, the couple's behavior during the intake interview usually provided some clues as to whether the husband and wife were Traditionalists (believed work and family roles should be divided strictly according to gender), Transitionalists (believed such roles are interchangeable up to a point), or Egalitarians (believed such roles should be equally divided).

I found Sue relatively easy to pigeonhole. Her combination of domesticity and egalitarianism suggested that she was what I came to think of as a Personality-Driven Egalitarian. The women who fell into this category—and we had a number of Project wives who did—often did not possess any special allegiance to egalitarianism or feminism as ideological concepts. They were Egalitarians for the same reason a painter paints or a writer writes: It was part of their nature. They just automatically expected to be treated as equals. Even though their abilities would have allowed them to operate in the more high-powered, competitive environment of a Philadelphia, New York, or Los Angeles, these women remained in central Pennsylvania because, like Sue, they were deeply attached to its neighborly, Sunday-dinner life-style. But their energy, talent, and drive automatically made them career-oriented. Small-town lawyers, store managers, nursing supervisors, teachers, and entrepreneurs, they may have chosen to work on a smaller canvas, but they almost always ended up trying to paint a big picture on it. This meant that they needed and demanded a significant spousal contribution in the division-of-labor and work (i.e., career sacrifices) categories. Strong-willed, these women also expected their demands to be met. The husband who told an Egalitarian wife he could not pick up their child at the center after work usually did so at his own peril.

Ron's gender ideology was harder to ascertain. When I arrived, he was in the kitchen washing the dinner dishes, and when Sue said, "Wouldn't it be nice to have some coffee?" it was Ron who got up and made it. But this kind of solicitousness could be deceptive. In prebaby days men often do almost as much around the house as their wives. But postbaby only egalitarian men remain as active in household chores. Transitional men usually cut back. Was Ron a Transitionalist or an Egalitarian?

At first I was inclined to classify him in the latter group. His large-family background and domestic skills (he loved to cook, and I gathered he was accomplished at laundry and cleaning) were characteristic of the egalitarian men I mentioned in the last chapter. And so, too, was his forthrightness in describing Sue's financial abilities. Because they were deeply in love with their wives, these egalitarian men took unusual pride and satisfaction in spousal achievements. And because they were unusually secure, they also were able to do what a great many other men have difficulty doing: show pride in those achievements without wondering what a friend, colleague, or stranger like myself might think. However, toward the end of the interview an issue emerged that led me to question my original assessment of Ron's egalitarianism.

I don't remember who first brought up the video store. But I do remember how surprised I was by the intensity of Ron's reaction. He had spent most of the interview stretched out on the sofa beside Sue looking very relaxed. But mention of the store suddenly brought him to its edge, where he was now perched, his face flushed, and his expression somewhere between tense and wary—the picture of a man in the midst of a flight-or-fight response, I thought.

I asked the Akerses whose idea the video store had been.

"Mine," Sue said. "People are buying VCRs by the cartload, but almost no one rents videos. We could have a real money maker."

"I take it you weren't very enthusiastic about the store," I said to Ron.

He shook his head. "I didn't see the point. I'm sure Sue's right; she usually is about these things. But we were trying to have a baby, we had enough money and full-time jobs. What was a video store going to do except create a lot of headaches and work?"

"It could have been a cash cow," Sue said.

"I'd rather have a wife."

I asked Sue if she'd abandoned the idea because of Ron's objections.

"Partly, but I couldn't find a good site either. You know what they want for rents these days! Between the two I decided to put the store on hold for now."

"For now?" Ron said. "Hello, Sue, we're going to have a baby."

"For now," Sue repeated sweetly but firmly.

Sitting in my car after the interview, I reviewed the Akerses' scores. I had given them pluses on five of our six domains: Expectations, Self, plus three other domains we'll look at in the next two chapters (Communication, Emotionality, and Conflict Management). Normally such a rating would indicate a smooth passage through the transition. But I thought the Akerses might be an exception to this rule. Whatever form

Sue's ambitions ultimately took, if she was like the other Personality-Driven Egalitarian women in our study, it was likely that they would be big enough and time-consuming enough to demand a very large division-of-labor contribution from Ron as well as significant career sacrifices. There were probably going to be many nights Sue would not be home by five or six. How would Ron respond? I would need to know more about his gender ideology before I could answer that question conclusively. But if he was a transitional and not an egalitarian man, as the discussion of the video store suggested, I thought it likely the Akerses would spend so much time fighting about work and chores that the other advantages they brought to the starting gate would be canceled out.

I listed Gender Ideology as a negative for Ron and Sue, then put a circle around it.

4

Jennifer and Calvin Renselear: The Burden of the Past

Jennifer and Calvin Renselear grew up within five miles of each other in Boston, but they did not meet until they arrived at Haverford College in the fall of 1974. During orientation week Jennifer and her new dormmate, a girl named Julie Romano, were on a bus on their way to a welcoming picnic for freshmen when a very tall boy a few rows behind them began poking fun at Julie, who was overweight. Jennifer thought the boy's humor cruel and adolescent, and when she saw tears welling up in Julie's eyes, she decided to tell him so as emphatically as she could.

A week later Jennifer saw Julie's tormentor again; he was in her freshman composition class. She was not sure he remembered her, but when class let out, the boy, whose name was Calvin Renselear, introduced himself, said they had met at the freshman picnic, and asked if Jennifer would like to see a movie with him. After correcting his memory, Jennifer said no and stomped off. Despite her annoyance at his cheek, Jennifer found herself thinking Julie's tormentor attractive, forceful, and in a quirky way charming. He also proved relentless. Four years later Jennifer and Calvin were married in the small Catholic church where Jennifer had been baptized.

When I met the Renselears in 1984, Jennifer, thirty, and Cal, thirty-one, were settling into their first real home, a converted farmhouse they had bought after Cal became assistant technical director of a small computer software firm in the Penn State area. Outside, the house, which lay in a clearing at the end of a long unpaved road, was gray-shingled and glass-paneled on three sides. Inside, its hall gave way to a large living room with a dramatically high ceiling and then a kitchen with exposed brick walls, a wood-burning stove, and a pair of French doors that opened onto a small garden that was bordered on three sides by trees. Cal, who greeted me at the door, seemed immensely proud of the house. While we waited for Jennifer, who was still upstairs dressing, he showed me around, pointing out its restored details and explaining its history, which dated back to the nineteenth century.

In a way the Renselears' presence in this handsome old house was an accident. Originally they had planned to remain in California. Both had fallen in love with Mill Valley, a small town just north of San Francisco, while Cal was at Berkeley getting his Ph.D. in computer science. They had planned to return there and make it their permanent home after he finished his postgraduate work at UCLA. But a few months before the program ended, the job offer from the software firm suddenly materialized, so the Renselears joined lots of other young professionals who were then moving into central Pennsylvania. Like Cal, most of these newcomers worked in computer and defense firms. Also like him they were notably different from the area's other older, more established professional class, academics like myself. The cars these newcomers drove were a little bigger and sleeker, the clothes they wore more fashionable, the accents they spoke in more worldly and, often the newcomers were more materialistic as well.

The Renselears were the first couple from this new group to join the Project, and Cal, in particular, struck me as a good example of it. He was articulate, self-assured, and extremely polished. Usually first interviews are a little awkward, especially at the beginning and most especially when one of the parties has not arrived yet. But Cal managed to keep the conversation flowing effortlessly from the moment I arrived until the moment Jennifer burst into the kitchen twenty-five minutes later, breathless and full of apologies. She had been on the verge of coming downstairs twenty minutes ago, but then her mother had called—didn't Cal and I hear the phone ring? Earlier that day her niece had fallen and broken her wrist.

Physically the Renselears could have been matching bookends. Both were tall with long faces, sharp-pointed features, and dark hair. Emotionally they were quite different, but in ways that seemed to make them a good match. Cal was every inch the professional manager—smooth, authoritative, self-contained. In his own quiet way he was forceful and even a bit intimidating, an impression that was intensified by his basketball-player's height and broad shoulders. Jennifer, who had a long-stemmed body and swanlike attractiveness, was breathless, animated, and slightly distracted. Beneath her fluttery charm I suspected she was also a bit vulnerable. I noticed that whenever she spoke, she referenced Cal, as if she were seeking his approval and support.

When I asked about her background, she said she had grown up in West Roxbury, a well-to-do section of Boston, in a "conventionally happy family." Her father, now retired, had been an attorney in a prominent Boston law firm, her mother a homemaker and a community activist. She had one sibling, an older sister named Carol, whose youngest child had just broken her wrist. Though she described herself as a good student, Jennifer said she had never had any serious career ambitions. "For a while in college I thought about acting. I love the theater, and God knows I'm always accused of being dramatic. But I knew I didn't have the drive to be a successful actor. By nature I'm domestic. I like to cook and sew and I've always loved children. When we lived in Berkeley, I used to go down to the little baby park near Shattuck Drive and just sit and watch. I always thought the women I saw there had pretty nice lives."

This self-description struck me as a bit modest for someone of Jennifer's background. And indeed later in the interview when she expanded on her vision of domesticity, it became clear she intended to be the kind of homemaker her mother had been: socially prominent, active in the community, and also active in her husband's career.

When I asked Cal to describe his background, at first only a few sketchy biographical details emerged. He said he had grown up in Dedham, a few miles south of West Roxbury, and was the only child of two academics, an economist and an art historian. But under Jennifer's prodding he gradually began to fill in the dots between these bare details. As he did, the picture that emerged was one of a frightened, lonely boy caught between two angry, bickering, mismatched parents. "In my family there were no good guys or bad guys," Cal insisted. "It was just that my mother was a little ahead of her time, and my father had a little difficulty dealing with that."

"Cal's parents fought all the time," Jennifer said. "Cal, tell Jay about the time you asked them to sign a peace treaty."

Cal reddened.

I thought Jennifer might be pushing Cal further than he wanted to go. "If you'd rather not, don't worry," I said.

Cal considered this for a moment, then began telling me the story of the peace treaty in a very quiet voice.

Cal was seven when this particular incident occurred. As usual, he said, the fight that inspired it was provoked by his father, and as usual it was about his mother's housekeeping, which Cal described as a constant source of friction between his parents. "My mother had very advanced views on everything, including housekeeping. Her attitude was, 'If a mess bothers you, pick it up. Don't wait for me to do it.' "

Cal thought what made this particular argument so ugly was that his father, whose views on housekeeping were considerably less advanced, had had nearly two hours to sit and stew. When he arrived home to a kitchen full of unwashed breakfast dishes, his wife was still out teaching a late class. Sensing his dad's volcanic mood, Cal fled to his room, where he tried to distract himself with a book, but he found it hard to concentrate. He had been through this scene dozens of times before, and he knew what would happen the moment his mother walked through the door.

His parents' argument that night seemed so violent to Cal, it almost felt as if a wild animal had been let loose in the house, one who moved in rapid and noisy succession from the hall to the kitchen to the living room and would soon be snarling at his door if he did not do something immediately. "I was terrified," Cal recalled, "so I ran to my desk and made out a peace treaty with two provisions: From now on my mother would agree to clear the kitchen table before leaving for work, and in return my father would agree not to raise his voice." However, Cal said when he showed this treaty to his parents, they immediately co-opted it into their argument. " 'Look at what you've done,' " he recalled his mother yelling as she waved the piece of paper in front of her husband. " 'You've got your son so terrified of you, he wants you to sign a peace treaty. Some father.' "

" 'Some father?' " Michael Renselear shouted, picking up and then dropping an unwashed breakfast dish on the table for emphasis. " 'Some mother.' "

Cal said scenes like that had taught him a lot about the value of self-control. "Fighting never solves anything," he declared.

"Sometimes it's better than just stewing and brooding. That's what Cal does when he's mad," Jennifer said, turning to me.

Cal shot her a not-entirely-friendly glance.

It seemed an opportune moment to play the Penny Game. I took out my boxes and placed them on the kitchen table in front of the Renselears and explained how the game worked. Inside each box were fifteen pennies divided into three containers marked Partnership,

Friendship, and Romance. I told Cal and Jennifer to remove the pennies and distribute them in a way that best characterized their relationship now. If they thought the Romance component was higher than the Friendship and Partnership components, their spending should reflect that. If they thought all three components were equally important, they should divide their pennies accordingly.

This time there was no inspection of the coins as there had been with the Akerses. Jennifer and Cal were brisk and businesslike in making their spending decisions. When they pushed their boxes across the table to me, I counted eight pennies in Jennifer's Romance container (plus six in Friendship and two in Partnership) and seven in Cal's Romance (plus six in Friendship and three in Partnership). I was surprised. Whatever else they might be, the Renselears clearly were not star-crossed lovers. But as we talked, it became clear that Cal's and Jennifer's expectations were romantic in a special way. Almost all couples approach the starting gate expecting the baby to bring some good things into the marriage and their lives, and the Renselears were no exception. Like a great many women with career-minded husbands, Jennifer hoped the baby would increase the time Cal spent at home. Like a great many men with stay-at-home wives, Cal hoped the baby would give Jennifer a new source of interest and engagement. And like most couples who come to parenthood after a long relationship, Cal and Jennifer both expected that within a year—maybe even less—they would be able to bring the baby along when they went biking or hiking or engaged in another activity they both enjoyed.

What made the Renselears' expectations overly romantic, then?

While they expected the baby to bring a good many relatively realistic things, they didn't expect that along with the good he also would bring some bad in the form of exhaustion, unsatisfying sex, and a host of other common transition-time complaints. During the transition such one-sided expectations can be as threatening to marital happiness as wildly unrealistic ones. When a couple anticipates only the good, they assume it must be someone's fault when they encounter the bad. So instead of taking the bad in stride as do parents who see trouble and strife as an inevitable part of the transition, they begin pointing fingers—sometimes at each other, sometimes at the marriage, sometimes at themselves, and sometimes even at the child.

When I asked them both if they saw any stresses or strains associated with becoming new parents, Jennifer became a bit brisk with me. "Obviously there'll be a lot of new work," she said, "but I'm getting a woman in to help me."

"Don't forget, we'll have to get up nights too," Cal reminded her.

"That doesn't bother me," she said. "I don't need much sleep. You know that. We're all going to be very happy. I'm sure of it."

Jennifer said this with some determination. On the long road to this handsome old house in the woods, she had dreamed a lot of dreams and she wasn't going to let go of them easily.

I listed Expectations as a negative for the Renselears. It was time to ask them about a major crisis.

Cal and Jennifer agreed that the most serious conflict in their marriage had occurred during Cal's last semester at Berkeley and was triggered by Jennifer's opposition to the UCLA move. Jennifer still remembered clearly the day Cal told her he wanted to do an additional two years of postgraduate work there. It was an unseasonably warm Saturday in December, and they were in Golden Gate Park having a picnic lunch. She also remembered very vividly her reaction to Cal's announcement. "I thought, 'Here I am, twenty-eight years old, I have no money, no baby, no home, a job I loathe, and a husband I hardly ever see. And now after five years of living a hand-to-mouth graduate student's existence, he wants me to go on for another two years.' I told Cal it wasn't fair, it wasn't fair at all."

Cal, who suddenly looked very defensive, insisted that he had wanted children, too, but he had looked upon these two years as an investment in his career. "And look," he said, making a sweeping gesture around the Renselears' living room, "they paid off."

Cal and Jennifer are very private people. So it was difficult to get a clear picture of exactly what happened during Cal's last semester at Berkeley. But from the few details I could piece together, they seemed to have drifted apart. Jennifer became sulky, provocative, and when she thought she had pushed Cal too far, dependent. Cal retreated into his work. During this period Jennifer said she barely saw him and when she did, "he had up that little wall he puts around himself when he's mad or upset." However, the Renselears did not seem to have fought much. Their antagonisms were expressed between the lines in sullen glances and sulky silences.

"We're not shouters or finger-pointers," Jennifer said. "When we disagree, Cal avoids, and I pout and cling."

The closest the crisis seems to have come to a confrontation was a conversation the Renselears had one April afternoon at Cafe Mediterraneum, a coffee house on Telegraph Avenue in Berkeley. Jennifer, who was in a sulk that day, had barely said a dozen words since sitting down. After three failed attempts to start a conversation, Cal decided he had had enough. "Look," he said in the quiet, controlled voice he used when he was very angry, "I'm going to do this thing. You can come along or you can not come along. That's up to you. But I'm going."

"That really frightened me," Jennifer said. "Cal never issues ultimatums like that."

Now Cal was looking guilty as well as defensive.

"I'm sorry, I didn't mean it. You know that."

"Well, you certainly sounded like you meant it."

I asked what happened after the ultimatum.

"What always happens when we disagree," Jennifer said. "Cal waited for me to come around."

Cal reached over and put his hand on his wife's.

The Renselears' handling of this crisis suggested that they also might have trouble with two other important transition domains and, in both cases, for the same reason: the burden of Cal's childhood memories. The first domain I thought might give them difficulty was Self, which mediates a couple's ability to join forces and work together during a crisis. Usually when a man fails to join the common cause during the transition, it is because of his intense self-focus. He is so self-involved that he fails to see how much his wife needs assistance. Or he ignores her needs because he considers his own more important. Cal's ultimatum suggested that he was not deficient in self-focus. But the way he totally absented himself from his marriage during the UCLA episode also suggested that he might be reluctant to link arms with Jennifer for another reason as well. His childhood experiences had made him conclude that the best way to deal with any kind of crisis was to do what his parents had not done—run away from it.

Cal's refusal to confront Jennifer about their differences also indicated that those experiences might make Conflict Management a significant negative for the Renselears. Studies show that the baby creates so many new differences between the parents—and crystallizes so many latent ones—that the incidence of marital conflict increases by between 30 percent (our figures) and 92 percent (those of a recent University of California study). At the start of the Project conventional wisdom held that the happiest new parents were ones who fought very little. But by the time of the Renselears' intake interview, our data indicated the opposite. Often couples who know how to fight constructively do quite well during the transition, whereas couples who do what the Renselears did during the UCLA episode—avoid confronting their differences—do not do well.

I listed the Self and Conflict Management as potential negatives for Cal and Jennifer.

During the interview I also scored three domains as significant pluses for them. The first, and in some ways the most significant, was

Gender Ideology. Cal and Jennifer were Traditionalists—or, perhaps more accurately in their case, High Traditionalists. I do not think either of them imagined that after the baby, Jennifer would spend all her time changing diapers, washing dishes, and baking cookies. No doubt she would do some of these things because she really did seem to enjoy domesticity. But she would also spend a lot of time playing the other roles she and Cal both wanted her to play (and their financial position allowed her to play): hostess, community activist, and charming, socially adept wife of a prominent young executive.

I know that these days Traditionalism of all kinds is in the ideological doghouse. But as I pointed out earlier and will again in some detail in Chapter Seven, our study strongly suggested that what makes Gender Ideology a plus for new parents is not whether the couple has a politically correct ideology, but whether, like Cal and Jennifer, they have a shared one.

I also thought the Renselears might score highly on the variable we called Emotionality. One subtle influence on marital satisfaction during the transition is the individual's perspective on events. If she tends to see the glass as half full—that is, if she tends to focus on all the positive changes the baby has produced—she becomes more tolerant not only of the problems and stresses the baby produces but also of her spouse and his failings. Conversely, if she tends to see the glass as half empty—that is, if she focuses primarily on the stresses and problems—she develops not only a lower tolerance for transition-time difficulties in general but for her spouse and his failings in particular.

Emotionality, a psychological predisposition, is what determines how the glass looks to a new parent. And our primary tool for measuring a participant's standing on it was a series of questions attached to the Marital Quality Questionnaire. But from what I had seen and heard during the Renselears' intake interview, I was fairly confident that their scores would place them on the positive side of the Emotionality spectrum.

I listed Emotionality alongside Gender Ideology as a potential plus for them.

The Renselears also had one other potential strength: their age. A lot of the things that happen during the transition can threaten self-esteem in a way that produces unhappiness with a marriage, a partner, and even parenthood itself. In the case of a woman these threats include unflattering physical changes, doubts about parental competence, and concern about lost career opportunities. In the case of a man they include concern about measuring up to new financial responsibilities and the experience of seeing oneself supplanted by the baby as the chief object of wifely affection. Age does not offer immunity from these threats. However, because of their greater maturity, parents age thirty and over are often less vulnerable to these upsets than younger couples.

Would Cal and Jennifer be able to draw on these strengths during the transition?

I thought that if they could, their marriage would very likely improve. But as I drove home after their interview, I also thought that their ability to take advantage of these pluses would largely depend on Cal's ability to confront and overcome the ghosts of his childhood.

5

Lem and Tina Carlson: The Choice

Lem Carlson remembered not wanting to go to the party. It was a Friday and he was tired after a week of teaching. Besides, it was a forty-five-minute drive from Hershey to Gettysburg, and the radio was predicting rain. But his friend, Nancy, who taught at the same junior high school, insisted that the party would be fun. On the drive to Gettysburg, she mentioned that it was being given by Tina Marshall, the younger sister of an old college roommate. Tina was a junior at Gettysburg College and, according to Nancy, "very pretty and very sweet. I think you'll really like her."

The party was in an old apartment building about two miles from the battlefield. When Lem arrived, he noticed a group of boys standing in a semicircle near the kitchen. It was not until one of them turned to put his glass on a table that Lem realized there was a girl standing in the middle of the circle, and it was not until another boy moved away to greet a friend that he realized how spectacularly pretty she was. She was tall and slim with delicate features and reddish-blond hair. "That's Tina," Nancy said, grabbing his arm. "C'mon. I'll introduce you."

When I met the Carlsons two and a half years later, they had been married for less than a year and were living on University Avenue, a few blocks from Penn State's main campus. Their apartment, a cluttered two-bedroom across from a mini-plaza, was decorated like most of the other student apartments in the area. Posters covered the walls, and books and albums were scattered around the floor. The furniture, which had been acquired mostly at garage sales by Lem, was functional. A red futon served as the living-room couch, and a card table as the dining-room table; most of the chairs were metal and collapsible. Tina, who greeted me at the door, seemed a bit embarrassed by the state of the apartment, which she blamed on Lem's frugality. "It has a low rent, and Lem hates to spend money," she said. On my next visit, she promised, I would find the Carlsons living a more grown-up life. They had just bought a new house and would be moving into it next month. When we arrived in the living room, Lem, who was sitting on the futon reading a book, got up to greet me. He reminded me a bit of Sam Sheppard, the playwright-actor. He was tall and lanky with longish brown hair, deep-set eyes, and chiseled features.

Like the Renselears and an increasing number of our other recent participants, the Carlsons were also newcomers to central Pennsylvania. Two years earlier Lem had moved from Hershey to take a teaching position at the local high school. Tina, who remained in Gettysburg to finish her senior year, joined him in June 1983, when they were married. Though it was now ten months later, the Carlsons were still celebrating their reunion. During intake interviews, it was not unusual for couples to occasionally touch and hold hands; Lem and Tina never stopped touching and holding hands through theirs.

The Carlsons were also different from our other couples in two other ways that intrigued me. First, they were notably younger. The average age for Project wives was twenty-eight; for husbands, twenty-nine. Tina was twenty-three and Lem was twenty-five. Second, they were entering the transition at a much earlier point in their marriage. Typically the period between wedding and parenthood for our couples was three years. Lem and Tina would become parents shortly after celebrating their first wedding anniversary. I was eager to explore these differences, but first I wanted to know more about each of them and their backgrounds.

Emotionally the Carlsons seemed similar in certain ways. Both were quiet, soft-spoken, thoughtful, and deliberative. Of the two, Tina appeared to be the more outward-going and, at least where the relationship was concerned, the more strong-willed. When the teaching job in State College materialized, she had not protested Lem's taking it. But in return for tolerating the separation it would involve, she did insist that he make the 250-mile round-trip commute to Gettysburg every weekend. And despite his complaints about equity, she prevailed. During their fourteen-month separation Tina visited State College once.

When I asked about her background, she said she had grown up in Harrisburg, the youngest daughter of two civil servants. Her father was an official in the Pennsylvania Department of Taxation and Finance, while her mother worked in the Department of Housing and Urban Affairs. Of the two, Tina described herself as closer to her father, who she said was very similar to herself in temperament. "Mom and Barbara [Tina's older sister] have these big, overwhelming personalities," she said. "Dad and I are more soulful and reflective. He had"—Tina corrected herself—"He has this wonderful ability to make you feel he understands you like no one else in the world."

Lem, who was even more soft-spoken than his wife, struck me as intelligent and shrewd. His answers to my questions were to the point and sometimes surprisingly insightful. He also appeared mature for his age. Younger men and women are frequently a little intimidated by the barrage of personal questions we ask during intake interviews. Lem handled my interrogation with poise and assurance, answering the questions he wanted to answer and deftly avoiding the ones he did not. Underneath his laconic exterior he also seemed to have a fair amount of ambition. During the interview he displayed a finely tuned knowledge of the academic pecking order at his school and what he would need to do to move up in it. It was only a suspicion at this point, but I had the feeling that Lem was the anchor in the Carlsons' marriage.

The background he described was a bit more modest than Tina's. He grew up in Hershey, had an older brother who was now a police officer, as Lem's father had been until his death in 1981. Academically, athletically, and socially he had been an outstanding student. He was a track star with statewide ranking his junior year and president of his senior class. When he mentioned this last position, Tina added one critical detail to her husband's biography. "In separate balloting," she said, "the senior girls also voted Lem 'sexiest boy.' "

I began the interview by asking the Carlsons to tell me about a major crisis in their relationship.

Their replies explained why they were entering the transition so early. Originally their plan had been to wait three or four years before starting a family. Lem wanted to build a financial nest egg first, and Tina wanted some time to settle into her new job as an administrator at a regional office of the Pennsylvania Department of Social Services. But then last September she found her menstrual period one, two, then three weeks late. Was she pregnant? Right up until the moment Tina placed a strip of litmus paper from a home pregnancy kit into a vial of testing fluid, she was inclined to doubt it. How could she be? She and Lem were always so careful. Fifteen seconds later when the mustard-yellow strip turned a bright pregnancy pink, Tina's mouth dropped open in amazement.

The Carlsons said the next four weeks were a period of great strain and turmoil in their marriage. But listening to them describe these weeks, it also seemed to me that they had been something else as well —a period of mutual discovery. Equally confused and uncertain, Lem and Tina helped each other sort out their very complex feelings about this unexpected new development in their lives. However, right from the beginning, both had been clear on one point: If Tina chose to have an abortion, Lem would support her. "Even if I ended up leaning the other way," he said, "I told Tina I wouldn't pressure her. I didn't think that would be fair."

Initially there seemed to be some fairly compelling reasons to consider the abortion option. Lem was worried about money. They were banking most of Tina's salary now, but if she continued to work after the baby, most of that money would go to a baby-sitter or day-care center; if she didn't work, could three people really live on the $22,500 he made per year? Either way they could forget about buying a house for the next few years. Tina was worried about her work. She was twenty-three years old. Could she handle a new baby on top of a new job? And both were worried about the new chores a baby would create. Did they really want to come home to a houseful of work after an eight- or nine-hour day? And what about the baby's disruptive effect on this wonderfully romantic time in their lives?

One day during a conversation Lem took a yellow legal pad out of his briefcase and wrote "Disadvantages" on one side of its top sheet. Under this heading he listed money, chores, time, and loss of freedom. On the opposite side he wrote "Advantages," put the pad on the coffee table where Tina could see it, and said, "Okay, why would we want to have a baby?" That afternoon the best and only really credible answer the Carlsons could come up with was fun. Tina thought the baby would be cute, Lem that it would make a good playmate. But in the discussions that followed, the Carlsons found their imaginations slowly starting to expand.

One night Lem told Tina that he found his perspective on his students changing. He had been surrounded by children since he began teaching, four years earlier, but now for the first time he was noticing the individual idiosyncrasies of his kids—the distinctive way this boy laughed and talked and frowned and the way that girl walked and furled her brow when she was puzzled. He wondered what it would be like to know that you were the source of those distinctive gestures and expressions—and the distinctive child they were a part of. He also told Tina that he had been thinking a lot lately about his father and the peculiarly proud way he used to say, "These are my boys," when he introduced Lem and his brother to strangers. Lem said that paternal voice did not sound funny to him anymore. He was beginning to understand the emotions behind it.

The Carlsons' discussion about what to do began to assume an urgency after an encounter Tina had one afternoon while returning home from work on the bus. Two stops after her a young woman got on with a child Tina guessed to be about fourteen or fifteen months old. He had on a pair of Osh-Kosh jeans so big that as the bus bumped along Route 322, his head kept popping up and down behind the bibbed front like a jack-in-the-box, and a pair of bright red high-top sneakers so tiny, they reminded Tina of the shoes she used to buy for her dolls. Seven months later Tina could still not articulate why this encounter had had such a profound impact on her. But when she got home that night, she told Lem she was leaning toward having the baby. He told her that he was too.

"We decided to go ahead with the pregnancy a week later," Tina said.

The Carlsons' handling of this crisis suggested that two transition factors might be important pluses for them. The first was the Self factor. Lem's and Tina's behavior during this episode indicated that each had a great capacity for setting aside individual perspectives and goals and joining together to work for the common good. The other domain I thought they might do well on was Communication.

One of my favorite metaphors for the transition is that of a storm-ravaged ship. One moment a couple is sailing along in calm waters, the next they and their ship are swept up in a tremendous gale. Hurricane-force winds rip at the sails and wave after mountainous wave crashes upon the deck, snapping lines and cables. In order to prevent the ship and all hands from going down at such a perilous moment, a high degree of teamwork becomes absolutely essential. But in order to coordinate their efforts under such difficult conditions, a couple must know how to communicate complex thoughts, feelings, and instructions in a way that is both economical and crystal clear. The reason why so many new parents complain about communication disruptions and breakdowns is that they enter the transition without stormworthy communication skills.

As we shall see in Chapter Ten, how a couple develops such skills is a complex process. But simply put, the key determinant is how much time and energy they devote to relationship building in the prebaby years. Husbands and wives who spend relatively little time trying to meld their individual selves into a larger Us—who, in other words, are content to lead largely independent emotional lives—often develop such weak communication skills that the storm overwhelms them and they fall into silence. By contrast those who devote a great deal of time to creating a larger Us often retain the ability to talk meaningfully under even the most chaotic of conditions. The Carlsons handling of Tina's pregnancy—the way they thrashed this issue out until they arrived at a mutually satisfactory solution—suggested that they fell into the larger category.

I listed both the Self and Communication domains as potential pluses for the Carlsons.

Lem's and Tina's scores on the Penny Game were the same. Each got a six on Romance, a five on Friendship, and a three on Partnership. Normally such numbers would make Expectations a significant negative for a couple. But in the Carlsons' case there was a countervailing factor: the nature of Tina's pregnancy. At the start of the Project we thought a planned pregnancy would be a plus for a couple because it reflected a certain degree of forethought and preparation. But to our surprise the opposite turned out to be the case. We found that couples like the Carlsons were somewhat more likely than planners to emerge from the transition happier about their marriage. The advantage of an unexpected pregnancy was not huge, but it was large enough to reach statistical significance. And more to the point the advantage appeared to have its roots in the way such a pregnancy subtly influences a couple's expectations.

Whatever their scores on the Penny Game, "unplanners," such as Lem and Tina approach the starting gate with great anxiety and trepidation. If they had wanted a child, they would have planned to have one. Now, for a variety of reasons, they have decided to proceed with the pregnancy, but that decision does not entirely lessen their ambivalence and doubts. Ironically these troubling emotions often end up having an unexpected salutary effect: They tend to boost a couple's standing on the Expectations domain in two ways. The first is by making the bad parts of the transition seem not all that bad. Not expecting paradise, unplanners are not unduly surprised when the baby turns out to have an almost infinite capacity for tears and when bills begin piling up with astounding speed. "What else could you expect?" the unplanner thinks. The other advantage of the unplanner's trepidation and ambivalence is that it makes the good parts of the transition seem almost transcendentally good. "Who would have dreamed I could love anyone like this?" or "Who would have dreamed the baby would make me feel so good about myself?" For a new parent who is expecting nothing but trouble and strife, such thoughts are especially resonant.

I listed Expectations as a potential plus for the Carlsons. Then I moved on to the next domain, Emotionality.

Our preliminary rating of participants' standing on Emotionality was based on the way they answered our questions about the pregnancy. The period leading up to the baby's birth, and in particular the last trimester before his arrival, is a roller coaster of highs and lows. There is the excitement of approaching parenthood, the sense of entering a new stage in one's life, and often a new sense of closeness in the relationship as well. The mother- and father-to-be feel bonded together in a newer, deeper way. But for a woman pregnancy can also bring great discomfort, unflattering physical changes, and puzzling mood swings. For a man it can bring intimidating new pressures. There is concern about money, about work, and, in the back of most men's (and women's) minds, about how the new baby will affect the marital relationship. The couple's sex life is also disrupted, as are many of the familiar routines they relied on to enrich and revitalize their marriage.

In answering our questions about pregnancy, participants always mentioned the highs and lows. Over time, however, we noticed that husbands and wives who tended to dwell on its gratifications usually ended up scoring on the positive side of the Emotionality spectrum. (As we shall see in Chapter Eight, emotionality occurs along a spectrum, and very few people are purely positive or negative; most are inclined in one direction or another.) Participants who tended to dwell on the problems and difficulties of the pregnancy usually ended up scoring on its negative end. Initially the Carlsons' status as unplanners made it hard to get a clear fix on their position. Was the fairly large number of doubts and anxieties they voiced a reflection of temperament or a reflection of Tina's unexpected pregnancy?

Toward the end of the interview I decided that in Lem's case these doubts and worries arose from his unplanner's apprehension, not a negative disposition. This decision was based on a number of factors, but the most compelling was Lem's talent for noticing the positive side of problems facing him and Tina. He displayed this ability first when we were discussing sex. Like most new participants the Carlsons were guarded in their discussion of this topic. But in passing, Lem did mention that while Tina's growing size had "complicated" their sex life, it had also inspired a creativeness. He displayed this ability for noticing the positive a second time when he was discussing his new feelings toward his students and his father. If the prospect of parenthood had suddenly confronted him with an array of unexpected and frightening problems, Lem noted with satisfaction, it had also deepened him as a teacher, a son, and a man.

This ability to find the silver lining in a problem is why, even at the worst of times, the glass always looks half full to a new parent with a positive disposition. Nothing can make a sleepless night with a baby fun, but if you are able to tell yourself, "At least we're getting some one-on-one time together" (and believe it), this gratification will help take the edge off your fatigue. Equally important, your talent for noticing the bright spots will also help protect your marriage. By feeling that you have received some compensation for your sleeplessness (time with the baby), at breakfast the next morning you will not be as contentious with your well-rested spouse as the parent who has no gratifications to set against her exhaustion and sense of being taken advantage of.

I listed Emotionality as a potential plus for Lem.

Tina's score on it was based on a story she told midway through the interview. She said that about four months ago she noticed something missing in her life and that one day last December while Christmas shopping she realized what it was.

"I wasn't being looked at anymore," she said.

Lem smiled. "You mean checked out."

"Don't," Tina said, suddenly looking very hurt. "I know it sounds childish. But it was something I was used to. I like being noticed. It's validating to know that you're found attractive." She stopped for a moment, then added, "I don't like being invisible."

"But you look beautiful now," Lem insisted.

Tina frowned.

"How does it make you feel not to be noticed?" I asked.

"Fat. Before when I walked down the street, I always felt a little slinky and foxy, especially when I was dressed up. Now I feel like Mr. Potato."

Many women share Tina's unhappiness about their appearance (though some like the Rubenesque aspect pregnancy gives their body). But her description of it was telling in two regards. She did not mention any offsetting compensations, for example that the end point of her temporary bulk would be a new baby, and she ignored Lem's compliment. This tendency to block out everything but the bad is as characteristic of individuals with a negative predisposition as a talent for noticing the bright spots is of individuals with a positive predisposition. And it can make those sleepless nights with baby and many other aspects of the transition more difficult to endure.

In addition to individual scores, we also gave a husband and wife a couple's score on the Emotionality variable. If both were positive, it was listed as a plus; if both were negative, it was a minus; if one partner was positive and the other negative, we put a question mark next to it, as I did with the Carlsons. Emotionality could go either way for Lem and Tina.

Social support wasn't one of the transition domains we studied intensively. But a couple's relationship with parents, friends, and family can often have a profound influence on their adjustment to life with baby. And tension between Lem and Tina's father, Frank Marshall, appeared to make social support a potential trouble spot for them. This being a first interview and Tina being present, Lem was fairly guarded in his description of this relationship. But from what he did say, I gathered that he found Tina's father stiff and formal (Lem was still expected to address him as Mr. Marshall) and also insensitive. He said his clothes and hair were frequent targets of Frank Marshall's barbs.

"Daddy's only teasing you," Tina said. "He doesn't mean anything by it."

"I'm a big boy. I don't need my father-in-law to tell me when to get my hair cut and how to dress, and I especially don't need him to tell me in front of my wife."

The latest episode in this smoldering conflict, which I suspect had its roots in each man's resentment of the other's position in Tina's life, was set off when Lem declared a house "financially out of the question for now," and Tina, refusing to accept his no, went to her father for financial help.

"Daddy's been very generous," she said. "He and Mom are going to pay our whole down payment."

"Your father is not the appropriate person to decide when we should buy a house," said Lem, who clearly felt more ambivalent about his father-in-law's generosity.

"At least you could show a little gratitude," Tina snapped.

Lem started to reply but then thought better of it. He did not want to air their grievances in front of a stranger.

When I got out to my car, I examined the Carlsons' score. They had four pluses—Self, Communication, Expectations, and Gender Ideology (both Lem and Tina were Egalitarians)—and two question marks—Expectations and Emotionality. In addition, Lem's in-law problems made Social Support a potential trouble spot for them. It was a hard score to read. But by this point in the Project I had begun to develop an intuitive feel for the domains that would matter most to a couple during the transition. My guess was that for the Carlsons the most critical domain would be Emotionality. Whether their marriage thrived or declined in the years ahead would depend on the depth of Tina's negativity and whether Lem could help her cope with it, and on how intrusive Frank Marshall would become.

However, as with the Akerses and the Renselears, at this point I was uncertain about how successful they would be in meeting these challenges.

PART THREE
THE TRANSITION DOMAINS

A word about the organization of the chapters in this section. For the most part, they are built around the one-, three-, and nine-month in-home observations we conducted with our participating families. This structure, I felt, would give readers an opportunity to follow our three Project couples through the critical first year of the transition in real time, experiencing the events of that period as the couples experienced them. But the chapters also include material from a series of follow-up interviews that I did with the Renselears, the Carlsons, and the Akerses in the summer of 1991. Time has a way of changing our perspective, and in these follow-up interviews, which frequently frame the chapters, readers get an opportunity to see how the problems and challenges of the transition look to each couple, now seven to eight years later.

6

Can We Work Together?

Jennifer Renselear remembers that the bright green numbers on the digital clock in the delivery room were flashing 7:30 A.M. when she first realized something was wrong. Her obstetrician, who had been so calm a moment ago, was suddenly talking to the nurse in a tight little voice. A second later he was standing over her. The umbilical cord was wrapped around the baby's head; an emergency cesarean would be necessary. The next moment Cal was by her side. "They want me to leave," he said. He bent down, kissed Jennifer, whispered, "Good luck," and was gone. Everything that happened after that seemed to happen at fast-forward speed. Another doctor appeared, there was a hushed conference in a corner of the delivery room, then a metal post with a bottle attached appeared from out of nowhere. "This will hurt a little," the obstetrician said, attaching a catheter to the bottle. A moment later Jennifer felt a sharp prick at the base of her skull.

When her grogginess cleared a half hour later, her only memory of the delivery was of her obstetrician saying, "You have a new baby girl." But where was she? The only other person in the room was a nurse. She was standing at the other end of the bed scanning Jennifer's chart. Gradually another memory emerged. "Alert the neonatal

ICU," someone was saying. Was her baby all right? "I'll get your doctor," is all the nurse would say when Jennifer asked about her new child. When the doctor and Cal walked into her room a minute later looking grave, Jennifer felt a surge of panic. She was sure something terrible had happened. But the obstetrician was reassuring. Her baby's breathing had been a little labored. The ICU was just a precaution; they had wanted to keep her under observation for a few minutes. Everything was fine now. The obstetrician paused and looked at Cal. When he turned back to Jennifer, he said there had been a minor complication. During the delivery the displaced umbilical cord had caused a cranial hematoma. "It's nothing to worry about. Basically it's just a black-and-blue mark. It'll heal over in a couple of months."

Cal placed his hand on Jennifer's. "I gulped a little when I saw it, but it's not that bad really."

While Jennifer and Cal were talking, a nurse came into the room with their new baby. This time the feeling of panic was so bad that Jennifer thought she would vomit. The entire right side of Allison Renselear's head was covered with a reddish-purple swatch of skin.

After Cal and the obstetrician left, Jennifer spent the rest of the afternoon sitting by the window. It was a gray January day, and she remembers that the trees in the park across the street looked bleak and bare in the pale winter light. Several times she felt an impulse to cry, but she managed to keep it in check until the nurse brought Ali in again around four. Then Jennifer began sobbing uncontrollably.

The one bright moment in the period following Ali's birth was the day she came home from the hospital. Waiting for Cal in her room that morning, Jennifer felt cranky and depressed. She had not slept well the night before, Ali had spit up twice during her early feeding, and there had been an unpleasant scene with her obstetrician. As the days passed, Jennifer's feeling that the hematoma was something more than just a "bad black-and-blue mark" had taken on the aura of a conviction. It had to be more serious. Anything that frightening could not be just a bruise. Jennifer wanted a specialist to examine Ali—a big-city specialist. But earlier that morning when she asked her obstetrician for the names of some, he had been almost insulting.

"Ali's fine now," he said. "Hematomas aren't that uncommon. It'll heal over in a couple of months. I've told you that three times now."

Jennifer decided she was too tired and on edge to bother with politeness.

"I want a second opinion. I have a right to a second opinion. You must have people in Philadelphia or Pittsburgh you can recommend."

Reluctantly the obstetrician wrote the names of two doctors—one in Harrisburg, the other in Philadelphia—on a piece of hospital stationery. Jennifer was putting their names in her Filofax when Cal arrived. In his own quiet way he had been as upset about Ali as she was. But this morning he seemed perky, almost bouncy. "How are my two girls today?" he asked, kissing Jennifer on the cheek, then Ali, who was asleep in her arms. On this grim January morning Jennifer found her husband's high spirits annoying, jarring, like chalk scraping on a blackboard. An hour later at the Renselears' front door, Jennifer felt annoyed at Cal a second time. As she was walking into the house, he cut in front of her and entered first. She was about to say something sharp when she heard a familiar voice—was that her mother?

Jennifer peeked her head in the door. Maureen O'Brien, arms outstretched, was standing in the middle of the Renselears' living room. Next to her was Jennifer's father, Tim; her sister, Carol; niece, Maura, and their next-door neighbors, Jim and Andrea Cavellano. On the table in front of them was a big cake with the words "Welcome home Jennifer and Allison" written on top.

"Surprise!" everyone shouted.

At the Renselears' follow-up interview Jennifer could still recall nearly every detail of that welcome-home party. How delighted and touched she was when she learned Cal had arranged it, how tender Maura was with Ali, and, as the party stretched into the early evening, how much it began to remind her of the parties of her childhood. The men standing in the kitchen, drinks in hand, their voices rising and falling in waves as they argued about sports and politics; the women sitting in the living room, plates on their laps, talking about children in voices so hushed, they might have been whispers. Going to bed that night, Jennifer felt for the first time since Ali's birth that everything would turn out all right, but that wasn't to be.

One afternoon a few weeks later Cal got a call from Jennifer's obstetrician. He said he was worried about her. "She's called me several times in the past few days."

Cal sighed. "About the hematoma?"

"Does she talk about it much with you?"

When Cal said yes, the obstetrician mentioned the name of a psychologist. "She's very good. Why don't you talk to Jennifer about seeing her."

Seven years later, when I interviewed them, both Cal and Jennifer dated the gulf that developed between them to the conversation they had that evening. Jennifer left it feeling unsupported and a little demeaned. Instead of accusing her of being neurotic, why couldn't Cal be more understanding about her fears? Cal came away from it feeling frustrated. What was the matter with Jennifer? he wondered. Why couldn't she accept her doctor's reassurances instead of driving herself and him crazy about the hematoma?

The sense of drift and estrangement that afflicted the Renselears after this conversation is a common by-product of the transition, and generally it baffles new parents because frequently it does not—as it did with Cal and Jennifer—seem to have a single center or cause. No one big disagreement is pushing the couple apart, and their feelings about each other remain unchanged in fundamental ways. Yet in some indefinable but still very palpable way, their marriage has changed. It no longer nurtures, no longer fills them up the way it used to. They begin to drift apart until at last they find themselves feeling, as one Project father put it, like two ships passing in the night.

A number of phenomena can cause this drift and estrangement. However, in most cases it is rooted in a challenge unmet. The husband and wife are unable to join hands and meet the crisis of the transition together. The term *crisis* in this context conjures up images of piles of diapers, unpaid bills, and unwashed laundry. But these are simply the manifestations of the deeper and larger marital crisis the baby's arrival triggers. Can the husband and wife surrender their individual priorities, concerns, goals, hopes, and dreams and transform themselves into a team?

At the start of the Project we hypothesized that a couple's ability to answer this question successfully would be largely determined by two factors. The first was the man's willingness to step into the marriage and provide his wife with physical and emotional support. The second was the wife's ability to continue providing her husband with a measure of affection, attention, and understanding despite her all-consuming love affair with the baby. We believed that when both challenges were met, a marriage would remain sufficiently nurturing to keep a couple together. When the challenges were not met, it would come to feel so lifeless and empty—there would be such a sense of mutual disappointment and betrayal—that, like Cal and Jennifer, the husband and wife would go their separate ways emotionally, if not physically. At the end of the study this hypothesis was borne out, as was a second one we had formed. We believed that the couples who would have the most success transforming themselves into an effective team would be those where the husband and wife had developed the ability to balance the first two components of the Self variable—autonomy and affiliation—within themselves.

The notion that these two tendencies might affect the marital satisfaction of new parents first occurred to me while reading the work of feminist scholar Carol Gilligan of Harvard University. Over the past decade Dr. Gilligan has been studying the various ways autonomy and affiliation manifest themselves in human behavior, and her research has supported a commonsensical observation: While both men and women share a desire to be independent (autonomy) and to be linked to others (affiliation), generally they do not share these impulses to the same degree.* In men the overriding impulse is toward autonomy. When an American man asks himself, "Who am I?" his answer is likely to involve some variant of the Gary Cooper figure in *High Noon*—a tall man in a tall hat who steps out onto an empty street to face his fate alone and unafraid. Only secondarily does a man see himself as a father, husband, brother, son—as someone connected to others.

In women the overriding impulse is toward affiliation. When a woman asks herself, "Who am I?" she is likely to see a mother, a wife, a daughter, a sister, or a friend. In other words, she is likely to define herself largely in terms of the roles she plays in a complex network of relationships and then, only secondarily, as an independent, autonomous agent.

A moral problem Dr. Gilligan posed to two eleven-year-olds, Jake and Amy, nicely captures the profound way these two impulses shape each sex's thinking. Dr. Gilligan's scenario: A man whose wife is critically ill learns that his pharmacist has acquired an expensive new medicine that can save her. What should he do if he cannot afford it?

Jake's answer to this dilemma was a tall-man-in-a-tall-hat solution,

* Why men and women attach different priorities to autonomy and affiliation is still not fully understood, but the work of another feminist scholar, Nancy Chodorow, suggests that one important factor may be the different ways little boys and girls acquire a sexual identity. For a little girl this acquisition involves drawing closer to her primary caregiver, mother. Because this experience is so satisfying, the little girl grows up cherishing connectedness. Dr. Chodorow believes the reason boys grow up prizing independence is that in order to acquire a masculine identity, a boy must push away from mother and identify with the father. Because this experience of separating is so painful, he develops a lifelong suspicion of relationships and a desire to be autonomous, to be "his own man."

an act of individual daring and courage: The man should break into the pharmacy and steal the medicine.

Amy, on the other hand, saw the man's dilemma as basically a relationship problem. First he should explain his plight to the pharmacist (in order to evoke sympathy and support), and if that failed to produce the needed medicine, he should explain it to the pharmacist's family and friends and have them talk to him.

Reading Dr. Gilligan's work and the other recent research on autonomy and affiliation, it occurred to me that a great many of the behaviors that produce marital drift and estrangement during the transition are rooted in one or both partners' inability to balance these two impulses within themselves. For example, many of the disaffected Project wives I spoke to blamed their disaffection on two behaviors that are common manifestations of an unbalanced autonomy drive. Either the man refused to surrender his independence and step into the marriage and share parental responsibility, or he remained so preoccupied and self-absorbed that even when he did step in physically, emotionally he remained outside of it.

Conversely many of the behaviors that can produce disillusionment in a man are often expressions of an unbalanced affiliation need in a woman. For example many Project husbands complained that their wives became so preoccupied with the baby that they and their concerns were all but forgotten. Complaints about maternal dependency and clinging were also common. "If I get one more call about a watery bowel movement . . . ," said one exasperated father.

Why don't these unbalanced autonomy and affiliation needs cause problems for a couple prior to the transition? Often they do, because marriages where one partner is perennially insensitive and the other perennially dependent are not very satisfying to anyone. But usually a childless couple has so many props and compensations available that neither partner must achieve a very precise balance to maintain a reasonably nurturing relationship. The woman may wish her husband did not spend so much time outside the relationship involved in autonomous activities such as sports and work, and she also might wish that he would show a little more sensitivity to her thoughts and feelings when he was present. But she usually has a network of friends available to provide that sensitivity, as well as no large, urgent needs that require immediate husbandly attention. As a result, for a childless woman these wishes usually remain what the pea was to the princess who eventually fell asleep atop the pile of mattresses—an irritating but tolerable discomfort.

A conversation I had with Jennifer Renselear provides a case in point. "It's funny," she said, "I saw even less of Cal when he was in graduate school than I do now, but I wasn't nearly as lonely. Most of the women I knew then were in the same boat as I was. We were married to these high-powered Type-A men, who spent all their time studying and plotting their futures. But we had each other. If I wanted someone to talk to or to go to a movie with, all I had to do was pick up the phone. Life sure is different now."

Similarly an unbalanced affiliation need is generally easier for a childless husband to cope with. He might wish his wife didn't spend so much time on the phone with her mother, sister, and friends and that she wasn't quite so dependent on him. But because she still has enough energy and time to meet his companionship needs and because he has enough energy and patience to tolerate a certain degree of dependency, these common manifestations of an unbalanced affiliative drive also remain pea-sized irritants.

"You know," Cal Renselear said to me once, "I don't know whether Jen's gotten more dependent or I've gotten less tolerant, but since Ali came along, I find her need for reassurance much more draining than I used to."

As Cal's remark suggests, once the transition arrives, things change dramatically for a couple. Now suddenly few if any friends are readily available to provide all the support and understanding that seems needed. And now nearly all of the time, energy, and tolerance that were available in prebaby days to accommodate spousal idiosyncrasies are gobbled up by the family's newest and most demanding member. Furthermore these props and compensations begin to vanish just at the moment when the marriage is thrown into a state of crisis. Usually after a week or two of coping with all the new problems and chores of parenthood, the man and woman begin to feel as tired, beleaguered, confused, and frightened as the storm-tossed couple I described in Chapter Five. Gale-force winds and thirty-foot waves lash at them out of a sea that offers no hope of relief or rescue. Rather quickly it is realized, as Bonnie Raitt sings, There is "no turning back this time." The baby and parenthood are here to stay requiring husband and wife to cooperate with one another in ways that leave no margin for unbalanced autonomy and affiliation needs. If they are to navigate their relationship to a safe port each must give up a part of their individual selves. And this creates challenges for both partners.

For example, in order to support the crew's most vulnerable and exposed member, the man must now be willing to surrender not just a portion of his independence, as he did in prebaby days, but nearly all of it. This will involve curtailing or giving up activities such as work, sports, and hobbies that are very important to someone who cherishes independence. Is the man willing to make this sacrifice in the name of the common good? He also faces a task that can be even more difficult for him, given his bystander status in the transition. Is he also willing to surrender some of his self-focus so that he can see his wife through the emotional ups and downs that are an inevitable part of living in the eye of the storm?

Seeing a marriage safely into port also requires large sacrifices from a typical wife. For example a high affiliation impulse can make the powerful feelings that a baby evokes hard to control. Can a woman learn to regulate these emotions sufficiently to provide her husband with a measure of attention and affection? And because the husband can also become exhausted and frayed by the storm, can the woman regulate her dependency sufficiently to handle minor problems and upsets on her own?

Typically in marriages where all these questions are answered positively, chores are divided in a mutually satisfactory manner and the baby's problems are not blown out of proportion. There is also a growing sensitivity to the wife's need for emotional as well as physical support and the husband's need for companionship as well as a respect and appreciation for his tolerance and patience. If you look at the literature on the transition, you will find that most studies describe these characteristics as the ones a marriage must assume if it is to remain nurturing to a couple not as parents but as husband and wife, man and woman. And we found this to be true too. But we also found that the hundreds of small acts of empathy, understanding, and self-sacrifice required to build such a marriage serve as grace notes that make their own individual contribution to marital happiness. A story Genell Marganau, a Project wife, told me provides a case in point.

One of the major issues in the Marganaus' marriage was husband, Bob's, gym schedule. Ever since his late teens Bob had worked out four evenings a week, and his devotion to this routine bordered on the religious. "There were times, right after Anna's birth, I'd get absolutely furious at him," Genell told me one day. "I'd rush home at five to be with her, then Bob would come rolling in around nine after a two-and-a-half-hour workout. But I always bit my tongue because I didn't think it would do any good to complain. I figured everyone has a cross to bear. Some people have to live with asthma, I have to live with Bob's gym schedule." But then one night about six months after Anna's birth, Bob Marganau surprised his wife. Over dinner he announced that he had decided to change his gym schedule.

"I know it sounds trivial," Genell said. "Your husband offers to cut back to two workouts a week. Big deal! But I knew what an enormous sacrifice that represented for Bob, and it really affected my feelings toward him. I thought, 'If he'll do this for me, he'll do anything.' I don't know, maybe knowing that has made me nicer to him, but since that night we're different with each other."

When I asked how they were different, Genell thought for a moment and said, "I think we're kinder to each other now. I know Bob likes his shirts folded a certain way, so when I do the laundry, I fold them that way. It takes a little more time, but it pleases him. And he reciprocates. He knows how much I hate it when the inside of the car is dirty, so he always makes sure it's clean for me."

Behavior such as Bob Marganau's helped to confirm another hypothesis we formed at the start of the Project. As we suspected, the participants who had the most success balancing their autonomy and affiliation drives were those like Bob who scored high on the third component of the Self domain, security. Those who had the most trouble balancing these drives were men and women who scored low on it.

How does security help a new parent regulate his or her autonomy and affiliation impulses?

Bob Marganau's story illustrates one way it helps a new father. Not only are sports a common expression of autonomy in a man (they take him out of the family), for most men sports are also a very important source of self-esteem. Performing a 200-pound bench press makes a man feel good about himself, so he goes to the gym three or four nights a week. Hurling a baseball eighty miles an hour makes him feel good about himself, so he joins a baseball team. What distinguishes the secure from the insecure man is not that he finds these activities less validating—he doesn't. But he also does not need them to pump up his ego because his security and the high self-esteem it produces already have given him plenty of reasons to feel good about himself. Hence when more important responsibilities arise, he is able, like Bob Marganau, to cut back or walk away from his sports activities with relative ease because he does not feel that he is losing anything big or important. The insecure man is in a different and much more difficult position. He does not have many reasons to feel good about himself to begin with, and if he gives up his sports, he will have one big reason less. Thus when faced with a choice between living with a complaining wife, whom he can escape, or living with low self-esteem, which he can never escape, often the insecure man will choose the former.

I suspect that if we had compiled a Project wife's wish list, at the top or very near it would have been a wish for more spousal sensitivity. Since even in homes where a man did surrender a great deal of his physical independence, often the woman still found herself confronting that other common by-product of an unregulated autonomy impulse—self-focus. The man remained so preoccupied with his own concerns that he offered his wife as little emotional understanding and support as the husband of the Project wife who told me the following story:

One day when this woman's son, Jason, was in the midst of his teething difficulties, the family sitter, who was Jamaican, suggested a remedy called Gripe Water. "Mothers at home use it all the time to calm irritable, cranky babies," the sitter said the next day as she removed a bottle from her purse. The Gripe Water, which was packaged like a medicine, worked as advertised. Within minutes of taking a teaspoonful the unsoothable Jason was asleep. When the mother read the label, she discovered why. Gripe Water's alcohol content is 4 percent. Jason had not fallen asleep, he had passed out.

"I was horrified at my sitter," the woman said, "for suggesting the stuff and at myself for not reading the label before I let her give it to Jason." But at dinner that night when she tried to tell her husband how guilty and depressed she felt about the incident, she bumped into his self-focus in the form of the Monday-night football game. In order to be in front of the TV by game time, her husband had to finish some work he had brought home from the office. Because a prolonged discussion of maternal guilt and depression would disrupt his schedule, he made his reassurances as brief as decency would allow. He told her not to worry, that Jason looked fine. It would make a funny story for their grandchildren. Before the wife had a chance to say another word, he was gone.

I suspect the self-absorption that produced this and many other acts of male insensitivity arises from male biology and upbringing. But a man's security level also has an important influence on his ability to control this impulse. Insecure men like Cal Renselear often become so preoccupied with their anxieties and self-doubts that they end up blind to their wives' feelings and problems. At the Renselears' one-month observation Jennifer complained that Cal was so self-absorbed, "If I dropped dead in front of him, I don't think he'd notice." Conversely a man with few inner demons to distract him usually develops enough outward-looking focus not only to listen to a wife's concerns and fears with a measure of empathy but also to begin making the kinds of observations that can keep the crew's most exposed member safely out of harm's way.

An example of this was a small but potentially telling change that a Project husband, Will Ostrow, noticed in his wife Suzanne's drinking habits. Prior to her pregnancy, Suzanne and Will would have a predinner glass of wine. But when the Ostrows resumed this little ritual after daughter Natalie's birth, Will noticed that on many nights Suzanne's one glass of wine was now two. Will's response to this subtle sign of stress was as sensitive as his observation of it. Knowing Suzanne would feel guilty if he said anything, he kept his observation to himself. But he did quietly eliminate his own predinner wine, and with no one to drink with, Suzanne eliminated hers.

There are two other ways a regulated self-focus can contribute to marital harmony during the transition. Being outward-looking, the man now begins to notice how the baby's vaporizer works and where the dishes and groceries go and how much his wife likes it when he cleans out the car for her without being asked. These are the characteristics of a good team player, but they are also something else: they are the grace notes that help enrich and strengthen a marriage because they tell the new mother how deeply committed her husband is to her and to their new family.

Typically an outward-focusing male is also better able to regulate the activity that takes more new fathers out of the family than any other—work. Because work is the one autonomous activity that palpably benefits not just a man but his family, and it is also a pursuit men are taught to equate with good parenting, often even a secure man has trouble curtailing his work schedule. But in time his ability to notice what is happening around him as well as inside him will bring his wife's needs into focus. Once that happens, he usually comes to realize that, for now at least, the team's interests are best served if he comes home at five at the end of the day, when he is expected, instead of lingering at work.

How does security help a woman balance her autonomy and affiliation needs?

Our exploration of this question helped debunk one common myth about American men: They are threatened by strong, independent women. In many cases we found the opposite to be true. Often the more competent and independent a wife, the likelier a husband was to emerge from the transition feeling better about her and better about his marriage. A graphic case in point is the experience of the Personality-Driven Egalitarian couples I mentioned in Chapter Three. Nearly two out of three of these marriages, which are based on a shared, almost intuitive sense of equality, ended up in our Improvers column, and one of the most remarkable features of these unions was the boldness and independence of egalitarian wives.

As we shall see in the next chapter, there were a number of reasons why these couples did so well during the transition. But one reason stands out: The men in these marriages were deeply in love with their wives. It is reductive to try to explain the roots of an emotion as complex as human love in terms of a handful of behaviors. But in conversations with egalitarian men we did notice that the spousal behaviors they singled out as being especially important to them were all expressions of a strong autonomous impulse. One was the wife's ability to deal with problems and difficulties on her own. If something serious happened to the baby or her, an egalitarian woman made sure her husband knew about it quickly. But she handled all the little bumps of day-to-day life in the transition on her own. Eventually the husband did end up hearing about many of these bumps, too, but usually at a time and in an atmosphere that was relatively congenial to them. Egalitarian husbands rarely if ever received frantic phone calls about minor upsets or were hit with a wish list of concerns as soon as they sat down to dinner. This respect for their patience and tolerance affected them the way knowing what a wife wants without having to be told affects her. Such spousal thoughtfulness made these men feel better about their marriages and their spouses.

The reason the egalitarian woman's self-restraint often eludes the less secure new mother is a lack of confidence. The woman does not believe she can handle even minor problems on her own, so when confronted with an upset or difficulty, she immediately loses control of her affiliative impulse and reaches out to her husband for help and assistance.

A story one of these egalitarian husbands told me illustrates another reason why a strong, independent woman makes a better teammate during the transition. A few months after his son's birth this man and his brother had a business falling-out. They owned a small cement business together. The brother wanted to buy a new portable mixer, and the man, who felt the mixer was too expensive for a small company, did not. One afternoon this difference led to an argument; voices were raised, fingers were pointed, and ugly things were said on both sides. Arriving home that night, the man was still replaying the afternoon's events in his head, as most people do after an upsetting encounter. Had he been too stubborn? Was he wrong to say the things he had?

Initially the only reply his wife had to these troubling questions was, "I don't know." She was too preoccupied with the baby to focus on her husband's concerns. After she disappeared into the nursery, the man resigned himself to rehashing the argument by himself. But then his wife did something that surprised and touched him. Reappearing in the living room, she apologized for her inattentiveness. "I know you're very upset. Just give me a few minutes to put Gavin down," she said, "then I'll be back. I want to hear what happened."

Men expect and want their wives to form a strong attachment to the baby. Indeed a recent study by a joint Harvard–Boston University team found that the stronger the woman's attachment to the baby, the happier the husband tends to be. But this expectation also has a flip side. While the average new father will put many of his companionship needs on hold, he does expect his wife to continue meeting some of them. He also expects that when he has a very big concern, as this Project father did, he will receive priority at least for a few minutes.

In homes where these expectations are routinely violated, it is usually because the woman lacks the security to regulate her feelings toward the baby. At bottom most forms of maternal preoccupation are a kind of overidentification. The woman loses control of her affiliation impulse and begins to see the child and herself not as separate individuals but as one and the same person. The contribution insecurity makes to overidentification is a weak self. The woman's sense of herself as "me," the independent, autonomous person is so underdeveloped that the boundaries between her and the baby easily blur in her mind. Usually this blurring puts her in a difficult position vis-à-vis her husband's companionship needs because in order to meet them, she must turn away not from another person but from someone she sees as a part of herself—and the smallest, most vulnerable part of herself at that. Faced with such a choice, a new mother feels she has no real choice. She may and often does feel guilty about saying no to movies and to dinners out and for ignoring her husband's concerns. But given the alternative, what else can she do?

Overidentification also leads to another problem we rarely encountered in egalitarian marriages: blowing the baby's problems out of proportion. If you see the child as a separate individual, for the most part you will be able to view his cries, whimpers, coughs, and regurgitations with a reasonable degree of objectivity. But if you view him as the overidentifying mother does, it becomes very difficult to view these and all the other little upsets of infancy objectively. Jennifer Renselear's inability to get perspective on Ali's cranial hematoma arose from such overidentification. Because on some level Jennifer saw her daughter as a part of herself, when she looked at the bruise, what she saw wasn't the self-healing injury her obstetrician described but rather a wound to the smallest, most fragile part of herself. And how could she possibly be objective about that?

Egalitarian husbands also rarely complained about being criticized for their parenting style. Paternal love is slower to take flight, less dramatic and compelling. But this more laid-back style of attaching to a baby does not trouble an autonomous woman because she is able to accept it for what it is—an expression of individuality. Everyone is different. She has one style of relating to the baby; her husband, who has a different biological relationship to him, another. Often, however, the male parenting style does trouble the overidentifying mother because to her it is not an expression of individual differences but a rejection.

Just as she sometimes confuses herself with the baby, such a mother also sometimes confuses herself with her husband. In a less dramatic but still notable form, the overidentifying woman comes to see the two of them as one and the same person. Therefore they should feel the same way about the baby and behave the same way toward him. Many Project husbands complained that it was deeply humiliating and alienating to have their parenting styles criticized. But in a sense the woman who chastises her husband for not spending as much time with the baby as she does or for not getting as excited about his little triumphs as she does cannot help herself.* Each time her husband responds differently than she would to the child, he is rejecting her notion of their oneness. And because this rejection hurts and threatens her, she complains about those differences.

What happens in marriages where autonomy and affiliation needs remain unbalanced?

In most cases these unions look like an upside-down version of a marriage where a reasonable balance is achieved. Chores and responsibilities are not divided in a mutually satisfactory way; the baby's problems are blown out of proportion; the wife does not receive adequate physical and emotional support; the husband does not receive adequate companionship, and his patience and tolerance are constantly tested.

The absence of the little acts of self-sacrifice, empathy, and understanding that are necessary to build a nurturing marriage often add to the couple's disillusionment and disenchantment. During the transition these grace notes are the equivalent of a little love song. Each tells the spouse it's sung to, "Here's how much you and this marriage mean to me." At the root of the drift and estrangement that afflict so many marriages during the transition is this lack of this music. In this —usually the couple's first real opportunity not to declare but to dem-

* It is important to make a distinction here. I am not talking about the woman who criticizes her husband for spending fifteen or twenty minutes a day playing with the baby. In these cases the problem is not female overidentification but male self-focus. The man is too self-absorbed to want to share any of his time with his new child. But the new father's different biological relationship with the baby means that a man often finds the baby a less compelling figure than a woman, and marital satisfaction is enhanced when this individual difference is recognized and accepted.

onstrate their love for each other in tangible and often demanding ways—they discover that no one is willing to understand, to empathize, to sacrifice, that no one is willing to sing a song for the common good.

Often this discovery is not made all at once; it is the result of a hundred smaller discoveries and the cumulative disappointment and disillusionment they produce. After a dozen failed attempts to explain how she is feeling, the wife concludes that her husband does not care how she feels. After a dozen attempts to initiate a night out, the husband concludes that his wife is not interested in spending time alone with him. Usually the drift that sets in following these discoveries is quiet. Initially there may be some heated arguments about the husband's insensitivity or the wife's obsession with the baby. But at a certain point both parents resign themselves to the fact that their marriage has ceased to nurture, ceased to be "a haven in a heartless world," and emotionally if not physically they go their separate ways. Increasingly the wife turns to her friends and family for support, or, if there are no friends or family available, she keeps her feelings to herself. And increasingly the husband saves all his energy for Saturday basketball games and work assignments.

Cal and Jennifer Renselear's past history as well as the results of their intake interview and Marital Quality Questionnaires suggested that they might be vulnerable to this kind of drift during the transition. But I was surprised at how quickly they began to part company after daughter Allison's birth and I was also surprised at the particularly virulent form of marital estrangement they fell prey to. But then I had no way of knowing beforehand about Ali's hematoma.

In fairness to Cal I should point out that initially he was as upset about this injury as Jennifer. The morning he called to reschedule the Renselears' first postpartum interview, he sounded tired, depressed, and a little frightened. "The bruise covers almost the whole right side of the head," he said. "Poor Ali looks like she's been mugged."

However, after visits to a specialist in Harrisburg and then a second in Philadelphia, he and Jennifer began to see the hematoma very differently. Cal accepted the reassurances of the doctors, who, like Jennifer's obstetrician, pronounced it harmless. But Jennifer did not. In her heart she remained convinced, in some obscure way, that Ali had been seriously injured. She also felt that if that damage remained undiagnosed, in time it would manifest itself in an irreversible disability. Ali would be a slow learner, or she would develop seizures, or her motor function would be affected.

One of the *what if*s in the Renselears' story is what would have happened if Jennifer had not had her sense of self so severely tested. The results of her personality scores suggested that she might have had trouble separating from her baby as a fairly large number of new mothers do. But without the hematoma, which made Ali look so fragile and vulnerable, I do not think she would have lost control of her emotions and begun to see herself and Ali as one and the same person. In a way Cal's willingness to consult a second specialist was an attempt to help Jennifer regain her emotional equilibrium. He imagined that if she heard one more expert pronounce the hematoma benign, she would stop obsessing about it.

However, in the weeks following the Renselears' visit to Philadelphia there were many signs that Jennifer's preoccupation with the hematoma and Ali remained unabated. There were, for example, the Polaroids. One night at dinner Jennifer surprised Cal by pulling two snapshots out of her purse and placing them on the table in front of him. It took Cal a moment to realize that they were photos of Ali's skull.

"I took the picture on the right last week and the one on the left this morning," she said. "Do you see any change?"

Cal was too upset by Jennifer's behavior to examine the photos. He pushed them away. "Don't you think taking pictures of Ali's head is a little bizarre?" As soon as he said it, Cal knew he had made a mistake. Jennifer felt humiliated.

"You're never going to learn to care about anyone but yourself, are you?" she said, snatching up the photos. "Goddamn you, Cal."

There was also the incident in the Italian restaurant. The Renselears' presence there represented a major victory for Cal, who had been lobbying for a night out for weeks. He felt housebound and thought time away from Ali might help Jennifer regain some perspective. But as soon as he arrived at the restaurant, Jennifer, who had agreed to the "date" with some reluctance, asked for change. She wanted to call the sitter. When Cal reminded her that it was only a twenty-minute drive from their home to the restaurant, Jennifer got annoyed. "Never mind. I'll get change from the cashier."

Seven years later at the Renselears' follow-up interview, Cal's memory of what happened next remained vivid. From their table he had a clear view of the phone, which was on a wall near the cashier's booth. After getting change Jennifer walked over and deposited a dime. A moment later her hand went up to her mouth in alarm. Cal recalled feeling simultaneously guilty and frightened as he watched her from the table. Jennifer would never have forgiven him if anything had happened to Ali in their absence. When she returned to the table, Jennifer had both their coats on her arm. "We have to leave now," she announced. "Ali just spit up."

Cal remembers that it took him a moment to process this information. When he collected himself, he said as calmly as he could that that did not sound very serious to him. Babies spit up all the time.

"It could be a sign of the flu. It might have something to do with the hematoma," said Jennifer.

"Jesus, Jen, don't be ridiculous." Cal had long since moved past the point of indulging Jennifer.

"We have to leave now," Jennifer insisted.

Cal said he wanted to have a sandwich first.

"They don't serve sandwiches here. Put on your coat."

A second *what if* in the Renselears' story is what would have happened if Ali had been born in Berkeley, where Jennifer had a large group of friends available to support and help her. But those friends were all a continent away now. Outside of Andrea Cavellano, the Renselears' next-door neighbor, the only other person in the area Jennifer could turn to for sustained support was Cal. As her concerns about Ali deepened, Jennifer's demands for both increased exponentially. These demands took many forms, but the ones Cal found most oppressive were the phone calls. In the weeks after her return from the hospital, Jennifer's one call per day became two, then three and some days four calls. Each was about one of Ali's little upsets, and each upset was reported in the same urgent voice.

One of Cal's other vivid memories of this period was of the afternoon an emergency operator cut into the middle of a phone conversation with a supplier. "Is this Mr. Calvin Renselear?" the operator asked. When Cal said yes, she said she had an urgent call. In the fraction of a second it took to put the other call through, a half dozen possibilities raced through Cal's mind, each one more horrible than the last. When Jennifer's familiar voice came on the line, he was so relieved, he almost forgot to get angry at her.

In some of the early research on the transition, behavior like Jennifer's was explained solely in terms of the woman's insecurity. Overwhelmed by all of the challenges facing her, the new mother loses control of her affiliation impulse and becomes overly dependent and clinging. But in his book *The Birth of a Family*, psychiatrist Jerry M. Lewis offers a more complex, subtle, and I think accurate explanation of maternal dependency and clinging. In many cases, he argues, it is vastly exacerbated by an unregulated male autonomy impulse. Instead of being responsive to his wife's neediness, the insecure man feels threatened by it, so he flees either into his self-focus (i.e., into the TV, a book, or a hobby) or into an independent activity that will get him away from her (such as work or sports). This then forces the wife to do something dramatic to get him to focus on her, such as calling him four times a day. In extreme cases, Dr. Lewis notes, a cycle of marital escalation and counterescalation called the Pursuer-Pursuee syndrome develops. Each time the woman pursues support, the husband burrows a little more deeply into some aspect of his autonomy impulse. Therefore the next time she pursues support, the wife is forced to up the ante and do something even more dramatic to get her husband's attention, such as resort to an emergency operator.

Like many pursuee husbands, Cal's favorite hiding place was work. One of Jennifer's most vivid memories of this period was a conversation she and Cal had one night. There was a fair in Belleville the next day, but when she suggested that they all go, Cal pleaded work. He had a pile of reports to sift through at the office. "Why don't you see if Angela wants to go?" he said. Watching Cal pull out of the driveway the next morning, Jennifer remembers thinking to herself that she might as well be a single mother.

At the time, Cal told himself that the Saturdays and Sundays he spent at the office were a sacrificial gift to his family. He was putting in such long hours for the same reason he had done those two extra years at UCLA—to ensure Jennifer's and Allison's future. He was putting their needs ahead of his own. However, seven years later at the Renselears' follow-up interview, with the events of the transition now safely behind him, Cal could be more honest about why he had spent so much time at his office. At home he felt no control over his environment. He never knew when Jennifer would make a new demand or what it would be. But at work he did feel in control. Once he was behind his desk, the universe again assumed a rational, orderly shape. There were no messy emotions lapping at him, no bewildering demands to cope with, no incomprehensible thoughts to untangle. There were only his own needs to consider, and they were as neat, as rational, and as well-behaved as they had always been.

From the time of our initial intake interview until about three months after the birth, we normally saw couples at eight- to twelve-week intervals. But because of Cal's rescheduling, which created a scheduling conflict for me, I did not see the Renselears again until the warm June afternoon I arrived for their three-month postpartum observation. When I came into the kitchen with their teenage baby-sitter, Denise, Ali was nestled in Jennifer's arms asleep. Despite the warm weather, she had on a blue-and-white-checked bonnet. I noticed a finger-shaped swatch of skin protruding from under its rim. The finger ran down her forehead and stopped at a spot just above the right eye. Jennifer caught me staring at it.

"The bruise goes all across the right side of the head. The skin's starting to heal over, but God knows what happened underneath."

At the intake interview I had noticed that the more stressed Jennifer felt, the more fluttery and animated she became. While we were sitting in the kitchen getting reacquainted, her hands never stopped moving. When Denise left, I discovered why. Browsing in a clothing store on College Avenue that morning, Jennifer finally had had the encounter she had been dreading since Ali's birth. She was waiting for a salesclerk when an elderly woman suddenly approached her and said, "May I see?" Before Jennifer had had a chance to reply, the woman was peering into the carriage at a bonnetless Ali. The presence of a stranger hovering over her startled Ali, who began to howl. But she did not seem nearly as startled as the woman, who lurched back from the carriage as suddenly as she had lurched into it. She stared at Jennifer for a moment in silence, then said, "I'm sorry for intruding," and walked away.

Cal came into the kitchen just as Jennifer finished her story. She looked up at him and smiled.

"I was just telling Jay about that dreadful woman in the store today."

Cal nodded and asked about dinner.

Jennifer, who suddenly looked very cross, said "Breaded chicken," and excused herself.

When we were alone, Cal explained that he already knew about the encounter. "I got two calls about it today," he said, raising two fingers. He walked over to the refrigerator and took out a beer. "Every time Ali burps, I get two calls about it. Sometimes I wonder what my secretary thinks." Cal took a long swig of beer. "Actually I know what she thinks, and it's not pretty."

A major portion of the first postnatal interview is devoted simply to observing the couple together. The observer does not ask questions or interact, he just sits and as unobtrusively as possible, watches and listens. But in the Renselears' case this proved difficult.

During dinner when Jennifer mentioned the woman in the store again, Cal, who clearly had heard enough about her, tried to change the subject. He began peppering me with questions about the Project. How far along were we? What were we finding? When I politely reminded him that I was there to observe, he said he understood and returned to his meal. The Renselears finished their dinner in silence. But it was one of those big, noisy silences that occurs when two people are furious at each other. As soon as he finished, Cal excused himself; he said he had some work to do.

Jennifer picked at her food for a few moments, then stood up so abruptly, she almost knocked over her chair. "Could you keep an eye on Ali?" she asked me and then disappeared into the back of the house where Cal's office was located. A moment later I heard his voice saying, "God, what is it now?" then Jennifer saying, "Why did you humiliate me in front of him like that?"

A jumble of muffled sounds followed, then the Renselears reappeared in the kitchen as abruptly as they had disappeared from it. "Could we cut the visit short tonight?" Cal asked. Jennifer was still upset about the incident in the store.

Our principal tool for tracking participants' marital satisfaction was the Marital Quality Questionnaires we left at the end of each observation. Based on the participants' answers to the questions on these forms, which were returned to us via mail, we would then rate them individually on four indexes of marital satisfaction: feelings of love toward spouse, feelings of ambivalence toward spouse, level of conflict, and level of communication. Within several days of my visit to the Renselears I received their latest scores. Between the one-month and the three-month postpartum observations, each had had negative changes in the 30 percent range on three of the four measures—feelings of love and ambivalence toward spouse and level of communication.

These scores were worrisome, but I wasn't without hope. Sometimes it takes a while for a couple to learn how to work together as a team. I thought if Cal could learn to be more supportive and Jennifer to curb her neediness, the rest of the transition would go more smoothly for them than the first few months had.

7

Common Ground

One day about six weeks after son Ian's birth, Sue Akers arrived home to a cryptic message on her answering machine. It was from a real estate agent; he wanted her to call immediately. Three hours later Sue was standing in a deserted store off Route 322, wondering what to do. The site was perfect: It was big; it was only a few minutes from State College; the McDonald's next door created a lot of traffic; the rent was reasonable and the lease long. On the other hand, there was Ron. What would he say? The memory of their last discussion about a video store made Sue hesitate. "I want to talk to my husband before I make a commitment," she told the agent as they said good-bye in the parking lot.

"Why don't you have him call me. I can show him the store tomorrow." The agent took a card out of his pocket and handed it to Sue. "But tell him he'll have to make up his mind fast. I have another client. . . ." The rest of the thought was left to speak for itself.

It's only a ruse, Sue told herself as she watched the agent walk across the lot to his car. *He doesn't have anyone, he's just trying to rush me.* This thought was interrupted by a shout. "Wait, wait," someone was yelling. Sue remembers it took her a fraction of a second to recognize the voice. It was hers.

By the time she caught up with the agent, he was standing by his car, out of breath. He was a heavy man, and the walk across the lot had winded him. He asked Sue what she wanted. As he spoke, she noticed his breath made little curlicues of white smoke in the cold February air.

"I'll do it now."

The agent looked puzzled.

"The lease. Give it to me. I'll sign it now."

Recalling this scene at the Akerses' follow-up interview seven years later, Sue attributed her impetuousness that day to the real estate agent's condescension. " 'Have your husband call me.' Who did he think he was talking to?"

"Maybe that's the point," Ron said. "He knew exactly who he was talking to."

Sue considered this for a moment and laughed.

"Maybe."

Sue's other vivid memory of that day was of the fight she and Ron had had at dinner. She knew Ron would be angry at what she had done, but she had never seen him as angry as he was that night. "How are we supposed to handle a new business and a new baby at the same time?" he shouted when she told him about the lease. "While you're at this store, who's going to look after Ian and do all the other things that have to be done around here?"

"Between you, Mom, and me we'll manage," Sue said defensively.

"Your father has angina now," Ron reminded her. "Your mother can't be here fifteen hours a day anymore."

"We'll work something out. Maybe we can get a teenager in."

Ron, who remembered this fight as vividly as Sue, recalled that at that point he flung down his napkin and stalked out. "I was so angry, I was afraid of losing it."

"We never fight like that," Sue said.

Ron nodded in agreement. In retrospect, he said, he realized his outburst that night had really been an expression of disappointment—of loss almost. Normally the early months of the transition are very difficult ones for parents. But Ron remembered this period as being quite wonderful. All the fears and anxieties about the pregnancy had lifted. It had gone to term and he had a big, healthy baby son. Sue was happier and more relaxed than she had been since the miscarriage two years earlier. Even the chores were not turning out to be as bad as Ron had expected. Ian created a lot of work, but with his mother-in-law at the house on an almost around-the-clock basis, the work went quickly.

During these early months he and Sue even managed to get away by themselves for a few day trips. One Saturday they drove over to Center Hall for a carnival, and the following Saturday down to New Hope. That day had been special to Ron. Seven years later he could still remember the little Greek restaurant where he and Sue had had lunch, the name of the barge that had carried the Akerses and a group of Japanese tourists along the old canal behind the town, and how after the boat ride he and Sue had sat on a bench beside the pier, talking and holding hands until it was time to go home. On that gray March afternoon the future seemed to unfold before Ron like a magic carpet.

"The reason I blew a fuse about the store," Ron said, "is I knew there wouldn't be anymore days like that one for a long time; there'd just be wall-to-wall work and a lot of grief. We'd never see each other." Ron stopped and turned toward Sue, who was sitting at the other end of the sofa. "A new baby and a new business. I don't know how we did it."

Sue smiled at him.

"We did it, though, didn't we?"

Ron did not smile back.

"By the skin of our teeth, we did."

The trace of anger in Ron's voice did not surprise me. If there are two nightmare issues for new parents, they are work and division of labor. Most studies, including our own, have found that when new parents fight, more often than not they fight about who does what or who makes the career sacrifices. Also like most of the other recent research on the transition, we found that a principal reason for the almost singular ability of these two issues to undermine marital happiness is their unrelenting nature. If a couple disagrees about sex or money or about how often to go out, at most they only have to confront those differences five or ten times a month. But if they disagree about a work issue, such as who gets to stay late at the office and who picks up the child at day care, they must face that difference on a daily or almost daily basis. And if they disagree about division of labor, they've got to deal with it every time the baby needs to be diapered or bathed or the dishes need to be washed, which is to say, they must confront it on an almost hourly basis.

As we watched our couples grapple with work and chore problems, however, we also found a deeper reason for the almost singular ability of these two issues to sow discord and unhappiness: They erode the common ground in a marriage. One of the chief bonds between a husband and wife is a sense of sharing a common vision. Feeling that they have similar ideas about fairness, a pool of common values, and a similar view of their obligations to each other and to the marriage strengthens a couple's sense of unity, of oneness. It makes them feel like "us" instead of "you and me."

Disagreements about chores and work erode this common ground because each disagreement reminds the husband and wife that they have conflicting ideas about fairness, conflicting values, conflicting visions of their obligations to each other and to the marriage, and conflicting views of each other's careers. Even in relatively happy unions the normal wear and tear of the transition usually erodes some of the common ground beneath a couple. But in marriages where there are big disagreements about chores and work the erosion rate can often be so rapid that by the end of the baby's first year the husband and wife are left wondering if they have anything in common outside of the roof over their heads and the baby in the nursery.

What determines how much common ground remains under a couple at the end of the transition is the second transition domain, Gender Ideology. And in a sense our discovery of its role in promoting or undermining marital unity was serendipitous. At the start of the Project we had no idea that gender ideology was such a key factor in determining how successfully new parents are able to resolve work and division-of-labor disputes. We were led to this discovery by our desire to fill in an existing gap in the literature. In the early 1980s when we launched our study, there were quite a few small-scale reports on work and chores. But what no one had yet done was examine these issues in a large group of new parents or look at how couples grappled with them not at a single point in the transition but through time. We decided we would.

One of the first things that struck us when we looked at division of labor is how inequitably labor continues to be divided in most new families despite a decade or more of egalitarian rhetoric. Our data on baby chores offers a graphic Exhibit A.

About an hour of the one-, three-, and nine-month visits we made to Project couples were devoted to observing four parental behaviors: (1) playing with baby; (2) kissing and hugging him; (3) tending to his basic needs (i.e., feeding, diapering, bathing, etc.); and (4) reading the newspaper and watching television in his presence.

On the first three measures our mothers' scores were 40 to nearly 300 percent higher than our fathers'. For example at one month our average mother scored a 63 on basic baby care, our average father a 23. Translated into percentages, this means that at one month our average mother did roughly 275 percent more of the feeding, diapering, and bathing than our average father. This difference narrowed somewhat as time passed, but at nine months our wives were still doing 100 percent more of the basic baby care than our husbands. The only measure where men outscored women was reading the newspaper and watching television in the baby's presence. At one month men's scores were 100 percent higher, and at nine months, 50 percent higher.

In the case of what might be called managerial chores, the disparity between Project husbands and wives was even greater. The average father's 23 on basic baby care might be much less than his wife's 63, but it did reflect a fairly significant level of involvement. It was rare to visit a home where the man did not do some diapering, feeding, bathing, or soothing. However, even very committed, dedicated husbands and fathers like Ron rarely assumed responsibility for managerial chores. I don't think I encountered a single male participant who regularly scheduled pediatrician's visits, monitored diaper usage (so he would know when a new package was needed), or otherwise involved himself in the managerial aspects of parenting, such as knowing how to operate the baby's vaporizer or where to put it, or how much and what kind of medicine to give him when he got sick.

We found household chores to be divided somewhat more equitably. New mothers did roughly 20 percent more of the laundry, vacuuming, dishwashing, and bedmaking than new fathers. But we also found that in most cases the man's contribution to household chores was smaller than it had been prior to the transition. More often than not, in prebaby days he did half or nearly half of these chores. In postbaby days he was doing 25 or 30 percent of them. There are a number of reasons for this retreat. But the key one seems to be that after the baby's arrival many men engage in the same kind of logic as that new father I quoted in Chapter Two, the one who said, "Pretty soon 'breast-feeding Jenny is Brenda's responsibility' became 'Jenny is Brenda's responsibility.' " In the case of domestic duties the logic seems to go, "The baby is my wife's responsibility, ergo the house is her responsibility too."

When we looked at how the 45 percent of our couples who were in dual-income families grappled with work issues, the first thing we noticed was that having an employed wife did not seem to measurably change a man's attitude toward baby and household chores. Often a new father would do a bit more in the kitchen and nursery when his wife went to work. But for the most part the woman was still coming home to 250 percent more of the baby chores and 15 percent more of the household chores. The way work intensifies division-of-labor problems in a family is delineated in a study by Berkeley sociologist Arlie Hochschild. She found that in the average working family, including household and child-care duties, the woman's work week exceeds her husband's by fifteen hours. Annualized, Dr. Hochschild notes, this difference means that the typical woman works a month longer per year than her husband, and each of her extra thirty workdays is twenty-four hours long.

In families where the wife's job is not simply a job but also a career, we found that the equity issue extended beyond chores to the question of who makes the career sacrifices. A new baby requires a vast amount of parental time and energy. Which parent was going to put his or her career on hold in order to provide it? With the notable exception of couples like the Akerses, we found that 80 to 90 percent of the time the answer to that question was the wife.

What is the most important factor in determining a couple's ability to resolve work and division-of-labor conflicts? The standard answer to this question is equity. Many authorities, including Dr. Hochschild, argue that the more evenly divided the household and baby chores, the less a husband and wife will fight about division of labor; the more evenly divided the career sacrifices, the less they will fight about work. Our data supported this view up to a point. We found that usually when a husband did a little more in these spheres, it made his wife a little happier and their marriage a little better.

But one of the first things we noticed when we began examining these two issues is that what constitutes a satisfactory arrangement of work and chores varies enormously from couple to couple. In some of our homes the man's 23 on baby chores was viewed as intolerable; in others as just about right; and in still others the wife was a little intimidated by it because she felt her maternal prerogative was being encroached upon. We also had families where a simple request to pick up the child at the day-care center provoked a fight, and others where a wife's three-day business trip was accepted as perfectly reasonable and justifiable.

These findings suggested that the conventional wisdom overestimated the role equity alone plays in a couple's ability to resolve work and chore differences successfully. But what did play a key role in their successful resolution? When we looked at the marriages with the most mutually satisfactory arrangements, a pattern emerged. Typically in these unions there was a great deal of common ground. The question of who does what and who makes the career sacrifices produced relatively little friction because the couple had similar ideas about what constituted a fair division of labor, saw the roles and responsibilities of motherhood and fatherhood the same way, and agreed on whose work was the most important. In other words, we found in such marriages a shared vision of how the new family ought to operate. At the heart of this shared vision lay a shared gender ideology.

In the simplest sense gender ideology might be described as how an individual defines appropriate male and female behavior. And three factors usually influence our choice of a particular ideology: the larger culture and what it happens to be saying at the moment about men and women; our parents and the behaviors we saw them model; and finally our own personal experiences, needs, and desires. For example we found that the memories of overburdened, frustrated mothers led many of our Project wives to adopt an egalitarian or transitionalist ideology; they did not want happening to them what they had seen happen to their mothers. But we also found something else that has been less commented on: Behind the ideological choices many of today's men have made are memories like the one Ron recalled for me one day.

"Once when I was about eight or nine," he said, "my dad offered to take me to a movie. I was thrilled. We never did anything together. The whole next week I looked forward to our date, but when the big night arrived, Dad called just before supper and canceled. Something had come up. Something always was coming up with him. 'Don't worry, though,' he told me. 'You're still going.' It turned out that our neighbor, Ed, owed my father a favor, and Ed's repayment was taking me to the movie. You know, in a lot of ways my dad wasn't a bad guy. But whenever I think about him, that phone call is the first thing I think of. I don't want Ian remembering me that way."

At the moment there are three major gender ideologies: Traditional, Egalitarian, and Transitional. And one way they influence attitudes toward work and chore issues is by determining which activities a new parent does and does not find validating. For example, often a Traditional woman will happily do 70 to 90 percent of the housework because her ideology says homemaking is a validating activity for a woman. An Egalitarian woman will not contribute this amount, because her ideology defines homemaking in a less flattering way. The receptiveness of Egalitarian and Transitional husbands to wifely expectations of participation in what are commonly regarded as traditional female chores illustrates another way gender ideology influences spousal attitudes. Even if a man dislikes diapering, cooking, and the night shift, if he is a Transitionalist or an Egalitarian, he will often do his fair share of these chores because his ideology says fairness demands that a man do 30 percent (Transitionalist) to 50 percent (Egalitarian) of everything.

Often gender ideology also influences how much emotional support one partner extends to the other. A Project husband named Michael

Fishman provides a case in point. Four times in the nine months since son Ben's birth, Michael's wife, Lotte, who is a fairly high official at the university, traveled on business, violating Michael's Transitionalist view that while women may work, motherhood should come first. During our three-month observation of the Fishmans, Michael did not mention Lotte's absences. However his frequent and fairly pointed praise of a family friend who did not leave her baby's side at all during the first year made it pretty clear to me—and to Lotte—how Michael felt about her absences and also her mothering.

I thought Lotte held up well under Michael's silent assault that day. But when I returned to the Fishmans' six months later, I saw that it had had an effect. Lotte spent the first hour of the observation engaged in a nonstop, strenuously athletic attempt to amuse Ben. She tossed him, she turned him, she got right up into his face and made funny faces. She did all the things that Dr. Sarale Cohen of the University of Michigan found working women often do when they are suffering from a bad case of maternal guilt. Watching his wife and son roll around on the floor that afternoon, Michael looked quite pleased. I suppose on some level he imagined he had won. But Dr. Cohen also found that an overly energetic maternal play style can hinder a baby's development. So Michael had lost, Lotte had lost, and of course the biggest loser of all was Ben.

What might be called the diaper question illustrates a third way gender ideology shapes parental attitudes about work and division of labor. It determines what an individual will not do as well as what he will. Almost all of our fathers would change a wet diaper without complaint, but a poopy diaper pushed some to the ideological limits and beyond. Very few men pleaded ideological conflict in backing away from this particular chore, but beneath the thousand excuses they did offer was a burning ideological conviction that changing a poopy diaper was woman's work.

Egalitarians, Transitionalists, and Traditionalists are often made to sound like conscious idealogues the way that, say, Democrats and Republicans are. But in fact most of our beliefs about male and female behavior remain buried or half buried until we bump into something big enough to force us to begin thinking about them in a clear and sustained way. During intake interviews, for example, few of our participants could clearly define their ideology or their spouses'. A husband might say he "sort of" disliked his twice-weekly stint as the family's cook, but because he had no reason to, he had not thought about what his dislike said about his gender ideology. Or his wife might say she "sort of" enjoyed her work, but because she had no reason to, she had not thought about what that said about hers.

At the one- and particularly the three- and nine-month observations, things were different. Now our couples were more conscious of their ideological leanings. Few used terms such as *gender* and *ideology* of course. Instead husbands and wives talked about making "discoveries." In the man's case these often involved parenting. Like some of our men, for example, Ron Akers found fathering more fun than he had expected so he became more involved with Ian than he thought he would. Alternately we had men who found it more burdensome than they had expected; usually they spent less time with their new children than they thought they would. Many of our mothers' discoveries also involved parenting. Like Sue, for instance, some Project mothers ended up asking for more of a contribution from their husbands than they thought they would because they found the baby unexpectedly demanding. Others found him so delightful, they wished their husbands would contribute a little less. (Admittedly this group was not large, but we had a number of women who felt this way, and they tended to be Traditionalists.) Some mothers also found that they missed work less than they had expected. Others, such as a Project mother named Betty Dorris, found they missed it more than expected.

Betty had always thought of her teaching career as a kind of prelude; her real life would begin when she had a child. But three months after daughter Darlene's birth, Betty found herself beginning to question this assumption. While she loved Darlene, without her work she felt a little empty and unfocused. She missed the intellectual stimulation of the classroom and the companionship of her students and colleagues. At the Dorrises' three-month observation Betty said she felt guilty and a bit ungrateful. She finally had everything she had always believed she really wanted out of life. Yet instead of being happy she was complaining. "I feel disappointed in myself," she said that night. By the nine-month observation Betty's guilt had passed; she was teaching again. And while there were mornings she felt a sharp pang when she dropped off Darlene with a neighborhood woman who provided child care for her, on the whole, she was beginning to feel like her energetic, focused self again.

What produced Betty Dorris's change of heart was not a change in beliefs or values; her feelings about work had been there all the time. However, in the transition she had finally encountered, as most parents do, that big bump that forces an individual to do some clear, sustained thinking about gender ideology. One reason for the transition's crystallizing effect is all the new chores it creates. The man who knew he sort of disliked meal preparation and house cleaning now gets enough time at these tasks to think through the implications of his dislike. At heart he is a Traditionalist who believes that cooking and doing related domestic duties are woman's work. The tendency of the baby to divide chores along gender lines also has a crystallizing effect on ideological beliefs. In the first months after the baby's birth almost all women are at home involved in diapering, cleaning, shopping, and other domestic duties. Usually during this period the woman who sort of enjoys her work has an opportunity to think about why she does in a sustained way. While she loves her baby, at heart she is an Egalitarian who finds her job more rewarding than domestic life.

The discovery of the important role that gender ideology plays in mediating a husband's and a wife's ability to resolve differences about work and chores raised two questions in our minds. The first was about marital satisfaction. Did the ability to settle work and chore disagreements with a minimum of friction make for a better marriage? We were not surprised to find that it nearly always did. But we were a little surprised to find why it did. Initially we imagined the principal reason would be a lower incidence of conflict. Seeing maternal and paternal responsibilities and obligations the same way and having similar ideas of fairness, couples with a shared gender ideology would argue less. And we found that they do, but we also found that even in homes where there are fairly profound differences about work and chores, shouting matches are fairly uncommon. Rather than waste precious time and energy (both of which are at a premium during the transition) arguing, one partner (usually but by no means always the wife) will quietly decide to "eat it" and do the contested chore.

A calculation we did brings us closer to the real reason why a shared gender ideology is such an important element in marital happiness during the transition. We estimated that even if a couple only bumps heads three or four times a day about diapering, the day-care pickup, or responsibility for the night shift, by the end of the first year they will have received between 1,000 and 1,500 reminders that in their marriage there are two sets of values, two different ideas of fairness, and two different attitudes toward each partner's career. And with each of these reminders the couple will feel more and more like "you and me" and less and less like "us."

The second question our research raised was: How do different ideologies fit together during the transition? Do all forms of ideologically mixed marriages enhance the volatility of work and division-of-labor issues to the same degree? Or do some enhance their volatility more than others? And what about ideologically matched marriages? Were they all equally beneficial in helping a couple preserve marital common ground, or were some more beneficial than others?

We did not, as we did with our domains, explore these questions via statistical analysis. However, from our observations and discussions with our couples—in other words, from our impressions—we concluded that most marriages today involve one of six forms of ideological couplings. In terms of how they do and do not facilitate the resolution of work and division-of-labor conflicts, these matchups fall into three general categories.

MOST DIFFICULT IDEOLOGICAL COUPLING

Traditional Man–Egalitarian Woman

Because Traditional men are anathema to Egalitarian women and vice versa, this combination is uncommon. When it does occur, it is usually because neither partner has yet encountered that big bump that makes an individual think hard and clearly about gender ideology. On occasion, though, another factor is also at work in these matchups. The man whose culinary skills end with grilled-cheese sandwiches and whose apartment looks like it belongs to a third-grader often has a bumbling, hapless, Woody Allenish quality that can make him quite endearing. In a recent column *New York Times* columnist Anna Quindlen described the traditional man as a kind of "bear with furniture" and despite her own feminist leaning, she confessed that in many ways she found him a winning figure.

Bears with furniture, however, become that way because they believe domestic life is a woman's sphere. During the transition this attitude makes division-of-labor questions a constant source of friction between the bear and his wife. Typically in these marriages there is a 40 to 45 percent gap between what the Egalitarian woman feels she should do (50 to 55 percent of everything) and what her Traditional husband feels she should do (90 to 95 percent of everything). And because the baby requires around-the-clock care, nearly every time they turn around, this couple is reminded of how little common ground they share. On occasion these reminders lead to fights. The woman asks for help putting the baby into his snowsuit, the man says he is busy, and they argue. But more commonly they do not. The woman decides to bite her tongue and manages the snowsuit herself. But every one of these little reminders of how differently she and her husband see things affects her feelings toward him and toward their marriage.

Sometimes as the transition progresses, the Egalitarian wife and the Traditional husband do begin making concessions to each other, but their opposing ideologies rob these concessions of their healing power. The wife who at six months finds her husband now doing 25 percent of the chores instead of 10 percent still feels betrayed because her gender ideology makes the 75 percent she is still doing feel like too much. Her husband feels similarly frustrated because: (a) given his ideology, the 25 percent he is doing feels like 2,500 percent; and (b) even this 2,500 percent does not make his wife happy.

Paid employment is also a divisive issue for this couple. The Traditional woman is happy to stay home if she can. Usually the Transitional woman is more ambivalent. But because a part of her also enjoys homemaking and "being a mom," if she has to stay home for a year, generally it will not lead to a major drop in self-esteem. We found the Egalitarian woman to be different. Her attitude toward her work is—for lack of a better term—masculine. Work is a critical source of validation and self-esteem to her, and when it is removed, she tends to feel as empty and bereft as a Project wife called Kathy McNamara.

Kathy, who had been a reporter for a Pittsburgh newspaper, was not happy about leaving what she regarded as a dream job when husband Bob was transferred to central Pennsylvania. But she told herself that writing was portable work; she could start a free-lance career from her new home. However, the lack of contacts and outlets made writing assignments infrequent. So Kathy spent most of her days looking after son Jeffrey and while she enjoyed that immensely, it was not enough to fill her up. "The dreams I used to have for myself . . ." she said to me one day, "and look what I've become. My own worst nightmare of myself."

Egalitarian and Transitional men are both, to varying degrees, sensitive to the Egalitarian woman's attitude toward work. But the Traditional man tends to feel like Kathy's husband, who felt that once she had a baby, Kathy would stop thinking about her work. That his wife's attitude toward a career might be similar to his own does not get on a Traditional man's radar screen. Eight months after leaving the Project the McNamaras separated, and Kathy and Jeffrey returned to Pittsburgh and her job on the newspaper.

MANAGEABLE BUT DIFFICULT IDEOLOGICAL COUPLING

The couples who fall into this category are usually able to come up with work and division-of-labor arrangements that are viable. However, their different gender ideologies make these arrangements a constant source of friction.

Transitional Man–Egalitarian Woman

If upon meeting, the first thought of an Egalitarian woman and a Traditional man is "Never," the first thought of the individuals in this category is "Well, maybe." The Egalitarian woman may wish that the

Transitional man were more enlightened, and the Transitional man that the Egalitarian woman were more flexible. But they share enough ideological similarities to make this combination fairly common. And typically until the baby arrives, it operates fairly smoothly. Occasionally the husband and wife find themselves bumping into each other's beliefs, but usually not in major ways.

One reason things change during the transition is that no matter how many ways they cut the division-of-labor card, these individuals still find themselves coming up with a 15 to 20 percent gap. This is the difference between the 25 to 35 percent the Transitional man expects to do and the 50 to 55 percent his Egalitarian wife expects him to do. In itself 15 to 20 percent is not a large gap. However, these couples often have trouble bridging it because it is full of chores and responsibilities the Transitional man is psychologically unprepared to fulfill. As I pointed out earlier, he will do his "fair" share, but he still thinks of things in terms of "helping" a wife, not being her partner. If the diaper box is empty, he will run out and buy a new one; sometimes he will cook or vacuum the rug without being asked. But like his father and grandfather before him, he still expects his wife to take full responsibility for all managerial and overseeing chores. Which is to say, if the baby gets sick, he expects she will know what to do.

However, in some big ways a Transitional man is different from his father and grandfather. He not only does more at home and with baby than they ever dreamed of doing, more critically he is emotionally involved with his family in a way they would have found incomprehensible. The Transitional man's ideology says that a woman has a right to a career, so he tries to support his wife's work; it says that a man should be involved with his child, so he tries to give his new son or daughter what he might not have had—an involved, tender father. Usually, though, the Transitional man feels he does not get enough credit for these differences. "Why isn't my wife more grateful?" he wonders. But from the Egalitarian wife's perspective this complaint is unjustified self-pity. Why should she be grateful? If the child-care arrangements break down, is her Transitional husband the one who will risk his boss's ire by taking time off to arrange new ones? Is he the one who will have to stay up half the night doing the work that piled up while he was off inspecting child-care arrangements? And if the baby gets sick, is he the one who will have to miss an important meeting to take the child to the pediatrician?

When this couple fights about work—and they do fairly often—it is usually because the Egalitarian woman's attempts to divide her emotional energy fairly equally between motherhood and career rub up against the Transitional man's belief that while his wife's work is important, the baby should be her overriding priority at all times. The experiences of Jim and Laura Blakenship offer a case in point.

At first Jim, who is a professor at Penn State, tried to be understanding when Laura, who is a doctor, said she wanted to return to her job as deputy chief of emergency medicine at a local hospital. Going back to work three months after son Alex's birth seemed like cutting it a little thin to Jim. But because, like most Transitional men, he wanted to support his wife's career, he told Laura it was all right with him. However, when Laura resumed her twelve-hour work shifts, Jim became less understanding. I think one reason for his change of heart was inconvenience. Because the sitter left promptly at five o'clock and refused to work weekends, which Laura did, Jim felt house- and baby-bound. But in fairness to him, this was not the chief reason for the change. Like most Transitional men he also believed that a father, no matter how devoted, is no substitute for a mother and he felt that Alex was not seeing enough of his mother.

Midway through Alex's first year Jim's concerns led to a confrontation, the details of which are not entirely clear to me because neither he nor Laura was eager to talk about it. From the little they did say, though, I gathered that some hard words were exchanged during it, including an accusation that sometimes Laura put her work ahead of

Alex. Two months later she put in for a demotion to part-time emergency medicine physician. The new job allowed her to spend more time with Alex, but it also changed her. Laura, who had always seemed so bright and vivacious to me, became subdued and a bit distant.

Traditional Man–Transitional Woman

This combination is also fairly common and for the same reason as the last one: a certain degree of ideological kinship. Traditional men and Transitional women, for example, often agree that the baby should have an overriding claim on a woman's emotional energy and time. But like a Transitional husband and Egalitarian wife, this couple's sizable ideological differences become much harder to finesse once the baby arrives.

Like many couples in ideologically mixed marriages, for example, the Traditional man and Transitional woman approach division-of-labor questions with two different sets of assumptions. The woman expects her husband to do roughly 40 percent of everything, the man 20 percent, which leaves a 20 percent gap—big enough to ensure that the transition will erode a lot of the common ground of their marriage.

Work is also a problem for them because the Traditional husband's off-limits attitude toward domestic chores puts his Transitional wife in a bind every time she needs domestic support to meet career obligations. Say the obligation is an early meeting at work and the help she needs is someone to get the baby ready in the morning. In this situation she is confronted with three options, each of which is likely to leave her a little less happy about her Traditional husband and her marriage. She can ask him to take care of the baby in the morning and risk a fight if he resists. She can try to beg, cajole, and bribe the sitter into coming an hour early. Or she can "eat it"—get the baby and herself up an hour early to care for him before she leaves for work.

Even when the Transitional woman does stay at home, however, work remains a constant source of friction in her marriage because she and her Traditional husband will see what she does very differently. Someone once said, "If men got pregnant, pregnancy would be a sacrament." Something like that has begun to happen with housework now that more and more women are coming to it after pursuing a career. Having learned to put a dollar value on their labor, today's new mothers know that the chores and the housework they do have a concrete market value. Their cooking, cleaning, and shopping are worth *X* amount because that is how much it would cost the family to have a housekeeper do them; their baby chores are worth *X* amount because that is how much the family would have to pay a sitter or a day-care center to do them.

The Traditional man takes a different view of what his wife does at home. He knows that housekeeping and parenting are not easy, but he does not regard them as work in the way that, say, operating a forklift, planning a marketing campaign, or selling life insurance are work. One place where these conflicting attitudes cause problems for a couple is in the area of worker privileges. Does the Transitional woman get an occasional Saturday and evening to herself? Like her fellow workers in more glamorous professions, she feels entitled to time off from her job. But when she asks her Traditional husband to cover for her, he will resist because he regards himself as the family's sole worker. And whether his resistance provokes a fight or not, it will make the Transitional woman feel a little less happy about her life and her husband.

Transitional Man–Transitional Woman

The chief characteristic of this couple is a loyalty to both the old and the new. For example, like her Egalitarian counterpart, the Transitional woman often wants a career and a husband who is an involved parent. But she also is Traditional enough to want to have a larger voice in the baby's care. Similarly the Transitional man shares his Egalitarian counterpart's desire to be a New Father and to support his wife's work, but he is also Traditional enough to feel that when push comes to shove, his work should come first.

In our study population we found the Transitional marriage to be the most common form of ideological matchup, as I suspect it is in the general population. The high volume of complaints we heard from these couples, however, also make them the one exception to the shared-ideology rule. Typically Transitional couples have as much trouble with division-of-labor and work issues as husbands and wives in ideologically mixed marriages.

Why?

One virtue of being at either end of the ideological spectrum is the clarity it confers. Because they attach their allegiance to a fairly well-defined idea of what it is to be a wife and mother or husband and father Traditionalists and Egalitarians know what they will and will not do in a given situation. Transitionalist couples agree that the wife should be responsible for 60 to 70 percent of everything and the man 30 to 35 percent of everything. But with their allegiances divided between two diametrically opposed ideals, they have trouble making up their minds about everything else. This indecisiveness creates two problems that couples with other shared ideologies avoid. The first is that Transitionalists often disagree about who gets to do what with the baby. The man says he would feel more like an involved father if he could do some of the feeding, but the wife resists because she does not want to stop breast-feeding yet. The other, more insidious, problem they face is a vulnerability to frequent changes of mind and heart. One day, in an Egalitarian mood, one spouse will suggest to the other, "Why don't you take responsibility for chore *X*?"; then a week later, in a Traditional mood, that spouse feels a pang of regret for so blithely surrendering chore *X* and longs to have it back.

An example is the Project mother who asked her husband to share bathing duties, then decided bathing the baby was so much fun, she did not want to share it. Sometimes when this happens, the Transitionalist parent will ask to have the chore back. But more commonly he or she will do what this Project mother did: begin sending mixed messages. She did not ask her husband to stop bathing the baby, but she was there for every bath and full of unsolicited advice about what to do and what not to do during this relatively simple task. Since she was, as parents in her situation often are, acting unconsciously, at first this woman was stunned when her husband accused her of wanting to retrieve the bath chore, but as she thought about his charge, she realized he was right—she did.

The Transitional man also sends mixed messages about child care. He says he wants to be an involved, committed father. However, he puts so many qualifications on his commitment—he will drop the baby off at the sitter's but he won't help his wife find a new one if this one quits, or he will get the baby's vaporizer but won't learn how to operate it or where to put it—that his wife begins to question the seriousness of his commitment. This skepticism often intensifies the couple's division-of-labor difficulties because frequently the Transitional wife then begins to behave in ways that tell the husband, "I don't trust you." For example, now when he cares for the baby on his own she gives him the name of a half dozen people to call in case of an emergency, and now when he packs the baby's bag for an outing, she monitors him to make sure he has done it right; that is, the way she usually does it!

Work is also a high-tension issue for a Transitional couple, and again the problem is divided loyalties. The Transitional man is quite serious when he says he supports his wife's work. However, because he continues to see himself as the family's primary breadwinner (and because he usually earns more than his wife, he feels justified in this perception), his support of her career is contingent upon the imperatives of his work. In other words his support is unpredictable. Transitional men often make breakfast for their children and take them to day care, but if a work commitment demands that they get to the office early, they will insist that their wives take over these duties—and at a moment's notice. Their career comes first.

RELATIVELY SMOOTH IDEOLOGICAL COUPLING

The shared gender ideology of couples in this group allows them to settle work and division-of-labor differences with a minimum of friction and unhappiness.

Traditional Man–Traditional Woman

People with an ideological cast of mind can find much to criticize in this combination, which is so ingrained in old gender roles that it might be called *Leave It to Beaver Redux*. But it works relatively well for couples who share a loyalty to those old roles because transition issues are settled in a way that dovetails with their expectations and assumptions. For example Traditional couples rarely have trouble with work issues because the woman is content to stay home if she can, and even if she cannot, she is happy to put her husband's work first. With one major exception the Traditional wife is also satisfied with the 90 percent–10 percent division-of-labor split that is common in such marriages. Putting a high priority on domesticity, the Traditional wife wants and expects to assume the lion's share of the chores.

The significant qualification involves her tiredness. Shouldering 90 percent of everything all the time is exhausting, so Traditional women do look to their husbands for some support and help. For example when the man comes home at the end of the day, the wife will often want him to take the baby for a half hour or forty-five minutes. But because child care is not on the Traditional man's ideological map, this request frequently leads to scenes such as the one I witnessed one evening at the home of Phil and Barbara D'Amato.

Phil, who had gotten home about a quarter of an hour earlier, was sitting in an easy chair sipping a Coke and watching the news when Barbara came into the living room with thirteen-month-old Celeste in her arms. "That's right," Barbara cooed to her daughter, "Daddy's dying to see you. Why don't you sit and watch Peter Jennings with him?" Phil did not look happy about this idea, but, perhaps because I was sitting next to him, he did not protest when Celeste was deposited into his not-altogether-willing arms. About ten minutes later a light bulb appeared to go off over Phil's head. It had just occurred to him that two could play this game. "What?" he said to a startled Celeste. "You miss your mommy and want to go into the kitchen and help her make dinner?" Before Phil was out of his chair, Barbara cut him off. She was planted in the doorway between the kitchen and the living room. The large spoon in her hand made her look like a Spartan guarding the pass at Thermopylae.

"I just thought . . . ," Phil began uncertainly.

"Do us both a favor, Phil," Barbara said, "don't think."

That night Celeste stayed with her father until dinner was ready. However, because not many women—or men—possess an aroused Barbara D'Amato's power of intimidation, typically what happens in this situation is that after ten minutes of play the baby is handed back to the frustrated and exhausted mother. There are many other times when the Traditional man's unwillingness to help also disturbs his Traditional wife—on Saturdays, for example, when he vanishes to the park for a basketball game, and on a weekday evening when he plays cards with his buddies. Watching her busy husband, the Traditional wife wonders why he gets to do all of these things when she has not been to an aerobics class since her second month of pregnancy.

For an Egalitarian or Transitional woman such spousal behavior would be so far off the ideological map, it would produce a permanent disruption in the marriage. The woman would either begin to withdraw emotionally from it or, like Kathy McNamara, file for divorce. The unhappiness such spousal behavior can cause a Traditional wife is more like a summer squall. The woman gets angry at her husband's insensitivity and selfishness, but because his behavior is on her ideological map and because most of the time what she does fills her up emotionally, it does not sour her on her husband or on her marriage in an irrevocable way.

Egalitarian Man–Egalitarian Woman

This kind of marriage comes in two forms. Ideological Egalitarianism is based on a view of masculinity and femininity that sees the sexes as so alike in talents and capabilities that most roles, including the roles of breadwinner, nurturer, and homemaker, can be played interchangeably by men and women. Typically the husbands and wives in our study group who shared this view were educated professionals. They tended to be academics who lived in or near State College (the home of Penn State) or managers or technicians in relatively New Age industries, such as computers. And as with our Traditionalist couples, a shared ideology allowed them to divide chores and career sacrifices on an equal (50–50) or roughly equal (40 to 45 percent to the man, 55 to 60 percent to the woman) basis with a minimum of friction. But we found that as the transition progressed, some of these couples had difficulty maintaining this equality, and usually the problem was caused by the husband.

While all the women in our ideological group were emotionally as well as intellectually committed to egalitarianism, some of the men were not. They agreed to an equal division of labor because it sounded fair and they wanted to please their wives. But because they were unable to transfer their intellectual commitment into an emotional one, in time they began backsliding. Their minds were no longer able to drive their not-altogether-willing bodies. Instead of getting up every other night with the baby as promised, these men began getting up every third or fourth night; instead of making dinner three or four nights a week, they began ordering Chinese takeout and pizza.

Egalitarian husbands who fell away from their commitments offered many excuses, but in most cases the reason was the same. At a certain point the magnitude of what the man had committed himself to hit home, and then his not-altogether-willing body rose up and said, "Enough." Joe Cronin, one of our Project fathers, remembers the moment he reached this point. It was five-thirty on a Tuesday afternoon and he was sitting at his desk at work preparing for a final meeting of the day when the Cronins' baby-sitter, with two-year-old Moria Cronin in tow, appeared apparitionlike before him. Wife Ann had to work late that night, the sitter explained, and because she could not stay late, Ann had told her to drop off Moria at Joe's office. "That was the final straw," Joe told me.

The second form of Egalitarian marriage is personality-driven. In our study population the men and women who had such unions were much less stereotypical. This group had a sprinkling of professionals, but it also included nurses, salespeople, purchasing agents, secretaries, store managers, and police officers. Like their friends and neighbors in central Pennsylvania, many of these individuals were relatively conservative on cultural matters. Though their lives had been touched by the last twenty years of social change, as a group they were not committed to complete egalitarianism as a social principle.

Their form of Egalitarian marriage predates the ideological variety. If we had done our study in the 1950s, or indeed earlier in the century,

I am sure we would have found a certain percentage of such unions in our sample. This is not to say we would have found anything like an equal division of labor in these marriages (though, for the time, the man's involvement in the family probably would have looked radical), but we would have found an emotional parity. The man and woman would look upon each other as equals and afford each other the respect one affords an equal.

This is the chief characteristic of this form of egalitarian union, and to a large extent it seems to be a function of the wife's personality. For the most part the women we saw in these marriages were intelligent, unusually energetic, and as emphatic as firecrackers. Often they were also natural leaders. If their community did not have a paramedic service, they would—as one of these wives did—organize one. Many were also ambitious. Sometimes this manifested itself in a high level of community involvement, other times in money-making activities. In addition to their full-time jobs, a number of these women also had part-time jobs or ran small businesses on the side. During the first two years of the transition a Project wife called Libby Buchanan actually held three jobs. Four nights a week Libby worked full-time as an emergency medical technician, two nights a week as a cashier in a 7-Eleven. Days, in between being a full-time mother to daughter, Sheila, Libby operated an Amway dealership out of her home. Women like Libby might best be described as temperamental Egalitarians. They win equality in a marriage through sheer force of personality. Quite simply, they are too indomitable to settle for anything less.

Temperamentally the men in these marriages were very different from their wives but in ways that made them good counterparts. When the woman's balloon threatened to fly off into the stratosphere, the man was always there to put his finger on the string. Low-key, easygoing, less impulsive, and very secure, these men enjoyed, loved, and were proud of being married to such intelligent, ambitious, and energetic women. This remained true even when, as sometimes happened, the woman's intelligence and ambition won her a bigger paycheck and a better job. Typically these men were also more domestically skilled than most husbands. Sometimes it was because they had come from large families where even boys were expected to know how to soothe a baby brother or sister, sometimes because they liked cooking, cleaning, or other domestic activities. We even had one Egalitarian husband (but only one) who liked to iron; he claimed it relaxed him.

The most notable characteristic of these men, however, is not one that easily submits to scientific analysis, but it is a big part of the reason why their marriages were successful: They were all deeply in love with their wives. Having an energetic, intelligent (if sometimes unpredictable) partner lit up their lives, and they were self-aware enough to realize it and self-confident enough to be grateful. Their other notable characteristic, sensitivity, flowed directly out of this love. If a wife was unhappy about her stretch marks or her figure, the man would know it without having to be told and would try to find ways to make her feel better about herself (such as touching her a little more). The willingness of these men to sometimes put their wives' happiness above their own is another mark of their unusual sensitivity (and love).

I do not want to idealize these couples. While a disproportionately large number ended up in our Improvers group, division-of-labor and especially work issues loomed large in their marriages too. But their gender ideology gave their disagreements a different twist. Usually when a couple with a shared gender ideology fought, what they were fighting about was ideological betrayal; someone was betraying the tenets of his or her ideology by not doing as much as he or she was supposed to do, and had led the other to expect they would do. When Egalitarian couples fought, at issue was something more fundamental and potentially volatile—the loss of love or at least the risk that it might be lost. An Egalitarian man was usually happy to do whatever he was asked to do. When he objected to a chore or to a career sacrifice, it was because in one way or another it threatened to give him less of what he wanted most—time with his wife.

At the end of the Akerses' intake interview I already knew that Sue was a Personality-Driven Egalitarian, but I had been less certain about Ron's gender ideology. The responses he gave on our questionnaire and the Akerses' one-month observation began to bring this question into focus. Their three-month observation gave the focus a final, conclusive twist.

During the observation itself neither Ron nor Sue said much about her encounter with the real estate agent three weeks earlier. But in a sense that encounter was all they talked about. I felt two conversations were taking place that evening—one between the Akerses and me about Ian and life in the transition, the other between Ron and Sue about the video store and its consequences for their marriage.

I got one glimpse of this other conversation when Sue offered me a cup of coffee. Ordinarily Ron offered to get it for us. But this time he remained in his chair, silent. Sue was surprised.

"You're not going to make coffee?"

Ron shook his head. "Why don't you this time?"

Sue gave him a tight little smile and got up.

I got another glimpse of it later toward the end of the observation. Even after they got to know us, couples remained fairly guarded in talking about sex, and they almost never fought about it in front of us. But sometimes when a husband and wife were both riled by a troubling issue, as Ron and Sue were this evening, they said things they did not intend to say. I don't remember who initiated this particular exchange or why it spiraled out of control so quickly, but I do remember how angry both Akerses sounded as they described a confrontation they had had the previous Saturday.

Ron had been pushing Sue to go upstairs all afternoon, and just before dinner she finally gave in. "I did it more to keep him quiet than anything else," Sue said, "but when we were in the bedroom, I got really mad. I said, 'I've got a million things to do, I don't feel like making love, and I'm not going to let you bully me into it. If sex is so important to you, find someplace else to relieve yourself, mister.' "

Ron made an attempt to change the subject, then his anger got the better of him. "You know what I'd really like to know?" he said. "Exactly where do I stand on this list of a million things to do? At the bottom?"

"Don't be silly." Sue was getting defensive.

"I'm not being silly."

When I got up to leave a half hour later, Ron, who had been relatively conciliatory during the last part of the observation, offered to walk me to my car. "I'm sorry about what happened in there," he said when we were outside. "We're both sorry. We're a little on edge."

"The store?" I asked.

Ron nodded.

Since my last visit I noticed that most of the homes around the Akerses' had been landscaped. On this soft May evening their lawns looked a lush, almost extravagant green.

"I gather you don't want to do it?"

"My family thinks I'm absolutely crazy."

I knew there was a certain amount of tension between Sue and Ron's family, especially his mother. There had already been one open conflict between the two women, though it had not been about Ron. The previous Thanksgiving Mary Akers had gotten annoyed at the way Sue had treated her own mother, who had been enrolled to help out with the dinner. Neither Ron nor Sue had been eager to elaborate on this incident, but from what little they did say, I gathered that Mary Akers, who could be as outspoken and forceful as her daughter-in-law, had accused Sue of being disrespectful and high-handed toward her mother, and that had led to an exchange of words in the kitchen after dinner.

Now the video store had apparently revived tensions between the two women, which Ron had spent the entire winter trying to smooth over. "I was at my parents' house last Sunday," he said. "When I told them we'd need a forty-thousand-dollar loan to open the store, my mother hit the roof. She said, 'You're crazy. You'll spend the rest of your life paying for her harebrained idea.' "

Ron smiled ruefully. "That's just what I need now, another fight between Sue and my mother. God."

I am sure family tensions and the financial risk contributed to Ron's anxieties about the video store, but I suspected his real objections lay elsewhere. A story he told me a few minutes later confirmed my suspicion. One evening toward the end of their senior year Sue casually mentioned to Ron that she had sent off applications to three Philadelphia brokerage houses. "I'm only fishing," she had said. "I just want to see what my market value is." However, three weeks later, when one of the brokerage houses wrote back offering a summer internship, Sue told Ron she was taking it. "I'll spend the rest of my life wondering 'What if?' if I don't." Often during that summer, Ron said, he found the same two images revolving around in his mind. One was of Sue coming down the dorm steps in that blue dress the night they met, the other was of the June morning she stepped on the train to Philadelphia with her aunt's borrowed pearls around her neck and a straw hat in her hand.

"She came back that time, and now you're afraid you're going to lose her all over again," I said.

"Something like that. It's funny how things work out. One night about a month ago we were having dinner at McTigue's over in Huntington when this middle-aged couple came in with their two teenage sons and sat down next to us. They were really a neat-looking family. Watching them, I thought, 'This is going to be Sue and me. One day we'll have another child, then ten or fifteen years from now we'll be this middle-aged couple with these two terrific boys.' " Ron picked up a stone and threw it up into the evening sky; a moment later there was a *plunk* on the other side of the lawn.

"I want Sue to have everything she wants. I just want to make sure there's an 'us' too."

When we finished talking, it was almost dark. As I pulled out of the driveway, I caught a glimpse of Ron in my rearview mirror. He was standing in the driveway. He remained motionless for a moment, then bent down and began smoothing over the area of the lawn where we had been standing.

Six days later I received the results of the Akerses' latest Marital Quality Questionnaires. Since the one-month observation Ron's scores on three of the indexes we used to track marital satisfaction—ambivalence toward spouse, conflict, and communication—were down 10 to 15 percent. The only index that remained unchanged was love.

A shared gender ideology is an important plus for a couple, but it is not a guarantee of marital happiness. As I considered the Akerses' scores, I thought that what happened to their marriage from this point would largely depend on Sue and her sensitivity to Ron's concerns.

8

The Good Companion

When Tina Carlson walked into the ladies' room, the woman was standing in front of the mirror. She applied the lipstick in her hand with a few swift strokes, then leaned into the mirror. As she did, her dress, which was very short and tight, rose almost to the top of her thighs. *What a breathtaking figure,* Tina thought. The woman pursed her lips to remove the excess lipstick, pushed back a stray blond hair, then abruptly moved away from the mirror, giving Tina, who was late in her eighth month, an unobstructed view of herself.

As soon as she got home from the restaurant that night, Tina took the Carlsons' wedding album out of the bedroom closet and removed a photo of herself. The next morning it was taped to the refrigerator door when Lem came down to breakfast. He smiled when he saw it. He remembered it well; he had taken it on the Carlsons' honeymoon. But what was a picture of Tina in a bikini doing on the refrigerator door?

"Inspiration," Tina explained when she came into the kitchen. She said that if she had to look at that near-perfect version of herself every time she turned around, she wouldn't cheat on her diet when she came home from the hospital.

Once the baby was born, Lem told himself, Tina's concerns about her weight would vanish. But this hope evaporated the morning after the delivery, when Tina stepped on the scale in the maternity ward. She was expecting it to tell her that she had lost ten or twelve pounds. But it said 127. How could you go through a ten-hour labor, have an eight-pound baby, and only lose seven pounds, Tina wondered. It did not seem mathematically possible. She stepped off the scale, removed her slippers and arm bracelet, and stepped back on: 127 again. Tina vowed to lose 4 pounds by the time she left the hospital. But when she stepped on the scale just before checking out, it had barely budged: 126½.

The next morning when Lem came down to breakfast, he found the bathroom scale sitting in front of the refrigerator under the picture of Tina in the bikini.

"You're going to drive yourself crazy," Lem warned her.

Tina shook her head and said she did not care. "What drives me crazy is looking like a blimp."

Late in her pregnancy Tina also had a premonition of the other concern that was to preoccupy her after son Will's birth. Sometime in the middle of her third trimester Tina began having a recurring dream. It was six o'clock, she had just come home from work and was about to call her baby, when she was struck by a horrifying thought: She forgot where she had put him that morning. Tina's obstetrician smiled when she told him about the dream. "You're just a little anxious about becoming a mother," he said. "Try not to worry. You're going to do fine."

However, Tina's initial experiences with Will were not reassuring. She found him hard to read and hard to soothe, and no matter what she did, she could not seem to get him on a regular feeding and sleeping schedule. Worse, others seemed to notice her difficulties. One day while she was trying to get Will to smile for her sister, Barbara, she was gently criticized for being overstimulating. "You're trying too hard," Barbara said. "Relax. He's just a little baby."

A few weeks later Tina had an even more humiliating experience in the baby park. About twenty minutes after she arrived, Will got really upset, and everything Tina did only seemed to make him cry louder. To add to her distress, the three women on the bench opposite hers seemed to be scrutinizing her every move. "Why don't you try a teething ring," one of them finally suggested. When Will spit out the ring, the other two women began offering suggestions. Pretty soon Tina felt that every one in the park was staring at her.

That afternoon when she got home, all of Tina's frustrations about Will, about her weight, and about every other aspect of her new life finally erupted in a thunderous explosion. Seven years later at the Carlsons' follow-up interview, Lem still recalled that outburst vividly. He was sitting in the living room reading a magazine when he heard a crash. Thinking that Tina had fallen, he rushed into the kitchen, where he found her standing naked in front of the refrigerator. At her feet, smashed in a half dozen pieces, was the bathroom scale.

Tina looked at him and shouted, "Shit," so loudly, Lem was certain everyone in the neighborhood heard her.

At the follow-up interview Tina said she had been convinced that no one had ever felt as incompetent, unattractive, and overweight as she had that afternoon. But several years ago, when Dr. Candace Smythe Russell of the University of Minnesota asked a group of new mothers, "What aspects of the transition do you find most stressful?" three of their top five complaints were similar to Tina's. The women said they were very unhappy about their figures and general appearance and very concerned about their parental competence. (Their other two top concerns were tiredness and unpredictable mood swings.) Dr. Russell also found that, like new mothers, new fathers tended to worry about the same things. In one way or another nearly all of the men she interviewed cited intrusive in-laws, lack of sleep, loss of free time, and all the new chores the baby had created as their top transition concerns.

Studies show that new parents are in as much accord about the transition's top satisfactions as they are about its top stresses. Among the gratifications that turn up in report after report on this topic are "the baby and all the new love he has brought into my life, the way he has changed my feelings about myself, the new sense of closeness I feel toward my spouse and toward my own mother and father."

Where new parents differ enormously, however, is on which of these two aspects of the transition—the positive or the negative—they focus on. Most mothers and fathers imagine that what they notice after baby's arrival is arbitrary and highly changeable. If the day-care center calls about an overdue bill, they will spend a few minutes worrying about how poor they have become, and if the baby suddenly produces a radiant smile, they will spend a few minutes thinking about how lucky they are to have him in their lives. But when we began talking to new parents in the early 1980s, we found that, unconsciously, mothers and fathers do a great deal of selective looking, and noticing. Like Tina, some parents tend to focus on the transition's stresses. The new joys baby has produced do not go by unnoticed, but in any given situation these individuals focus first and most intently on problems and difficulties. We also found that there is another group of parents who unconsciously do the exact opposite. In any given situation they focus first on the satisfactions and gratifications. Where others see lemons, these mothers and fathers see lemonade.

I had a graphic example of this one snowy day as I watched one of our mothers wrestle her nine-month-old into a snowsuit. As soon as the child was inside the suit and zippered up—a process that took about three or four minutes and looked to be as entertaining as wrestling a snake—an odor filled the air. A diaper change was required immediately. Under the circumstances a little parental frustration, even teeth gnashing, would have been understandable. But this mother was so transfixed by how cute her baby looked in the snowsuit that it barely registered that she was now going to have to go through the whole agonizing process a second time.

"Maddy's unbelievable," her husband said with a smile while she was upstairs getting a fresh diaper. "If Ned pulled down the roof, she'd be so thrilled by his strength, she wouldn't notice we were homeless."

Incidents like this one suggested to me that where a parent looks during the transition might have two important but still largely unappreciated consequences. The first involves the capacity to handle stress. This woman's ability to offset a fairly large negative (wrestling her baby out of his snowsuit, then having to wrestle him back into it again) with a positive observation ("But he looks so adorable, how can I be upset?") indicated to me that a talent for noticing a cloud's silver lining probably enhanced a parent's ability to cope with transition stresses. The other consequence involves marital satisfaction. It is easy to imagine the snowsuit incident developing in ways that might have undermined that satisfaction. For example, in her frustration the woman might have gotten annoyed and yelled at her husband for not offering to go upstairs and get a fresh diaper for her. But she was so thrilled by her baby's cuteness that she did not do either. This suggested to me that a positively focused mate would probably wear a lot better during the long, dark nights of the transition than one who was constantly finding fault and constantly complaining about the faults she (or he) found.

At the start of the Project these observations produced two hypotheses. We believed a parent's ability to handle stress during the transition would be determined by which aspect of it she unconsciously focused on—the positive or the negative. And this ability would also, for better or worse, influence marital satisfaction. Our data provided support for both hypotheses. Project participants with an eye for the positive were 75 percent more likely to emerge from the transition with a happier marriage than participants with an eye for the negative. Our data also supported another hypothesis we had formed. Where a parent looks during the transition—and hence the ability to handle stress in a way that hurts or helps a marriage—would be determined by Emotionality.

This is our third transition domain, and in the simplest sense it might be described as a feature of temperament that controls our emotional predisposition. People who score on the plus side of the Emotionality spectrum tend to have more positive than negative emotions; people who score on the minus side, more negative than positive ones; and people who fall in the middle tend to be equally inclined to positive and negative feelings. Emotionality is important during the transition because it affects where a parent looks. Upbeat things are more likely to catch the eye of people who tend to be upbeat, optimistic, positive, and gregarious. For the same reason problems and stresses more quickly catch the eye of individuals who are inclined toward anxiety, depression, and hostility.

It is important to emphasize that Emotionality is only a predisposition, not a form of predestination. Being slightly anxious and prone to depression will not blind a parent to all of baby's little triumphs and successes any more than being positive protects a parent against all the stressful effects of intrusive in-laws, unpaid bills, and stretch marks that will not go away. Nonetheless one's emotional set does matter during the transition, because it creates characteristic ways of thinking, looking, and even remembering that can have an important effect on a new parent's ability to handle problems and difficulties.

At the top of the stress-coping totem pole are people with positive emotionality. Because their eye for the silver lining makes them very skilled (if unconscious) self-comforters, often they are able to function well in situations that would cause other parents to lose hope and heart. A Project father named Joe Puillo provides a case in point. The troubles that were to beset Joe after the birth of daughter Anna had their origins in Vietnam eleven years earlier. One night in 1972 Joe's platoon was ambushed by a squad of Vietcong, and in the ensuing firefight he had a good part of the left side of his head shot away. Two years and three hospitals later Joe was discharged from the Marine Corps with a Purple Heart, a metal plate in his head, and a 75 percent chance of a full recovery. According to the doctors, 25 percent of those with his type of head injury subsequently developed seizures and headaches.

By the time Connie Puillo became pregnant in the summer of 1983, Vietnam and the head wound both seemed safely in the past. Joe and Connie assumed that if complications were going to develop from the wound, they would have done so by now. But one evening that summer while driving home from work, Joe felt a sudden, sharp pain in the side of his head. A moment later his hands began shaking on the steering wheel. By the time he got the car to the side of the road, his legs were starting to tremble too. The doctors at the Veterans Administration Hospital in Philadelphia told the Puillos that a new medication could help control the seizures, but because it was not 100 percent effective, Joe would not be able to operate machinery of any kind, including a car. He was warned that if he got behind the wheel, he would be a danger to himself and to others.

When Joe told his sales manager about the doctors' warning, the sales manager said he would try to get Joe transferred from his current position in outside sales, which required a lot of driving, to inside sales. But no openings were available. Four days after Anna's birth Joe surrendered his driver's license and his job. With the exception of the Vietnam period the next twelve months were the bleakest of his life. There were dozens of job rejections, the loneliness that every stay-at-home parent feels, and constant economic pressure (the Puillos were now living on Connie's much smaller salary plus Joe's monthly disability check). And hanging over everything was the ever-present fear that the medication would not work and the seizures would increase in intensity and severity.

Joe's salvation in these months became Anna, or perhaps more accurately his ability to take comfort in his little triumphs and successes with her. One way parents with positive Emotionality unconsciously self-comfort in moments of stress is by doing what that mother I mentioned earlier did: use a positive observation ("My baby looks adorable in his snowsuit") to take some of the sting out of a problem ("Now I have to go through the changing process all over again"). Another way is by using their little achievements with the baby as balms and soothers. At the Puillos' three-month observation Joe did this. He was legitimately proud of having gotten Anna on a regular sleeping and feeding schedule and of understanding her cries and moods better than Connie. But as he talked about these successes, I realized that he was also using them to stroke himself and his wounded ego. In these months every little triumph with Anna gave Joe another candle he could light against the dark.

At the Puillos' twelve-month observation I got an example of another way people like Joe self-comfort. That night he was almost bubbling over with relief. A week earlier a local market-research firm had hired him to do telephone canvassing. That night Joe was full of memories. He spent nearly the first hour of the observation recounting the events of the past year to Connie and me. Every once in a while I noticed Connie shaking her head in disbelief as she listened. Joe was painting a very bright picture of what had been a very dark year. All his little triumphs and successes with Anna were remembered and recounted in great and loving detail. But not remembered or mentioned were all the defeats and little humiliations he had endured—the jobs he had been turned down for, the five thousand dollars he had had to borrow from his brother, Alfred, the phone calls from friends asking if he had found work yet.

"You know, you're distorting things," Connie said when Joe had finished. "There were a lot of times you felt pretty awful. I know, I was there."

I was there, too, and Connie was right. Joe was guilty of selectively misremembering. But just as people with positive Emotionality notice selectively, they also remember selectively. Such individuals are much more likely to remember good rather than bad things, and when they do remember an upsetting event, they tend to recall it as not being as bad as it really was. During the Project we found that this kind of recall is also a form of unconscious self-comforting. The individual uses it to remove some of the pain and the upset from a past defeat or setback. And that was what Joe was doing. He was about to face a new challenge—a new job—and unconsciously one of the ways he was preparing his battered ego for the challenge was by giving himself a better, more rewarding year than he had experienced.

When Connie turned to me and said, "Jay, don't you think he's exaggerating?" I lit my own candle for Joe. I lied and said no.

There is a postscript to the Puillos' story, and it is worth mentioning because it illustrates another reason why people like Joe are good at handling problems and setbacks. About two months later Connie and Alfred threw Joe a combination back-to-work and birthday party. A few weeks later when I ran into Connie in a hardware store on College Avenue, she reported that the party had been a big success. "Everyone in Centre Hall [the Puillos' hometown] was there," she said. I was not surprised. Because their optimism and sociability make them so pleasant and likable, when people with positive Emotionality run into difficulty, a great many helping hands are usually extended in their direction.

Individuals with negative Emotionality are like an upside-down version of those with positive Emotionality. Where the latter can see sunlight in a cloud-filled sky, the former can see clouds in a clear blue one. For example, where one mother may only see a few weeks' more of dieting when the scale says she is still ten pounds above her prepregnancy weight, a new mother with negative Emotionality may see the threat of marital calamity (her husband will lose interest in her if she does not lose the weight now) or another reason to feel bad about herself (she still looks like a blimp). Similarly, where one mother may see the baby's temper tantrum as a request for soothing and comforting, the mother with negative Emotionality may see it as a sign of failure (she still does not know how to soothe her baby) or she may see it as a source of public humiliation. Like the witches in *Macbeth,* the other parents in the baby park have gathered around the caldron and are cackling to one another about her inadequacies and incompetence.

At the start of the Project it was fairly clear why people with negative Emotionality gravitate toward stresses and problems. A predisposition toward anxiety, depression, and hostility place a kind of invisible halo around stresses. "Invisible" because while the problems and difficulties cannot always be seen by others, the negative-minded man or woman almost always can see them. At the start of the Project, however, what was not clear was why these individuals had such difficulty dealing with the stresses they did notice. We found there were two principal reasons. The first might be called the Velcro effect. Instead of noting a problem and moving on as most people do, these men and women got stuck on it. Exhibit A of the Velcro effect is Tina Carlson's refusal to remove the photo of herself from the refrigerator door. Taping it up there was not unusual; other Project wives used prominently displayed prepregnancy photos of themselves as dieting aids. But at a certain point if the weight refused to come off, the photo came down. The transition created enough problems and difficulties, why go out of your way to add to them?

Lem made this point to Tina several times. But she was adamant;

the photo would stay where it was. So over time it metamorphized. Instead of being a source of inspiration it became a standing rebuke. Every time Tina turned around, it was there to remind her of how slowly the weight was coming off and how far away she still was from being the perfectly proportioned young woman in the picture.

A second reason why people like Tina have trouble coping with stress is what might be called the magnifying effect. Unwittingly they often turn a little stress into a medium-size one, and a medium-size one into a big one. Exhibit A of this phenomenon was Tina's destruction of the scale. Before she flung it to the ground, she already had two reasons to feel bad about herself. Her maternal competence had been called into question by Will's crying jag in the park, and her dream of being the young woman in the photo again by the scale. Throwing the scale to the ground gave her a third fairly big reason to feel bad about herself. On top of everything else she was behaving immaturely.

A Freudian might say that Tina's last wound had been self-inflicted. She felt bad about the incident in the park and about not losing weight as quickly as she wanted to, so unconsciously she decided to punish herself by doing something that would make her feel even worse. But the recent research on Emotionality suggests that some of the roots of Tina's outbursts lay elsewhere—in biology. People with negative Emotionality have what physiologists call reactive nervous systems; they are innately high-strung in comparison to others. And in moments of stress, hostility and anxiety cycle through them in ways that turn this reactivity into overreactivity. The individual blows up and does something to make a bad situation worse.

A conversation the Carlsons had that evening at dinner illustrates another important point about negative Emotionality: It can be controlled. Just as a secure person is better able to regulate her autonomy and affiliation drives, she is also better able to regulate her anxiety and proneness toward hostility and depression, because her security makes her confident enough to reach out for help when she feels upset. Talking through a problem with a sympathetic spouse can remove a lot of its sting. And as soon as Lem sat down to dinner that night, Tina told him about the incident in the park (which he did not know about), her frustrations about her weight (which he did), and how stupid and immature she felt for breaking the scale.

At the Carlsons' follow-up interview Lem did not recall this conversation. But it was still very vivid to Tina, who said that the opportunity to ventilate her frustrations to a sympathetic spouse left her feeling better than she had in weeks. Unfortunately, she added, "I had to ruin it by going out the next day and buying a new scale."

One of the major surprises to emerge from the Project was the number of people who have emotional dispositions that are an almost equal mixture of positive and negative. Conventional wisdom holds that one is, to varying degrees, either upbeat and optimistic or anxious and hostile. But a significant number of our participants were both upbeat and downbeat. And often this combination gave their responses to transition stresses a self-correcting quality. A conversation I had with Barbara D'Amato provides a case in point.

The morning of this particular talk Barbara was in a foul mood. Just before I arrived, she had gotten a phone call from the Central Pennsylvania Light and Power Company about an overdue electric bill. Unless it was paid immediately and in person, the D'Amatos' electricity would be shut off the next day at noon.

"What a nincompoop," Barbara said as she poured me coffee.

"Phil?" I asked.

"Who else? He was supposed to pay that bill last week. Now I have to waste the whole morning waiting in line."

Phil's latest transgression put Barbara in mind of all of Phil's other transgressions. She began complaining about his lack of help with Celeste, moved on to his unfulfilled promise to fix the leak in the basement, and ended up with her favorite bête noire—Phil's dogs.

Phil raised bull terriers in the D'Amatos' backyard, and in her darker moods Barbara would convince herself that Phil was fonder of his dogs than he was of her. "Do you know that every time we have a fight, Phil goes out back and talks to those goddamn dogs? Maybe he should have married one of them."

At that point Celeste D'Amato, disheveled and still heavy with sleep, wandered into the kitchen with her teddy bear and asked for breakfast. Her impact on her mother was as dramatic as a rainbow at the end of a summer squall. Barbara was aglow. I'm pretty sure Phil got an earful that night about his forgetfulness, his dogs, and the leak in the basement. But I'm also pretty sure that earful would have been much more caustic and the woman delivering it much unhappier if she lacked Barbara's ability to filter husbandly transgressions through the joy she took in her child.

Our decision to include Emotionality in our study of new parents' marital satisfaction was influenced by the emergence of what is known as family systems theory. In the early research on the transition, and indeed on marriage in general, each partner tended to be treated as a distinct and autonomous unit. What the husband said and did and felt was thought to raise one set of research issues; what the wife said and did and felt, another. In the 1970s husbands and wives were finally brought together under the microscope. This joining together is called family systems theory and it is based on a commonsensical but important observation: A marriage is more than a union of two autonomous individuals; over time it also becomes a distinct self-contained system, and like all such systems, what happens to one person in it ends up affecting the other person in it, whether it is intended or not.

In transition research, family systems theory has often been used to study parenting. A number of investigators have examined how and in what ways one partner's parenting is influenced by the other's support and encouragement. As we shall see later, during the Project we also did some of this research. But we went beyond parenting and applied family systems theory to Emotionality. What we found was not surprising: How one partner copes with stress affects the other partner, whether it is intended or not, which is to say that how one partner copes with stress affects both partners' marriage, whether it is intended or not.

The principal reason for this is companionability. During the baby's first year especially, when a husband and wife must rely largely on each other for companionship and the ability to cope with stress, companionability can be affected in two ways. One involves contentiousness. As I have already pointed out and as we shall see in some detail in the next chapter, a certain amount of fighting is actually beneficial for new parents. But a spouse who yells at her mate every time she is frustrated or frightened by a stress makes a much more exhausting companion than one like Barbara D'Amato or Joe Puillo, who can use their ability to notice and savor gratifications in order to comfort themselves when something distressing happens.

The other reason involves the even more fundamental issues of pleasantness and civility. Loneliness is a common complaint among men and women with negative Emotionality. They often complained that they did not get the attention they wanted, needed, and felt they deserved. But when we talked to their spouses, they would usually plead self-defense. The transition is hard enough, they said, why make it harder by spending your precious free time with a mate who does nothing but complain about the state of the house, the baby, the bills, your parents, and you? I remember the wife of one complaining husband telling me that out of self-protection she had taken to hiding herself during the evenings. When dinner was through, she busied herself with the baby, and after he was put down, the woman took a handful of magazines and went into the bathroom. "It's not much of a life," she said, "but it is better than listening to Bill complain all night about how poor we are and how terrible his job is."

Family systems theory also suggested that how big a plus or minus Emotionality became for a couple would depend on how both partners, not just one, scored on it. Not surprisingly we found that the marriages that got the biggest lift from this domain were those where the husband and wife were both positive. Also not surprisingly we found that the marriages most threatened by it were those where both partners were, to varying degrees, negative. We found that marriages where one partner was positive and the other negative could move in either direction. If the positive partner stepped into the marriage and used his sunny disposition to navigate himself and his partner through the storm, a marital decline was usually forestalled. But if he (or she) kept the sunshine to himself, usually the marriage declined—sometimes as precipitously as Larry and Monica Marchands'.

At intake interviews I frequently could not predict where a new parent would fall on the Emotionality spectrum. But I did not have that trouble with Larry, who is a professor at the university. At the Marchands' intake interview he was charming, funny, upbeat, and engaging. That night he also seemed very supportive of Monica. But after daughter Christine's birth Larry suddenly began spending many evenings at work. He insisted that the late nights were a professional obligation. He didn't want to spend the rest of his life as an associate professor, he told Monica. But as the months passed, Monica began to feel that Larry's late nights had less to do with his desire for professional advancement than with his desire to get away from her. "I think he's just using work as an excuse to get away from me," Monica told me at the end of the Marchands' three-month observation.

I was not sure whether this remark was an accurate reflection of Larry's intentions or simply the imaginings of Monica's negativity. But my concern about her, which had been growing from observation to observation, leapfrogged into something like alarm the drizzly March afternoon I arrived at the Marchands' for the nine-month observation. On these occasions it was very rare for me to be offered anything stronger than coffee, but almost as soon as I sat down in the kitchen, Monica took a bottle of wine from the refrigerator and asked me if I would like to join her in a glass. When I declined, she poured herself one, then a second. By the time I left two hours later the bottle was nearly empty.

Three weeks later Monica called to say she and Larry would be leaving the Project. They were separating. She spent a few minutes telling me about her plans. She and Christie were moving back to Hagerstown (Maryland), where she had grown up. Her parents had bought "a lovely little house for the two of them," she said. I had the feeling that what Monica really wanted to tell me was why she and Larry were separating. Although she never clearly said so, I got the distinct impression another woman might be involved.*

I never got the chance to speak to Larry again. One day I saw him crossing the campus, but he saw me first and ducked into the Old Main Building. But one of my graduate students, who worked as an observer on the Project, did talk to him. She ran into Larry one afternoon in the bookstore and they spent several minutes chatting. She said Larry felt guilty about the way the Marchands' marriage ended. But he also felt that the breakup had been more Monica's fault than his; she had driven him to it. According to the student, Larry said that in the last months of his marriage he had begun to feel as if he was drowning. "I felt that if I didn't get away from her, I'd end up becoming as sour as Monica," he had asserted.

Driving home from the Carlsons' intake interview, I found myself thinking about the Marchands. Like Larry, Lem also scored high on the positive end of the Emotionality spectrum, and like Monica, Tina

* How common are extramarital affairs during the transition? Larry Marchand's was the only one in our cohort of 250 couples. Carolyn Pape Cowan and Philip Cowan, who followed 72 couples, reported three in their group. But these numbers may significantly understate the incidence of affairs in this period, because neither we nor the Cowans were specifically looking at this issue. In both cases the affairs surfaced more or less spontaneously.

was fairly negative. Would Lem behave like Larry or would he put his optimism at the service of his marriage? I came away from the Carlsons' one-month observation still unsure about the answer to this question. Tina, who had taken a four-month maternity leave, was clearly beginning to feel overwhelmed by the demands of her new life. But I had not gotten any inkling of how her upset was affecting Lem, or what if anything he was doing to help her. He had been held up at school by a conference and did not arrive until much later than scheduled.

During the Carlsons' three-month observation, however, the level of Lem's support began to become apparent. This was my first visit to their new home, which, like Ron and Sue Akerses', was located in one of the new and rather bleak-looking housing developments that had sprung up around Penn State. No trees were visible when I pulled onto the main drive, and outside of a solitary child on a tricycle, there were no people either. The houses that stood at the end of each neatly manicured lawn looked empty and still. Lem's and Tina's home was in a cul-de-sac called Pine View Drive and, like the surrounding houses, was a split-level raised ranch with brick on the bottom and white siding on the top. Tina was standing by the bay window when I pulled into the driveway. She had the phone in one hand and was gesturing wildly with the other. She looked upset.

"Jay, let yourself in," she shouted when I rang the doorbell. "I'm on the phone."

I went into the kitchen and unpacked my briefcase. I was surprised to see a new bathroom scale sitting in front of the refrigerator.

"I'm sorry," Tina said when she joined me a few minutes later. "That was the bank. There's been a screw-up with our mortgage." She said the Carlsons had calculated their mortgage payments at $400 a month, but when their coupon book arrived in the mail this morning, $475 was printed on each coupon. Tina did not know how she and Lem had miscalculated, but she did know they did not have the extra

$75 a month. "We're already up to our eyeballs," she said. "I can get the money from Daddy, but Lem will have a fit." Tina frowned. "I may have to ask him anyway."

Just then Will began to cry. He had woken up from his nap.

One of the things we notice about parents like Barbara D'Amato and Joe Puillo is that the ability to derive joy and comfort from a child produces a kind of synergistic effect. The joy the baby produces flows inward, bounces off the parental heart, and then flows back out in the form of warm, energetic, zesty parental behaviors. A twelve-week-old cannot identify much, but she can identify a hug or a warm tone of voice that says, "I think you're absolutely terrific." Parents who lack this facility for joy often respond to the child the way Tina responded to Will as she removed him from the crib. Everything she did was technically correct. Entering the baby's room she murmured, "Good afternoon, Mommy's little boy." And as soon as she had Will in her arms, she gave him a hug. But her gestures and tone of voice lacked the music, the zest that reflects a capacity to be inspired, to be lifted up by the baby.

Particularly in moments of stress a parent like Tina also has trouble reading the child's moods and cues. When he cries, spits up, or does something else upsetting, the parent's reactivity produces an all-consuming, all-preoccupying distress that hinders her ability to analyze the situation calmly and determine the cause of the upsetting behavior. I suspect this phenomenon was at the root of Tina's difficulty in the park that day, and I am certain it was at the root of what happened on this visit. As soon as Will was sufficiently awake, the three of us repaired next door to the bathroom. Tina wanted to give him a bath. But the moment Will hit the water, he began howling. At first Tina thought perhaps the water was too hot for him. But when she removed Will from the tub and began rocking him, he cried louder. "He just woke up," she said, "maybe he's still a little grumpy."

After putting Will back in the tub Tina picked up a rubber bunny from the floor and began waving it in front of him. But that only produced more tears. Tina began to panic. "Do you think he's hurt?" I told her I didn't know. "Let me see if he's hungry," she said. Will was removed from the tub a second time. But when Tina lifted up her blouse and put him to her breast, Will turned away and cried still louder.

At this point the cavalry arrived. Lem, who had just gotten home, walked into the bathroom and rescued the three of us. "I think Will's got some water in his eye."

"Those are tears," Tina said.

"It's easy to miss," Lem said, taking Will out of her arms. "But look, see how he's squinting? I'll bet he has some water in his eye." Lem pulled out his shirttail and began dabbing the area around his son's left eye. A few seconds later Will's crying had subsided to a series of intermittent whimpers and sobs.

I was struck by Lem's skill in managing this intervention. He had made himself a helpful, even forceful presence in a moment of difficulty without humiliating Tina. He had done nothing to make her feel inept or inadequate. I was also struck by how quickly he turned his attention to her once Will was under control. "Why don't you go downstairs and throw your feet up for a few minutes?" he said. "I'll take Will into the bedroom with me while I change."

Sheets, pillows, and a comforter were still scattered across the top of the Carlsons' bed when we arrived. "I have a good idea," Lem said to Will. "Why don't we make the bed." That task accomplished, Lem put Will on top of the comforter and began tickling him with one hand while he took off his shirt with another. A constant stream of mostly nonsensical chatter accompanied all of this motion. Lem asked Will if there was any truth to the rumors about him and Christie Brinkley and what did he think the Phillies would do this year? He also reminded his son that there were only twenty-five days until his sainted dad's birthday. Out of the corner of my eye I saw Tina standing in the doorway. For the first time since the observation began, she was smiling.

After the three of us came downstairs, Lem got another smile out of his wife.

When Tina, who was wearing a pair of bicycle shorts, bent down to pick up a pillow that had fallen off the couch, Lem said, "Mmm." It was not the same kind of "Mmm" produced by freshly baked bread.

Tina giggled and threw the pillow at him.

"Fresh. We've got company."

Lem picked up the pillow, walked over, and kissed Tina on the cheek.

"I just remembered; I forgot to kiss you."

Tina's behavior with Will during the rest of the observation was a good example of one of the family systems theory's main tenets: The more supportive and encouraging a man is to his wife, the better parent she is to their child. Lem's presence in the house was akin to plugging a light cord into an outlet. Tina lit up. And the principal beneficiary of her brightness was Will. When Lem handed him to Tina a few minutes later, suddenly her voice and gestures had all the music, all the zest and excitement that had been lacking before.

Two weeks later when we received the Carlsons' latest set of Marital Quality Questionnaires, Lem's and Tina's scores on all four of the indexes we use to track marital satisfaction were up by 5 to 10 percent.

9

Constructive Fighters, Destructive Fighters, and Avoiders

It began raining just as the Renselears' Saab pulled out of the O'Briens' driveway. "Be careful, you two," Jennifer's mother shouted from the porch. Then she reached inside the white quilt nestled against her chest, took her granddaughter's hand, and made a waving motion with it. Jennifer smiled and waved back, but there was not much enthusiasm in her gesture. At the end of her parents' street she turned around and tried to get a final glimpse of Ali. But from that distance all she could see through the rain-streaked back window was a white blur in her mother's arms. She turned around and slumped into her seat.

"You promised me you'd try to relax," Cal said without taking his eyes off the road.

"I know. I will." Twenty minutes later the Renselears were out of Boston and heading west along the Massachusetts Turnpike.

Spending Memorial Day weekend in the Berkshires had been Cal's idea. If they could get away by themselves for a few days, he thought, maybe they could start sorting out their lives. But as they headed west that wet Friday morning, Jennifer seemed to slip deeper into the funk that had begun at her parents' house. Glancing over at her, Cal found himself wondering if it was always going to be like this: two people so estranged they could not even make small talk. He knew that Jennifer had been through a great deal with Ali, and for that he had much sympathy. But the hematoma was gone now, healed without a trace. Why couldn't she shake off her sullenness and depression? Sometimes Cal felt that Jennifer almost willed herself to be unhappy. At the Sharon exit about forty miles east of Stockbridge, he suggested stopping at Howard Johnson's for lunch. It was the first time either of them had spoken in an hour.

Seven years later at the follow-up interview, Cal's memory of what happened next was still very vivid. He was sitting across from Jennifer examining his menu when he heard a low whining sound, almost like a puppy's whimper. When he looked up, he saw that she had begun crying.

"What is it? What's the matter?"

"I don't know," Jennifer said, shaking her head. "But I can't help it." For a moment she seemed to regain control of herself, but then the tears began again. This time her sobs were so deep and loud that heads started to turn. Cal felt self-conscious.

"Please, Jen," he whispered. "People are staring at us."

"Do you think I'm doing this on purpose? For God's sake, give me a hanky."

"I don't have one."

"Here." An elderly woman leaned over the booth divider and handed Cal a handkerchief. "Is she all right?" the woman asked, pointing at Jennifer.

Cal felt an irrational impulse to grab the woman's finger and bend it back until it snapped. Instead he thanked her for the handkerchief and said his wife was a little overtired. She would be fine in a moment.

The woman did not look convinced.

The restaurant was very quiet now. "Take a deep breath," Cal said.

"Maybe that will help." But Jennifer could not hear him. She was crying so hard now, she had begun to shake.

Once when he was nine, Cal had seen his mother fall into a similar crying spasm. "I'm sorry," she kept saying. "I don't know what's wrong with me today." But Cal was already old enough to know what was wrong. His mother was crying about all the hurt and humiliation in her life. Her anguish had seemed too big, too frightening for a nine-year-old to deal with, so Cal had remained in his seat, a silent bystander to the pain of someone he loved. This time he decided he would not be. Ignoring the elderly woman, the other diners, and his own acute embarrassment, he slid over to Jennifer's side of the booth, put his arm around her, and sat there holding her until she had cried herself out.

At their follow-up interview both Renselears indicated that after their return from the Berkshires that weekend slowly, tentatively things began to change between them. Jennifer recalled being surprised and touched by a conversation they had one evening a few weeks later as they were sitting in the garden behind the kitchen. Suddenly Cal, who normally shied away from talk about "the relationship," evidenced a deep concern for it. "It's kind of crazy if you think about it," he said. "My energy goes into work, yours goes into Ali, and we just let the marriage float along on its own. We have to start being smarter about ourselves."

At the follow-up interview, Jennifer also recalled getting another pleasant surprise a few days later at breakfast. They were looking through the newspaper for a movie to see when Cal pointed at an ad for *The Terminator* and said, "Hey, this looks like fun." The thought of spending two hours with Arnold Schwarzenegger did not exactly thrill Jennifer, but Cal usually made the Renselears' movie choices, so she shrugged and said, "Okay, if you want."

"You don't look like a happy camper."

"No, no, *The Terminator*'s fine with me," Jennifer insisted. "Honest."

"Uh-uh," Cal said, picking up the paper. "You've suffered through enough of my movies. Let's find something we both want to see."

Touched by such solicitousness, Jennifer began to reach out toward Cal, and as she did so, a sense of intimacy began to return to their marriage. "It's hard to explain," she said at the follow-up interview, "but after the Berkshires it felt as if a weight had been lifted from us, from the marriage."

"Maybe because the hematoma wasn't there anymore to divide the two of you," I suggested.

"I think that was a big part of it," Jennifer replied. "I was so tense and worried in the first few months after Ali's birth that even if Cal had been kinder, I wouldn't have appreciated it. But by that Memorial Day the hematoma was gone, and I was relaxed enough to be touched by his attempts to make amends and get us back on track." For a while that summer, Jennifer said, the Renselears' sex life began to regain some of its old energy and excitement. She and Cal even began talking about a subject they'd both been consciously avoiding for a long time—the future. Maybe they would go to Europe next summer, or maybe they would buy a new house. While neither was ready for it yet, there were even a few exploratory discussions about another child.

Because we did not see our couples between the third and ninth month postpartum, I did not have an opportunity to witness these changes firsthand. But I did get one brief indication that something important had altered between the Renselears. Coming out of Vesuvio's, an Italian restaurant on College Avenue, one afternoon late that June, I heard someone call my name. When I turned around, I saw a tall, sleek, stylish young woman approaching me. It was Jennifer, but it took me a moment to recognize her. She looked like she had lost twenty pounds and nearly as many years since the Renselears' last observation in March.

We did not do much more than exchange pleasantries that afternoon. Jennifer had an aerobics class to go to, and I was on my way to an observation. But the dramatic change in her appearance and manner—she was the fluttery, animated Jennifer of the intake interview again—suggested a very major change in her life. And the warmth in her voice when I asked about Cal suggested this change had something to do with him. Of all the *what ifs* in the Renselears' story, the biggest is how their reconciliation might have fared if what happened next hadn't.

One morning about a week after we ran into each other, Jennifer woke up with what felt like a terrible hangover. She was nauseous, woozy, and light-headed. She thought it was a summer flu. But when the hangover returned the next morning and the morning after that, another possibility crossed her mind. There had not been any morning sickness with Ali, and God knows she and Cal were always very careful. Still, as a precaution, she decided to have a pregnancy test.

"Should I congratulate you?" her obstetrician asked when he called her to tell her it was positive.

"I don't know," Jennifer recalled telling him. "I have to sit down and think about it for a minute."

At the follow-up interview Cal dated the end of the Renselears' reconciliation to that phone call. "Jennifer decided she wanted the baby, I decided I didn't, and bang," he said, slapping his hands together for emphasis, "we ended up flying apart all over again." I did not challenge Cal's explanation. But I knew that at best it was an oversimplification. What ended up pushing him and Jennifer apart again was not the sudden appearance of a big disagreement in their marriage—that happens all the time during the transition. It was rather that they, and especially Cal, had never learned to fight constructively about big disagreements.

The notion that fighting, or what we called Conflict Management, might be among the most important skills new parents possess first occurred to me while reading the work of Dr. John Gottman of the

University of Washington. One of the oldest truisms of marital research is that fighting about differences makes them worse. But in the 1980s Dr. Gottman's work began to challenge this notion. His studies of married couples showed that arguing can often make differences less divisive rather than more so. It gives a couple an opportunity to share thoughts and feelings that, unshared, can lead to future misunderstandings and to ventilate grievances and frustrations that, unventilated, can produce destructive acting-out behavior.

Dr. Gottman's theory of marital conflict was based largely on work with middle-aged couples. But reading it over, I found myself thinking that if he was right, his findings might even be more relevant to the couples I was about to study. After all, Project families would be living through an especially challenging period in the marital cycle—one in which the diverging priorities of His and Her transition risked putting them at odds about money, sex, division of labor, and a dozen other issues that his largely middle-aged subjects most likely had already resolved—or at least had learned to live with.

That became one of our major hypotheses about Conflict Management. At the start of the Project we conjectured that, for all the reasons I outlined in Chapter Two, the transition would increase the incidence of conflict among new parents. Our second hypothesis about this domain was based on another piece of Dr. Gottman's research: his identification of three common styles of conflict management, which we called Constructive Fighting, Destructive Fighting, and Avoidance. We conjectured that how well new parents were able to handle the increase in disagreements would be determined by which of these three styles they employed. And our careful analysis of individual families tended to support both hypotheses. Overall, the diverging priorities of the transition increased the incidence of conflict among our subjects by 20 to 30 percent, while their ability to handle this increase was determined by which of Dr. Gottman's three fighting styles they employed.

Most successful were our Constructive Fighters. These couples did not always get what they wanted in an argument, but they often seemed to get what they needed: the sense that their thoughts and feelings on an important issue had been heard, understood, and if not agreed with at least respected. Less successful were our Destructive Fighters. Often arguments gave these couples so little of what they wanted and needed that they were at each other again an hour later. Also unsuccessful in managing conflict were our Avoiders, whose aversion to locking horns about differences often ended up making those differences much more divisive than they had to be.

How did we explore these three styles of marital fighting?

Our principal tool was what we called the Conflict Experiment. At a certain point during their stay in the Project we gave our couples a list of six hot-button issues (sex, work, religion, division of labor, the relationship, and money) and a tape recorder. Then we asked them to pick what they considered to be the two most contentious issues on the list, go into another room, and discuss them for ten minutes with the tape recorder on. Our instructions said nothing about conflict or fighting. But our expectation was that at a certain point, the discussion of volatile issues would provoke a disagreement, perhaps even an argument. Eventually many of our couples ended up fighting. Our analysis of these "conflict" tapes supported another recent finding about marital disagreement: Men and women tend to argue in very different ways.

Typically women play the more assertive role in disagreements. On our tapes, for example, usually it was the wife who first raised the hot-button issues. How did her husband think they could resolve their differences about sex, work, or religion? However, since men seem as eager to avoid disagreements as women are to confront them, these attempts to initiate a discussion often did not succeed. The male voices on our tapes frequently were flat, unemotional, and above all wary. They all but screamed, "I don't want to talk about this; let me out of here." The pattern of escalation and counterescalation that characterizes extreme marital conflict tends to be triggered by this male stonewalling, which so frustrates the wife that she raises her voice, which then gets the man so annoyed, he drops his passivity and begins to strongly defend himself.

Constructive Fighters, Destructive Fighters, and Avoiders all employ this basic form of marital conflict: The wife is typically the confrontational partner, while the husband tends to be wary, self-contained, and hesitant to engage in open disagreement. But Constructive Fighters are the only ones who know how to use conflict to promote long-term marital happiness. To the untrained eye and ear their fights may look and sound like everyone else's. But in the midst of serious disagreement each partner gets an opportunity to air his or her thoughts on important issues and to ventilate frustrations and grievances.

I suspect that what makes Constructive Fighters virtuosos of the form is their mutual affection and regard. Simply put, they both love and like each other, and during arguments these feelings serve them in two important ways. One is by preventing them from crossing the inviolate line that transforms an argument from a forum for airing and resolving disputes into a street fight whose only aim is to inflict punishment. The recent research shows that both men and women emit certain distinct signs when they feel they have or are about to be grievously injured in a fight and want it to stop. In men these warning signals include whining, defensiveness, and agitated attempts to withdraw—instead of slowly backing away toward the door the husband lunges for it. In women these signals include sadness and fear. Studies also show that when these signs are ignored, often the injured partner "loses it" and the fight spins out of control. Constructive Fighters will argue right up to these warning signals, which provides both partners with plenty of room to air frustrations and upsets. But once one of these signs appears, the attacker, unconsciously sensing danger, backs off and gives his or her opponent room to make a graceful retreat.

The second characteristic of Constructive Fighters also arises out of their high mutual regard. For most husbands and wives the chief priority in an argument is winning. While this is also important to Constructive Fighters, just as important is the desire to end the interruption of their happiness. And research by Dutch psychologist Cas Schapp shows that this desire makes Constructive Fighters different from other squabbling couples in a second important way. Even in the midst of the most heated arguments they continue to offer olive branches to each other in the form of concessions and compromises.

During the Project I witnessed very few actual fights. For obvious reasons our couples preferred to settle their differences privately. But one I did see illustrates how the ability to fight constructively can keep even differences about very volatile issues such as religion from spinning out of control. During their early years together Paul and Rebecca Trintano considered their religious differences largely beside the point. If anything, Paul rather liked it that Rebecca was Jewish, and Rebecca liked it that Paul was Catholic. Both considered it a mark of their worldliness, of how far they had traveled from the provincialism of their families that they were with a partner of a different religion. But as often happens, once Rebecca learned she was pregnant, the Trintanos found old loyalties, old habits of the heart stirring.

Rebecca had never paid much attention to the Jewish Community Center she passed each day on her way to and from work. But during the pregnancy suddenly that building became like some wrathful Old Testament prophet, which rose each morning at eight-thirty and each evening at five-thirty to point an accusing finger at her and remind her of where she came from, who she was, and the heritage she was about to deprive her child of. Paul's reawakening was hastened by his immigrant Sicilian grandmother, who warned him that if his child went unbaptized, it would bring eternal dishonor on the Trintano family.

The fight I witnessed represented the first serious breakdown in the agreement Paul and Rebecca had made to deal with their complicated new feelings about religion. A few hours before I arrived for an observation, Paul had come home with a Christmas tree, which greatly upset Rebecca. Wasn't the agreement that they would expose their son equally to the symbols of Judaism and Christianity? There had been no Hanukkah bush that year, she said, so there should not be a Christmas tree either.

I'm sure that Rebecca had no desire to share her sense of grievance with me. But sometimes big upsets become so big and hard to contain that they spill out into the conversation, even when the person does not want to talk about them. And that's more or less what happened at dinner.

When Paul got up and announced he was going to water the tree, Rebecca looked up from her plate and snarled his name as if it were an epithet. Unaware of the Trintanos' earlier exchange, I was stunned by this sudden outburst of anger. But Paul, who managed to look both embarrassed and frightened, was not.

"Look, I don't know why you're making such a big deal about the tree," he said. "I told you, it's like Santa Claus. It doesn't mean a thing."

"You should have discussed it with me."

"What? Now I have to clear everything with you?"

"We agreed . . ."

"We agreed what, Becky? Do you really want to deprive your kid of a Christmas tree? C'mon."

The next few exchanges were so sharp, I was sure the argument was about to spin out of control. But then, unexpectedly, Paul's voice softened. "You're right," he said. "I should have talked to you before I bought the tree."

At first I attributed this sudden peace offering to my presence. I thought Paul did not want me to see them fighting. But when I turned around and looked at Rebecca, I realized he had noticed something I had not: Her expression had changed from angry to sad. A moment later he displayed the second characteristic of a Constructive Fighter.

"You know, we could still get a Hanukkah bush," he said.

When Rebecca declared, "It's too late now," Paul offered her another compromise. "You said you'd like to have a Passover seder at the house. Maybe we could do it this year."

I don't think this suggestion entirely mollified Rebecca either. But knowing that her concerns had been heard and understood did. That night when I said good-bye to the Trintanos, they had their arms around each other.

What qualities characterize Destructive Fighters?

Their arguments also follow the basic form of marital conflict. Usually the wife initiates the discussion of problems in their relationship and the husband tries to withdraw. But the feelings Destructive Fighters bring to their disagreements lead them to do very different things with the form. Typically there are a lot of grudges and resentments in their marriages and insufficient mutual regard or affection to temper these. Among other things these negative feelings make them much more likely to ignore the warning signals of spousal distress or even notice indices of spousal consideration and understanding. This tends to be especially true of Destructive Fighting wives. On our tapes they can be heard ignoring their husbands' olive branches and signs of distress, such as whining, defensiveness, and withdrawal, and getting increasingly irritated in the process.

A few years ago when Dr. Jessica Bell of the University of California asked a group of such wives why they pressed home their attacks so ferociously, she got a surprising answer. In almost every case the women reported that their aggressiveness was really an expression of powerlessness. They said their husbands subtly controlled the pace and tempo of arguments through their stonewalling. Frustrated at not getting through, these wives said they often upped their attacks in hopes of breaking through that wall and evoking some kind of human response—some kind of connection. Typically at some point in the conflict the Destructive Fighting wife does get through, and just as typically the result is a cycle of escalation and counterescalation. Annoyed that his distress signals have been ignored, the besieged husband launches a fierce counterattack, producing sadness and fear in the wife, who after regaining her momentum then launches an even more ferocious counter-counterattack. At that point the argument usually spins out of control and becomes about nothing but inflicting misery and pain on each other.

It will probably not come as much of a surprise to learn that this kind of fighting undermines marital happiness by making divisive issues even more divisive than they already are, as well as eroding whatever positive feelings a couple have for each other. But a recent study by a husband-and-wife team from Ohio State University indicates it can also threaten a couple's physical health. Over the last few years animal research has shown that high levels of stress can impair the functioning of the immune system, the body's first line of defense against disease. This work raised a question in the minds of Drs. Janice Kiecolt-Glaser and Ronald Glaser: Do marital conflicts produce enough stress to affect a couple's immune systems? In the case of Destructive Fighters the answer turns out to be yes. Round-the-clock physiological monitoring of such couples shows that the hostility and negativity in their arguments produces so much stress that for a full twenty-four hours afterward they experience a drop in eight key measures of immune-system functioning.

Often the ten minutes we allotted for the Conflict Experiment was not enough for Destructive Fighters, who would just be hitting their stride when I came to collect the tape recorder. But couples who employed Avoidance, the third common Conflict Management style, frequently had as much trouble filling up their ten minutes of discussion time as Michael and Lotte Fishman, the Project couple I mentioned in Chapter Seven.

I think it was a measure of the Fishmans' nervousness about the procedure that the night I arrived to conduct it, we spent nearly fifteen minutes negotiating about where to do it. I suggested the den, playroom, and bedroom, but Michael and Lotte finally decided they preferred the kitchen. "That's where we do most of our talking anyway," Michael said. But because the kitchen did not have a door, what would they do about me? Eventually we decided I would station myself in the front hall, which was forty feet away. From that distance I could hear the murmur of the Fishmans' voices but not what they were saying. After placing a tape recorder and our hot-button list on the kitchen table, I took my position by the door and began flipping through a magazine. A few minutes later I started to feel vaguely uneasy. There had been a subtle change in the house while I was reading. But what was it? It took me a moment to realize there were no more sounds coming from the kitchen. Lotte and Michael had fallen silent. I looked at my watch. They had nearly five minutes left. What happened? I knew the Fishmans did not lack for things to disagree about.

One of the issues on our hot-button list was work, and I knew from previous observations as well as from their Marital Quality Questionnaires that work remained a very hot-button issue for the Fishmans. Lotte was growing increasingly unhappy with Michael's criticism of her business trips and even more unhappy about his refusal to help out more with nine-month-old Ben.

At the end of the taping I found the Fishmans where I had left them —sitting across from each other at the kitchen table. Michael was looking through a newspaper, and Lotte was staring at a Laura Ashley print on the wall. The silence in the room was oppressive and a little sad.

"You two finished early," I said.

Lotte looked at me and smiled uncertainly. She was not sure if this was good or bad. Michael put down his newspaper and asked me how I thought Penn State would do against Michigan the following Saturday. In some instinctive way he seemed to sense that he and Lotte had just revealed something telling, something damaging about themselves and their marriage. And embarrassed by it, he wanted to change the subject as quickly as possible. The three of us sat at the table for about fifteen minutes exchanging small talk, then I announced it was time for me to leave. But the Fishmans seemed reluctant to let me go. They began peppering me with questions about the Project. It almost seemed as if they dreaded being left alone with each other. That could have been my imagination of course. But often, being alone is a frightening prospect for Avoider couples because it means being alone with all the unspoken resentments, hurts, and frustrations in their marriage, and with the deafening silence those unvoiced feelings create.

Why are Avoider couples so reluctant to confront disagreements?

One chief reason is fear. One or both partners believe that confronting marital differences will make them harder to resolve than they already are. Maybe if we don't talk about them, Avoiders—and Avoider husbands in particular—think, our differences will just go away. Sometimes this fear arises from personal experience. Men and women such as Cal Renselear, who have lived through a childhood of parental conflict, often conclude that the worst way to deal with differences is to argue about them. Other times the fear arises from a sense of vulnerability. The couple feels that their marriage is too fragile to withstand the rough and tumble of argument. Another factor that can promote avoidance is upbringing. One reason this style of conflict management is more common among men than women is that little boys are taught to control their emotions, little girls to express them.

Ironically couples who elect to avoid rather than confront differences often end up seeing their worst fears realized. Their mutual resentments build and build until, like a rubber band stretched to its limit, one day the husband and wife snap and go at each other in the take-no-prisoners style of Destructive Fighters. Toward the end of the Fishmans' first year in the Project, Lotte told me that she and Michael had fallen into this trap. "Things have gotten pretty bad between us lately," she said one day. "Michael raises his voice, I raise mine, and the next thing we know, we are screaming accusations and threats at each other."

Besides Destructive Fighting, Avoidance has another, even greater danger: The other partner can perceive it as a form of emotional disengagement. The Avoider does not care enough about the marriage to lock horns on issues critical to its future. And because such ducking tends to produce a lot of anger and resentment as well as a sense of abandonment, in time it usually ends up pushing a couple apart.

Exhibit A of this phenomenon is the impact Cal Renselear's evasions concerning Jennifer's pregnancy had on the Renselears' marriage. At the seven-year follow-up interview Jennifer recalled that initially she was as confused and upset as Cal by her obstetrician's news.

"After he hung up that afternoon," she said, "I just stood there staring at the phone wondering, 'What now?' "

But over the next few days, a little to her surprise, Jennifer found herself warming to the idea of a baby. "I wanted another child, and at thirty-two I thought now might not be a bad time to have one." However, she also recalled that she would not have been terribly upset if Cal had felt differently.

"I had a lot of reservations too. I wasn't sure if I wanted to go through a second pregnancy so soon after the first, and I didn't want to do anything to hurt the marriage. That summer we were happier than we'd been in years." Jennifer stopped and looked at Cal. "Mostly what I wanted was just to know that whatever decision we made about the baby, we made together."

However, that wish was never fulfilled because the obstetrician's news had confronted Cal with the classic Avoider's dilemma. He thought another child now was a bad idea. He wasn't at all sure Jennifer or the marriage were up to it. But he thought drawing a line in the sand and saying no was an even worse idea. His parents spent their marriage drawing lines in the sand, and look what they'd done to each other and to him. So the most Cal would say was that while he had some reservations about proceeding with the pregnancy, ultimately it was Jennifer's call. She was the one who would have to carry the baby, so she could do what she wanted.

The response these evasions produced is a good example of a point made by those Destructive Fighting wives I mentioned earlier. Often a man subtly controls the pace and tempo of a disagreement through his withdrawal. At the follow-up interview Cal complained that in the weeks following the obstetrician's call Jennifer's behavior grew increasingly irrational, as it had during the hematoma incident. But much of this irrationality was provoked by his own refusal to confront the pregnancy, because it forced Jennifer to keep upping the intensity of her pressing. Like the partners of Avoider spouses, she'd thought, *Maybe if I do something really dramatic next time, I can break through Cal's silence.* A case in point was what, seven years later, the Renselears were still referring to as the calendar incident.

It had its roots in yet another failed attempt to set a common course. The night before, when Jennifer brought up the pregnancy, Cal had snapped, "How many times do I have to tell you? I don't care. Do what you want." Then before Jennifer had an opportunity to say another word, he was halfway up the staircase heading toward the bedroom. The next morning in a fit of frustration Jennifer piled Ali into the Saab, drove into State College, and bought a calendar at a stationery store. That evening when Cal came into the kitchen for dinner, the calendar was lying next to his plate, opened to the month of September.

"What's this, Jen?" he said, picking it up. "Another one of your visual aids?"

Jennifer decided to ignore the sarcasm. "We have to make a decision by then," she said, pointing to September 18. To emphasize the importance of the date, she had circled it with a red Magic Marker. "Today's August eighteenth. That gives us four weeks."

The stunned look on Cal's face produced a twinge of guilt. Maybe the calendar was a cheap trick, Jennifer thought. "Please," she said. "I just want us to work together. I'm not trying to bully you."

"Yes, you are," Cal replied, tossing the calendar on the table. "And you love it. You love to beat the shit out of me."

A week later Jennifer thought she finally did get a brief glimpse of Cal's real feelings about the pregnancy. Getting ready for bed one night, he mentioned that a friend of his at work was having an affair with his secretary. Because Jennifer knew the man's wife had recently had another child, she did not think the remark was meant innocently. As evenly as she could, she asked Cal if he were threatening her.

"Don't be silly," he said with some outrage. "God, can't I even gossip now without being accused of something?"

Jennifer started to reply, then caught herself. What was the use? After Cal fell asleep, she went downstairs, took a shawl out of the hall closet, and walked out into the garden behind the kitchen. She sat there until one A.M. thinking about Cal's story, then went back into the kitchen, took a glass out of the cabinet, and filled it to the top with Scotch. The next morning she called her sister, Carol. They decided that the following Tuesday—the Tuesday after Labor Day—Jennifer would fly up to Boston and have the abortion done there. At dinner when she announced that she wanted to visit her family for a few days, Jennifer half expected to be interrogated. Cal could be relentless when he thought she was trying to hide something from him. But after she reassured him that Ali would be coming with her, Cal had no more questions.

Two years later he still felt guilty about his silence that night. I don't recall how the conversation came up the afternoon he brought Ali to our studio for a father-daughter videotaping session. But I do remember Cal saying that as soon as Jennifer told him she was going to Boston, he knew why, and he felt "slimy" for letting her go alone.

I asked him why he hadn't said something.

"God knows where that conversation would have led. Better to just have it over and done with."

The morning following Jennifer's announcement, however, Cal did try to offer Jennifer one small gesture of support. He told her he would drive her and Ali to the Harrisburg Airport on Tuesday. As they were saying good-bye at the departure gate, he tried to offer another. He told her he would wait at the gate until her plane took off.

"You don't have to," Jennifer said.

"I want to," Cal insisted. "Look for me when you get in your seat."

But the moment Jennifer and Ali disappeared into the plane, Cal felt an overwhelming urge to get away from the gate, the airport, and the shame he felt for abandoning his wife like this. Almost before he realized it, he was in the main terminal heading toward his car at a half run. A few minutes later when Jennifer looked out her seat window, there was an overweight man in a flight handler's bright orange jumpsuit standing in the spot where Cal promised he would be.

Jennifer's memories of the Boston trip are bracketed by two images. One is of that flight handler, the other is of a young woman she saw at the abortion clinic she and Carol visited the next day. The clinic reminded Jennifer of her dentist's office. Its walls were painted in the same soothing pastels, and the staff moved about with the same hushed efficiency. While Carol hung up their coats, Jennifer walked over to a counter at the center of the reception area. There were two young women behind it; one got up, asked Jennifer if she had an appointment, then handed her a medical history form. As she was explaining how to fill it out, Jennifer's eye went to the second young woman. It was lunchtime and the young woman had a piece of aluminum foil spread out on her desk. Jennifer watched as she removed a sandwich from inside, then reached into her handbag and pulled out a magazine. As she opened it, she unexpectedly looked up and smiled at Jennifer.

Jennifer tried to smile back but found she couldn't. She had begun to cry.

About six weeks later we received the Renselears' final Marital Quality Questionnaires. Scores from their earlier ones had suggested that Cal and Jennifer might end up in our Decliner group. But their scores on this questionnaire, which was filled out after the nine-month observation, were so low, it seemed likely that the Renselears would be classified among a special subgroup of couples we called Severe Decliners.

10

How a Baby Changes Communication

It is a crisp, cool Sunday morning in early September, and I am sitting in my den, TV clicker in hand. I press the On button expecting the avuncular Charles Kurault to appear on my TV screen, but instead a large, moon-faced man with an extravagant widow's peak and a cherubic smile materializes. The carnation in his buttonhole and the mousse on his slick-backed hair suggest a prosperous mortician, but a logo at the bottom of the screen identifies him as the owner of a car dealership in Altoona. I must have caught the concluding segment of the local business program that precedes "CBS Sunday Morning." While I'm deciding what to do next, an offscreen voice suddenly challenges the auto dealer's assessment of local economic conditions. In the Sunday-morning stillness of my den, the voice sounds like a firecracker exploding. It also sounds familiar. When the camera pans to the mysterious speaker, I see why. A logo at the bottom of the screen identifies her as Susan Akers, president of Penn Central Video.

Another firecracker. Sue is attacking the auto dealer with an un-Sunday-morning-like ferocity. It's almost as if she has a personal grudge against him. The moderator attempts to ease the tension with a little humor.

"Well, if our panelists' discussion is any indication, the local economy certainly is heating up," he says.

It doesn't work. Sue continues her attack. Now the moderator looks alarmed, the auto dealer even more so. I wonder what's got Sue so angry.

Seven years later, at the Akerses' follow-up interview, I learned that at roughly the moment I was contemplating this question in the quietness of my den, the phone rang in the Akerses' kitchen. Turning on the "Christian Power Hour" that morning, Mary Akers had also stumbled across Sue. Now she wanted to know why she had not been told about her daughter-in-law's TV debut. The truth was that Ron had been afraid to tell her. She already thought Sue was too ambitious for her son's and grandson's good. God knows what she would make of a TV appearance.

"I'm sorry. I forgot about it, Mom," Ron lied.

"I worry about you and Ian," Mary Akers said. "Does Sue ever spend weekends with the two of you?"

"We spend a lot of time together," Ron lied again. The last thing he needed now was for his mother to accuse his wife of neglecting her family. The thought of the explosion that would set off was too terrible to contemplate.

"Are you sure?" Mary Akers said.

Ron wanted to get his mother off the line. "I'm sure, Mom. I have to run."

"I understand. By the way, tell Sue to do something about her hair. It looks like a rat slept in it." Before Ron had a chance to reply, there was a click at the other end of the line.

Ron picked up the egg he had put on the kitchen counter when the phone rang and broke it over a skillet. He adjusted the gas jet and began to stir the egg listlessly. Pretransition, pre-video-store, Sunday mornings used to be one of the high points of Ron's week. He and Sue would wake up late, lie in bed for an hour or so reading the newspaper, then go downstairs and prepare a huge breakfast. Afterward they would usually make love. But now most of Ron's Sunday mornings were spent like this—standing alone at the stove scrambling himself an egg. By the time he woke up, Sue had already dropped Ian off at her mother's and was at the store.

The phone rang again. It was his brother, Darryl.

"So how does it feel to be married to a TV star?"

There was no need to lie to Darryl. Over the past few months he and his wife Denuda had become Ron's principal confidants.

"I don't see enough of her to know."

Darryl did not pick up on the remark. He knew when his brother wanted to talk and when he just wanted to ventilate. "Why don't you come over around twelve," he said. "We'll have lunch, then watch the game."

Ron hung up and began to set the table. Even when he ate alone, he always put out a placemat and cloth napkin. Sue used to tease him about his fastidiousness. "You're like a little old man," she would say. "You can't even have a sandwich without putting a lace doily under it." But lately Sue had done very little of this teasing. In truth the Akerses barely talked at all anymore. And the problem was not just a lack of time. Ron felt he and Sue were gradually losing their ability to communicate. They did not so much converse now as interrogate each other. "How are you?" "How do you feel about this?" "What are you planning to do tonight?" Thoughts and feelings that used to flow effortlessly out of both of them now had to be dug out with a pickax and shovel.

Ron knew that communication difficulties were common among new parents. Just before Ian was born, Darryl, who had a three-year-old, warned him about them. But he wondered if they were really as inevitable a fact of life as Darryl had implied. They had to have a cause, and sometimes Ron thought the cause was Sue. Between Ian and the store, she was so preoccupied that she had lost touch with him. Other times he blamed himself. Maybe he was not giving her enough help and in some subtle way that was undermining their ability to communicate. But he was certain about one thing: His loneliness would not abate until the marital conversation between him and Sue resumed.

Transition folklore has long held that the kind of intimate, engaged talk Ron found himself longing for on that long-ago Sunday morning becomes rare after the baby's arrival. And our data indicate that on this point transition folklore does not exaggerate. Almost all of our couples experienced a drop in the quality of their communication postbaby, and in almost half of the cases the drop became permanent. In these homes the music never came back to the marital conversation. This loss is a leading cause of transition-time alienation and dissatisfaction. When couples say they do not feel as close as they used to, in most cases what they mean is that they cannot talk to each other the way they used to. And it is also a leading cause of transition-time depression because couples often take their communication difficulties as a confirmation of their worst fear: The baby has pushed them apart in an irrevocable way and nothing can put them back together again the way they used to be.

Surprisingly very little was known about postbaby communication breakdowns at the start of the Project, despite the fact that they are one of the well-identified occurrences of new parenthood. A half dozen studies had documented their prevalence, but no one had yet looked at how and why they originated, whether some couples were more vulnerable to them than others, and if so, why. A series of pre-Project interviews with transition veterans suggested some tentative answers to these questions. Almost all the couples we spoke with said that not only did talk become less frequent after the baby's arrival, it also became much less satisfying. There was also a surprising degree of unanimity about the reasons for these changes.

One frequently cited culprit was the rapidly shrinking pool of shared interests. Many of the couples we interviewed said they approached the transition expecting the baby to expand this pool but found that he or she had had the opposite effect. They were left with fewer things in common and hence fewer things to talk about. A second often-mentioned culprit was rusty communication skills. No one actually used that term, of course, but many husbands and wives did say that as the transition progressed, they found themselves losing their ability to hear and understand their spouses. And this made conversation not only less satisfying for the spouses but for them too. A third obstacle many couples mentioned was a decline in the intimacy-promoting activities that often subtly lubricate the wheels of communication, such as nights out, just-being-together time, and sex.

These pre-Project interviews also produced another potentially important piece of information. Among the couples we spoke with, there seemed to be a correlation between the time and energy a husband and wife devoted to the autonomy-and-affiliation issue prebaby and the sturdiness of their communication system postbaby. At first this link surprised us. What did balancing one's autonomy-and-affiliation needs have to do with good communication? As we thought about it, however, a fairly obvious tie emerged. In storybooks a perfectly fitting "us" may spring full-blown from a couple's love. But in real life a relationship that fits both partners' needs for independence and connectedness is the product of an intense years-long conversation. Maybe, we thought, couples who spend a lot of time engaged in this conversation prebaby develop such a deep knowledge of each other and such finely honed communication skills that they are less vulnerable to communication disruptions postbaby.

At the start of the Project our interviews with transition veterans provided the basis for the two hypotheses we made about Communication. We conjectured that a first child poses certain inherent obstacles to good marital communication and that success in overcoming them is largely determined by when and how the autonomy-and-affiliation issue is addressed. Our data supported both hypotheses, but they also did something even more important: They provided the first detailed picture of how nature, nurture, and the press of events conspire to make meaningful talk difficult for new parents, and how pretransition experiences influence a couple's ability to overcome these difficulties. Read a certain way, our data could even be said to constitute a cautionary tale, because they indicate that couples who take on the frequently painful task of integrating their two individual selves into a larger "us" are often more successful in maintaining the marital conversation postbaby than those who put off this hard task until the last possible moment.

These findings about autonomy and affiliation were not documented until fairly late in our study. But almost as soon as we began our exploration of Communication, we discovered that the transition veterans we had interviewed were right about the obstacles the baby poses to meaningful marital talk. There are three major ones, and they are woven into the very fabric of the new-parent experience. We also discovered that many Project participants were already aware of the first obstacle. Due to a lack of time and money and also to diverging priorities, many of the shared interests that drove the conversational agenda prebaby begin to disappear. At intake interviews, however, many of our husbands and wives expressed confidence that they would be less vulnerable to this obstacle than their parents had been because recent social changes would give them at least one transition-resistant mutual interest to talk about—the baby. And up to a point this expectation was realized. The desire to be what their fathers had not been—an engaged, hands-on parent—did make it easier for many of our husbands to enter into their wives' involvement with the baby. And their role as workers made it easier for many of our wives to maintain the kind of outside interests that gave them common ground with their husbands.

But even in the homes of our most devoted new fathers and most career-minded new mothers, we found that the woman's all-consuming love affair with the baby would frequently end up putting a couple at conversational odds. Nothing so concentrates the mind and heart as a passionate love affair, so understandably most of our new mothers were bursting to talk about this affair. But at a certain point few things can be more boring than listening to someone else tell you about her love affair. Therefore at a certain point even our most dedicated new fathers would try to shift the conversation back to the subjects the couple used to talk about, such as books, movies, work, and friends. And in a great many cases the result was that familiar transition-time phenomenon: conversational gridlock.

I encountered the second obstacle many times during observations, and a good example of it is a conversation I witnessed one night between a couple suffering from a bad case of cabin fever. The husband and wife were eight months into the transition and not going out very much because the wife still found it difficult to separate from the baby. During the observation she did not try to defend this behavior; she just wanted to explain why her feelings about the child made separating so hard. But every time she tried to describe those feelings, her husband would interrupt to complain about her "obsessiveness."

Afterward the woman, who seemed more embarrassed than annoyed by her husband's behavior, pulled me aside to explain that it was of very recent vintage. Before the baby, even when they disagreed, he would let her explain how she felt. "All this interrupting and harrumphing of his is new, and I think it's because we don't talk enough." Her diagnosis was accurate. Like all other skills, communication skills are subject to the "use it or lose it" rule. The more you use them, the more supple and nuanced they grow; the less you use them, the rustier and more ineffective they become. And because the transition provides relatively few opportunities for intimate talk, often within a matter of months new parents begin to forget what they used to know about these skills (often without realizing they knew it). This might include how to be an understanding listener (you don't interrupt when the other person is telling you how he or she feels) and how to tell what is on your mate's mind even when he or she is unclear or speaking in a private code.

Unfortunately the "use it or lose it" rule takes a particularly large toll on what is the most important communication skill of all. There are not many generalizations one can safely make about a subject as big as communication, but one is that the better two people know each other, the easier talk becomes for them. And typically the way couples acquire this knowledge is by sharing their feelings. A lot of the stiltedness that creeps into the marital conversation postbaby arises from a decline in this sharing. Increasingly the husband and wife begin to feel out of emotional touch with each other, and because strangers have trouble talking, they find that they do too. Initially the chief culprit in this disengagement process is a lack of time. With a new baby to care for, who has a spare hour for emotional updates? But often as the transition progresses, a second culprit arises: a kind of inhibiting self-consciousness. Without practice, thoughts and feelings a husband or wife once would not have hesitated to share now begin to seem a little too intimate, too private, too self-incriminating, even for a spouse to hear.

A story a divorced friend told me illustrates the third reason why complaints about poor communication are so common among new parents. He had spent the previous Saturday with his eight-year-old and reported that during the six hours they were together, they had not had five minutes of honest, spontaneous conversation. For my friend the low point of the day came at dinner when he suddenly found himself in the middle of a long, rambling analysis of the movie he and his son had just seen. "As I talked," he said, "a part of me kept thinking, 'Why am I telling Bobby this? He's too young to understand or care about plot mechanics.' But I kept going on because I couldn't think of anything else to say to him."

I found myself thinking about this story when we began talking to Project couples about the ways the baby had changed their marriage because the third obstacle that emerged from these discussions is the same one that was responsible for my friend's—and many divorced fathers'—tongue-tiedness: a loss of dailiness. When two people spend a great deal of time together, whether they be father and child or husband and wife, that close contact creates a physical intimacy that helps enhance intimate conversation. It is hard to articulate exactly how and why it does, but anyone who has shared this physical intimacy with another person knows it does, just as anyone who has shared and lost it knows what that loss does to communication. Like my friend, you find that conversation with your once-intimate acquaintance becomes the emotional equivalent of a visit to the dentist's office.

In the case of new parents one leading reason for the loss of intimacy is of course a lack of time. The baby creates so many new demands and pressures that the husband and wife get almost no opportunity just to sit and be with each other in an engaged, focused manner. It is only a suspicion, but I think the transition's usually deflating effect on the libido may also subtly undermine communication. Again, the connection is hard to delineate. But sex is the most intimate kind of physical contact two people can have, and when it declines because of disinterest or exhaustion or both, an emotional distance develops that makes meaningful talk a little harder than it used to be.

Why does coming to terms with the autonomy-and-affiliation issue during the pretransition years make a couple less vulnerable to these obstacles?

As I noted earlier, prebaby there is really no compelling reason to address this issue. There are so many props available to a husband and wife in the form of abundant time, energy, and friends that they can have a reasonably satisfying relationship and still leave their autonomy-and-affiliation impulses flapping in the wind. Which is to say that prebaby a couple can have it both ways—someone to come home to at night and to go biking and antiquing with on Saturday afternoons and at the same time the freedom to live a largely independent life. Couples who resist this no-pain option are like prudent savers whose willingness to delay gratification is rewarded when that long-feared rainy day arrives. Resolving autonomy-and-affiliation questions is really an exercise in relationship building. The couple is learning how to integrate their two individual selves into a larger "us." And because finding solutions that satisfy both of "us" is a lot harder than finding solutions that satisfy just one of "us," this process inevitably produces a certain amount of aggravation, pain, and disagreeableness. But as they thrash through relationship concerns, a couple also shares feelings, develops communication skills, and learns about each other in a way that enhances their ability to overcome the obstacles the transition poses to meaningful talk.

A disagreement Larry and Helen Fahey had the night of their intake interview illustrates one reason why. The Faheys were exercised because a party invitation had arrived and conflicting work schedules made going together difficult. They could have simply decided to go separately and meet at the party, but because a sense of coupleness was important to them, the Faheys wanted to arrive together. So they did what a lot of couples in their position would not have done—they argued back and forth about their schedule conflict until they found a mutually satisfactory arrival time. Over the past few years communication researchers have spent a lot of time studying conflicts like the Faheys' and found that while they may appear pointless, often they have a very big point: They are an investment in the relationship. Every time a husband and wife spend fifteen minutes trying to find a party-arrival time or a movie or a weekend activity that suits both of "us" instead of one of "us," they are investing a little more of their individual selves in the relationship. And because prebaby couples such as the Faheys consider nearly every issue from the perspective of "us," by the time they become parents, both partners have made such a huge investment in it, "us" remains a conversational topic of riveting mutual interest, even though the couple's other interests and priorities have diverged.

Husbands and wives who take the time to squabble about party-arrival times and movies often benefit in another way as well. In the course of sharing their feelings about these and similar issues, a couple learns so much about each other's likes and dislikes, hopes and fears, and little idiosyncrasies that they do not need daily emotional updates to maintain the sense of connectedness that is the basis for informed, lively, mutually engaging talk. They already know each other so well and are so comfortable with each other that even if an opportunity to "really talk" does not arise for weeks—as often happens during the transition—their ability to converse remains unimpaired. Prebaby, couples who avoid relationship squabbles also avoid the aggravation they cause, but postbaby they often end up paying for exercising the no-pain option. Having not learned enough about each other, they do require daily emotional updates to keep in touch, and now that there's no time for them, their conversation begins to take on the awkward, forced quality of two people who have lost contact, who have become in a sense strangers to each other.

During my second visit to the Faheys I got an example of another way prebaby relationship building enhances a couple's ability to overcome transition-time communication obstacles. Toward the end of the observation Helen turned to Larry and said, "Later, remind me to call Mom. I'm supposed to go shopping with her tomorrow, but I've got too much to do."

Larry sighed and shook his head. "What did she buy Lisa this time?"

I was puzzled by this reply; it seemed like a non sequitur. But as the conversation progressed, it turned out to be anything but. Over the past few months there had been a number of heated mother-daughter conversations over what Helen felt was her mother's favoritism toward Lisa, who was her sister's two-year-old. Larry's reply reflected an observation he had made about this conflict. Whenever his wife threatened to break a date with her mother or complained about her for any reason, it was because her mother had bought something for Lisa without also buying something for their child.

Larry's ability to understand his wife even when she was speaking in private code is one of the two listening skills that make couples want to keep talking to each other. After all, who wouldn't want to keep talking to a partner who knows you so well, he knows what you're thinking even when you don't come out and say it? The other skill that enhances conversations is silence. Even when you don't agree, you let your partner state his or her thoughts and feelings free of interruptions. Prebaby most couples are aware of these two rules of good listening, but postbaby only couples like the Faheys who have spent thousands of hours listening to each other tend to remember them.

The big communication muscle that prebaby relationship building produces also confers another important advantage, and to a large extent it is a product of the three I have already mentioned. When you have both invested a lot of yourselves in the relationship, know each other well, and have good communication skills, you tend to be much less dependent on the props other couples rely on to foster their conversational skills, such as nights out and plenty of "just being" time. Marital communication is a form of music, and when you practice it all the time, your musicianship becomes such that you do not need a big-band backup to get you in the mood. You can sing anywhere, anytime, either with an accompaniment or a cappella.

Prebaby, what relationship characteristics distinguish new parents who become at-risk for major communication disruptions from those who do not?

Toward the end of the Project we realized we only had a very general answer to this question. While we knew what determined vulnerability to these obstacles, we did not know whether the decision to confront or to avoid the autonomy-and-affiliation issue produced different characteristics in a relationship. When we went back and reviewed our data, we found that indeed it did. Avoiders and confronters relate to each other in very different ways. And I think the traits that distinguish their relationships go a long way toward explaining why confronters can usually sail over transition-time communication obstacles with relative ease while avoiders cannot.

An example is the tendency of avoiders, prebaby, to use shared activities rather than shared feelings as a way of relating to each other. Our husbands and wives who did this often attributed the practice to like-mindedness. They discovered that they enjoyed a lot of the same things, so they spent a lot of time doing those things together. But there is also another explanation for this preference. Shared activities provide a neat solution to a dilemma faced by all couples who are not eager to share themselves. How can I be with you and at the same time not be with you? Hiking, biking, white-water rafting, and similar activities allow a man and woman to spend large amounts of time together and give them plenty to talk about but do not necessarily require either partner to surrender a single iota of emotional independence. After all, you can spend a whole day biking together, have a wonderful time, and still not share a single intimate thought or feeling with your partner or he with you.

Another pretransition characteristic of couples who become vulnerable to communication breakdowns is an "I'll go my way, you go yours" philosophy. If there are not any conflicts, these husbands and wives will do things together, but if, say, a scheduling problem arises, they will go to the party separately. Of course such flexibility can be seen as a mark of mutual respect. The husband and wife do not press, insist, or bully because they respect each other's individuality. And up to a point this is true. But when this philosophy becomes the central operating principal of a marriage, each partner ends up making a much larger investment in "me" than in "we." During the transition, instead of providing them with a bridge over their diverging priorities, this investment choice exacerbates that divergence.

Couples who become vulnerable to communication problems also often share one other trait. When the husband and wife do do things together, they do not make an effort to do things that please both partners. Like the last trait, often this one is a source of pride. The partner who gives in and goes to a movie she does not want to see or on a double date with a friend of her husband's she doesn't like often sees her acquiescence as an expression of love ("I care about you so much, I'll sacrifice what I want to do to please you"). And up to a point such sacrifices can deepen the marital bond. But when one partner acquiesces all the time, it indicates something else. The relationship is built around appeasing one of "us" instead of pleasing both of "us," and eventually this produces two types of communication problems—sometimes both at the same time. The first is a sullen, resentful silence, which arises from the appeaser's anger at being taken advantage of; the second is having nothing to talk about during the long, dark nights of the transition because the couple's knowledge of "us" is so thin, a five-minute conversation exhausts it.

Prebaby, couples who have built their relationship around these principles often do not encounter serious communication problems because neither partner is looking for much more than small talk, and their shared interests provide plenty of material for that. But postbaby, usually, they find what Marcus and Diane Arens discovered after the birth of their daughter, Hallie.

When I met the Arenses in the spring of 1984, they had been married for a year and a half and were, by central Pennsylvania standards, living a rather glamorous life. Like Sue Akers, Marcus also had timed the real estate market well, but in a much bigger way. His company had helped develop several new mini-plazas in the area. Given such success, I'd expected the Arenses' home to be imposing and I wasn't disappointed. From the driveway it looked like an airplane hangar that had somehow gotten stranded in the middle of the Pennsylvania woods. It was large, white, perfectly rectangular, and covered with odd, porthole-shaped windows.

In his own way Marcus turned out to be as avant-garde as his house. I don't know what I expected when I saw the term *building contractor* next to his name in the Project file, but I certainly did not expect the tall, intense figure in the black silk shirt who greeted me at the door the night of the intake interview. Marcus looked like a drama professor on his day off. He had a perfectly bald head, a long, aesthetic face, a leading-man's voice, and a flamenco dancer's figure. As the night progressed, I also learned he had a master's degree in philosophy, an encyclopedic knowledge of food and wine, and an offbeat spirituality that embraced everything from channeling to Zen.

Diane Arens was a schoolteacher, very petite and quite pretty in the fine-boned way of a Michelle Pfeiffer, whom she resembled a bit. At twenty-five she was also thirteen years younger than her husband. But at the intake interview Diane said she and Marcus had such a similar sensibility and liked so many of the same things that they had felt like peers from the moment they met at a cooking class three years earlier. That night both credited their shared interests, which in addition to cooking included travel, music, and the New Age movement, with giving them a deep bond. But as I got to know them better, I discovered that underneath that bond was a certain disengagement, a certain emotional distance in their marriage. And to a large extent it seemed to be an act of deference on Diane's part. After a lifetime of emotional independence Marcus, who had married at thirty-five, did not find emotional sharing easy. And Diane felt she could not insist. There were times where Marcus's aloofness made her feel less his partner than one of his life-style trophies, like their movie-star house and restaurant-sized kitchen. But the life he had given her seemed like a dream to a young woman who had grown up in a hard-scrabble Pennsylvania coal town. So if Marcus wanted to keep part of himself to himself, Diane felt she had to respect that wish.

The first indication the Arenses had that this distance would make them vulnerable to communication disruptions occurred eight weeks after daughter Hallie's birth while they were driving home from a reunion of their Lamaze class. Diane told me during the follow-up interview that what made this incident so memorable was the contrast. At the party there were so many people to catch up with, she and Marcus did not stop talking. But later in the car the mood changed abruptly. The party provided a few minutes of gossip, but after it was exhausted, the Arenses found themselves scratching around for things to say. Marcus mentioned a site he was thinking of developing, Diane her plans to decorate Hallie's room, but their conversation had the forced, artificial quality of two people who have lost all sense of emotional connectedness. "It was very depressing," Diane said when she told me about this incident later. "Here we were, alone for the first time since Hallie's birth, and we sit there talking about things neither of us is interested in because we can't think of anything else to say."

Two months later there was an even more upsetting incident in a restaurant in Bellefonte. After the reunion the Arenses' communication problems went from bad to worse, and as they did, something else began to change in their marriage. Before, even when Diane was alone in the house, she had never felt alone. Marcus's presence, the presence of their relationship, had always been there to keep her company. But now, even when Marcus was at home, she often felt as lonely as she had when she had lived by herself in that efficiency apartment in State College. The purpose of the visit to the restaurant was to discuss this loneliness and the sexual difficulties that seemed to be a part of it. The Arenses imagined that if they could get away from everything for a few hours—the phone, the housekeeper, and all their recent bad memories—maybe they could begin thrashing through their problems. But when they sat down at the table that night, they discovered what new parents like themselves often discover: Even when they have a great deal to say to each other, they still cannot talk.

In order to open up and explore a potentially volatile issue, a couple must know how to share their feelings with each other in a way that does not arouse defensiveness or embarrassment or produce misunderstanding. And because these are not qualities an emotionally disengaged relationship like the Arenses' fosters, when they tried to summon them up that night in the restaurant, they found there was nothing to summon. Diane never got an opportunity to talk in any detail about her loneliness because Marcus kept interrupting to say it was not his fault she was lonely. And Marcus never got a chance to talk about their sexual problems because Diane said she felt "funny" talking about sex.

Shortly afterward, Diane told me, "I don't know how two people can be together for nearly four years and not learn anything about each other. But somehow Marcus and I managed to do it." Eventually, as most marriages do at a certain point in the transition, the Arenses' began to stabilize. As Hallie grew older and there was time again for travel and cooking and music and the other things that Marcus and Diane enjoyed, the marital conversation resumed. But that conversation never regained its ability to heal, to nurture, to fill up a house in a way that keeps one partner from feeling alone even when he or she is. When couples say that a child makes a marriage different, it is often the loss of these conversational qualities that makes it feel so different. Communication continues to be a source of contact and, even to a degree, of sharing, but once its ability to heal, inspire, and nurture is gone, it ceases to be what it also once was—a source of magic.

What about new parents who maintain the ability to talk? What traits characterize their relationship in the pretransition years?

Given what I've already said, the first trait won't come as a surprise. We found that the more time a couple spends talking about the relationship prebaby, the more likely they are to continue talking to each other postbaby. Given the fact that some of this talk really is a form of low-level squabbling, however, what may seem surprising is that it does not have the opposite effect. After all, for a couple marital talk is not an exercise in building communication skills, it is about enjoyment. And one would think that squabbles about the shape and texture of the relationship would make talk so unenjoyable that the husband and wife would do less of it instead of more.

A few years ago a University of Michigan study provided an explanation for this paradox. Dr. Linda Acitelli and her colleagues found that even negative relationship talk has the seemingly topsy-turvy effect of increasing marital happiness. Less surprising, she and her colleagues also found that the happier a couple is, the more they talk. How do negative discussions about "us" perform the hat trick of making the husband and wife feel better about each other? The Michigan team found that in the case of women it is because a wife usually interprets even negative spousal comments about "us" as a form of caring and involvement. She sees her husband's complaints about the relationship as a sign that he also cares about its nurturance and well-being. And she sees his interest in its well-being as a sign that he cares about her. Husbands benefit from negative relationship talk for a different reason. It provides them with a way of ventilating. Men find it much harder than women to talk about "us," but when they do, they discover what the husbands in Dr. Acitelli's study did: Talk is such a good emotional release that you end up feeling better about your mate and your marriage.

Typically in marriages where communication remains easy, before the transition there also has been a great deal of reciprocity. Neither partner took from the other without also giving back. If, for example, the husband got his way on issue A, on issue B he would try to give his wife most of what she wanted. Research by Dr. Howard Markman of the University of Denver shows that such tit-for-tat responsiveness constitutes a form of marital investment. Because each partner is as careful to give at least as much as he or she takes, each ends up making a large investment in the other and in the relationship. And as noted earlier, when two people put a great deal of themselves into an enterprise, what happens to it remains of compelling interest to both of them, even at times when they have very little else in common. Dr. Markman's work also shows that what drives such reciprocity is a deep and abiding trust. Each partner gives readily because each is confident that at one point or another, even if not immediately, their concessions and sacrifices will elicit counterconcessions and sacrifices from a partner.

We also made a discovery about reciprocity. Couples who engage in a great deal of it before the baby arrives continue to do so afterward. Henry and Natalie Pritzkopf provide a case in point. When they found themselves at odds about the timing of daughter Amanda's weaning, the Pritzkopfs settled their disagreement the way they used to settle prebaby conflicts, such as what to do this weekend and where to go on vacation—through a process of give-and-take.

Their dispute about weaning arose because Henry began to feel excluded by Natalie's breast-feeding. He wanted to be an involved parent, too, and part of being involved was feeding his new child. Couldn't Natalie wean Amanda at six months instead of nine months as she planned? Natalie, however, did not want to be rushed into severing this last physical connection with her child. During our three-month observation of the Pritzkopfs these differences led to a sharp exchange. When Henry brought up Amanda's weaning, Natalie got very testy. "You didn't carry her," she snapped. "You can't know how I feel." Sensing the discussion was about to become an argument,

Henry let the matter drop. But saying good-bye to them that afternoon, I had the feeling he wouldn't let it drop for long and I wondered how the strong-minded Natalie would respond to his pressing.

At the Pritzkopfs' nine-month observation I found out. When I arrived, Henry was sitting in the living room feeding Amanda. Sensing my surprise, Natalie smiled slyly. "You didn't think I'd give in to him, did you?"

I laughed and said, "No. What happened?"

"The more I thought about it," Natalie replied, "the more I decided I was being unfair. Amanda's our baby, not mine."

I was a little surprised by Natalie's attitude. She did not seem at all angry or bitter about "losing." Later in the observation I discovered why. Another point of contention between the Pritzkopfs had been Henry's showering with Amanda. Every time he went into the bathroom with her, Natalie's heart stopped. What if he slipped and dropped her? Henry was certain he never would. Nonetheless about a month after Amanda went on the bottle, he told Natalie there would be no more father-daughter showers.

Reciprocal systems like the Pritzkopfs' provided the basis for a second hat trick some of our couples performed. Nineteen percent did not just maintain but in fact improved the quality of their communication during the transition. And in many cases it was because, like Henry and Natalie, postbaby both partners continued making large emotional investments in their shared interest. And at a certain point in the transition this created a snowball effect. The more of themselves a couple put into "us," the more interested they became in "us," and hence the more they wanted to talk about "us."

The last characteristic of couples who turn out to be good communicators is that, prebaby, they are friends as well as lovers. I know, that sounds like a greeting-card sentiment, but friendship is very important to new parents. If our data indicate anything, it is that romantic love is a very frail reed in the transition wind. A month of around-the-clock diaperings and feedings will take the stars out of anyone's eyes. Once romantic love ebbs, what happens to marital conversation pretty much depends on what else is left in the relationship. If a couple are friends, too, the conversation will continue because, like all friends, they will still have a lot to say to each other. But if they have been bound together by passion alone, once it dies, that conversation will gradually sputter to a halt.

I do not want to exaggerate the protective effect of these traits. Almost all new parents experience communication disruptions of one type or another. But husbands and wives who put a lot of time, energy, pain, and sacrifice into building their relationship also enjoy another advantage when they encounter these disruptions. Usually, prebaby, the quality of their communication was so good that when it goes into decline postbaby, both partners fight very hard to get it back. They had something wonderful and they want it restored. Despite all the contention and disruption the video store produced, this is what kept me optimistic about Ron and Sue Akers. From the decision to buy the plot of land on Route 322 through the miscarriage to the video store, their marriage had been one long struggle to build a sense of "us." And I was pretty sure that at a certain point Sue would begin to long for that "us" and the meaningful talk that was an integral part of it. But I didn't know how long it would take her to recognize this longing or where Ron would be when she finally did—irrevocably alienated by her impulse to put her hopes and dreams first or still deeply in love with her?

Before the Akerses left the Project, it was already clear that, for all the turmoil it had caused, the video store had little real effect on Ron's feelings: He remained deeply in love with his wife. But it wasn't until the Akerses' follow-up interview one night seven years later that I got an opportunity to satisfy my curiosity on the first point: When did Sue finally notice how much she missed her husband and the intimacy and companionship of their marriage? Sue dated her realization to a rainy Sunday morning when she was dropping Ian off at her mother's. But the more she talked that evening, the surer I was that her longing for both had been there a while before she finally recognized them. Often loneliness and unhappiness produce disruptive acting out, and two events that occurred in the weeks just prior to Sue's epiphany seemed to exceed even her admittedly large capacity for feistiness.

The first was a near accident in the parking lot of the TV studio the morning of her television debut. That evening when Sue told Ron about the incident, she attributed it to absentmindedness. Driving out of the parking lot, she said, she had been in such a fog, she almost hit her fellow panelist, the auto dealer, as he was getting into his car. "I never saw anyone look so frightened," she added.

"He was all right, though?" Ron asked. "You didn't actually hit him?"

Sue nodded.

"He saw me before I saw him. He leaped into the front seat. He's pretty light-footed for a big man."

"I hope you apologized."

"I didn't have time. I was already late."

Ron thought this lapse odd. But since Sue didn't seem eager to talk about the incident, he let it drop. Later that night, however, she unexpectedly returned to it—and with some gusto. "Do you know what that son of a bitch called me this morning?" she said as she and Ron were lying in bed. " 'Honey.' Before the show he came up, put his arm around me, and said, 'How are you today, honey?' "

It took Ron a moment to realize that Sue was talking about the auto dealer. But as soon as he did so, a very loud "uh-oh" went off in his groggy head. He bolted upright in bed. "Please don't tell me you tried to scare him on purpose."

" 'How are you this morning, honey?' " Sue said, mimicking the auto dealer's voice. 'Can I pat your bum this morning, honey?' The old lecher. That's what he wanted to do. He's lucky all I did was scare him."

The other bit of acting out occurred ten days later. Normally Ron made it a point to answer the phone in the evenings. It could be his mother, and the less she and Sue talked, the happier everyone, most notably himself, would remain. But on this particular evening Sue was standing next to the wall phone in the kitchen when it rang. As soon as he heard her say, "Thank you, but I'm very happy with the hairdresser I have," Ron knew who the caller was. At the follow-up interview Ron recalled that Sue's side of the conversation went something like this:

"I don't know how you can say that, Mary. I'm always home by seven at the latest."

Pause.

"My family doesn't complain. They are very happy with the amount of time I give them."

Pause.

"Well, that may be true, Mary, but why would I want to be like you?"

Ron also recalled that when he heard Sue say this to his mother, an image flashed into his mind. His head was caught in a vise and its two prongs kept getting tighter and tighter until finally the pressure became so great, his head exploded like a watermelon.

Sue's distress finally took a form she could recognize the following Sunday. She had just pulled up in front of her mother's house and was taking Ian out of his carseat when she felt a sudden pang—what she described at the follow-up interview as almost a pain. "I'd been feeling terrible for weeks, and sitting there in the car, I realized why. I didn't have a life anymore. I had given up everything that mattered to me to become this little worker bee. It was crazy."

At the follow-up interview Sue also said that the rest of that Sunday morning had been like a scene out of a movie. After leaving Ian with her mother, she drove home, and when she found the house empty, she drove to Elby's on Route 322, where Ron sometimes went on Sundays for breakfast.

"When I saw him, I felt awful," Sue said. "The restaurant was full of families. And there was poor Ron sitting alone in a booth at the back with the Sunday papers."

By the time the Akerses left Elby's that morning, they had made two agreements. The first was that Sue would hand over the day-to-day operation of the store to a manager until Ian was three. (A few weeks later Sue hired her brother, who had run a McDonald's near the big shopping mall in town, to oversee the store's day-to-day operations. This left her free to be creative: The following year Sue was the driving force behind its expansion to an adjacent building.) The other agreement was that Sue would make peace with Mary Akers, which she did dutifully if unenthusiastically the following Sunday at a family dinner.

Several weeks afterward, when we received the Akerses' final Marital Quality Questionnaires, I was surprised at the large improvement in their scores. On three of the four indexes we use to rate marital quality, there was a positive change in the 20 percent range, and on the fourth, Communication, a positive change in the 30 percent range. Ron and Sue had emerged as one of our Improver couples.

11

Be Careful What You Wish For

Lem had never seen a check as big before: $25,000. The thought of it almost made him giddy. That was more than he earned in a whole year. He took the check out of the envelope and looked at it again. How strange to see such a large sum of money written on a piece of paper with a rainbow on its face. "Twenty-five thousand dollars," he said out loud. It even sounded like a serious amount of money.

"I can't believe it either." Tina giggled. She was standing by the stove holding Will, the Carlsons' two-month-old.

"Twenty-five thousand dollars," Lem said again. "You know what we could buy with twenty-five thousand dollars? Fifty thousand Hershey bars, five hundred pairs of shoes, two hundred suits, and five trips around the world. You know what else?"

"A partridge in a pear tree." Tina was enjoying their little exchange as much as Lem.

He shook his head. "A down payment on a white raised ranch."

In the months following this conversation Lem would add one other item to the list of things his father-in-law's $25,000 could buy: his and Tina's privacy, their right to lead a life of their own. From the beginning Lem had feared that this would be the price he would pay for his father-in-law's financial help. He and Tina would get to buy the house they wanted but the quid pro quo would be more of Frank and Helen Marshall in their lives than Lem thought wise or healthy. That's why he had said no so quickly when Tina first suggested going to her parents for down-payment money on a house and why he had gotten so angry when she went behind his back and asked them for it anyway.

"You had no right to do that, no right at all," Lem shouted at her the evening she told him what she had done.

"But we need a house. And Dad wants to help. He really does."

"Never mind Dad. What about me?" Lem said, jabbing his chest with his forefinger. "I'm your husband. Doesn't what I think matter?"

But Tina knew Lem wanted a house as badly as she did. And over the next few months she played on this desire with a virtuoso's skill. At every opportunity she conjured up a picture of the wonderful life the Carlsons would lead in their new home. There would be no more efficiency kitchen, no more collapsible dining-room chairs, no more making love four feet from Will's crib, and no more neighbors playing Queen at four o'clock in the morning. There would also be no more of the Marshalls than there already was. Tina promised they would continue to be limited to one weekend visit every eight weeks and two phone calls every seven days.

By the time his father-in-law's check arrived, Lem had been won over. After a three-month search he and Tina had found the perfect house: a small three-bedroom raised ranch with a playroom in the basement. Now the couple could buy it and begin leading the wonderful life Tina had been conjuring up for Lem. Contemplating this happy prospect, Lem even found himself thinking more kindly toward his father-in-law. Maybe Tina was right, he told himself. Maybe all of Frank Marshall's unsolicited advice, unasked-for help, and humiliating criticism were really just the excesses of a big-hearted man who wanted to see his daughter and son-in-law start off life on the right foot.

"Boy, was that a big mistake," Lem said when I spoke with him at the follow-up.

"Did you say something?" Tina's head suddenly appeared in the kitchen doorway.

Lem shook his head. "No, Jay and I were just talking."

"Uh-huh." Tina did not sound very convinced. "The coffee will be ready in a minute." Lem waited until she disappeared back into the kitchen, then resumed the story of his big mistake. This time he spoke in a voice so low, I had to change seats to be close enough to hear him.

Toward the end of their first year in the Project the Carlsons' marital data had begun to indicate serious in-law difficulties. But the follow-up interview was the first time I heard about those difficulties in detail and the first time I learned what a central role Frank Marshall's $25,000 played in generating them. Even in his most euphoric moods Lem knew some strings would be attached to this money. He and Tina probably would have to see more of her parents and probably also tolerate more of their unsolicited advice. But he said the size, number, and strength of the strings his father-in-law ended up attaching to the gift had truly stunned him.

Feeling very upset and confused about them one evening about three months after the Carlsons moved into their new house, Lem sat down and made a list of all the things Frank Marshall seemed to think he had bought for his $25,000. The first item on the list was Lem's family loyalty. He and Tina used to see almost as much of his family as they did of hers. But now that was changing rapidly. They had only been down to Hershey once in the past five months, but whenever a Marshall had something to celebrate, his in-laws expected him to be in attendance no matter how distantly related that Marshall was to them. He and Tina had been to the wedding of her second cousin in Pittsburgh, the seventy-fifth birthday of her great-aunt in Baltimore, and the sweet-sixteen party of her first cousin in Reading.

The second item on the list had been unlimited visiting rights. Over the past ten weeks the Marshalls had spent three weekends with him and Tina. What was even more galling to Lem, his in-laws never asked if their visits were convenient or if the Carlsons had made other plans. They just came and camped out.

Tina was the third item on the list. Whenever Lem complained about the frequency of her parents' visits, she would tell him he was right to be upset. "They have to start giving us some breathing room," she'd say. But the truth was she seemed to enjoy their stays as much as they did and was just as sorry as they were to see them end. Not once in the year and a half Lem had spent visiting Gettysburg every weekend had Tina cried when they said good-bye. But every time her parents said good-bye, she acted as if it were their last. There would be a fervent hug in the living room before everyone went out to the car, a second hug in the driveway, then a stream of tears as the Marshalls' black Oldsmobile disappeared behind the tree line at the end of the Carlsons' street.

Lem's experience with his in-laws is a good example of violated expectation. A situation he thought would turn out one way (the Marshalls would be difficult) turned out another way (the Marshalls were impossible). Few events in life elicit so many expectations as the birth of a first child. And because nothing, including warnings from the new-parent grapevine, totally prepares a couple for life with baby, a significant number of these expectations end up being violated, such as Lem's. The child turns out to be more demanding than expected, or one spouse helps less than the other anticipated, or the marriage does not improve as much as the couple thought it would. Or alternatively —because these expectations can also be violated positively—the child turns out to be easier than anticipated, or one spouse ends up helping more than the other thought he would.

How do expectations in general and violated expectations in particular influence an individual's feeling toward parenthood, the baby, and the marriage?

As I mentioned earlier, my own interest in these questions grew out of an encounter I had with a divorced friend a few years before the Project began. He and his wife had separated midway through the transition, and according to him his wife's "monumental insensitivity" (his words) had been at the root of his marriage's undoing. However, listening to him describe that undoing, I found myself thinking that the real reason for his unhappiness was not his wife but one of his own very romantic expectations about the transition. Like many men and women, he had approached parenthood thinking the baby would make his marriage better, richer, happier; but unlike many men and women, he had also expected these changes to occur instantly, painlessly, effortlessly. And because that expectation was impossible to realize, he had set himself up for disillusionment and disappointment.

As I reflected on my friend's experience, it occurred to me that if his response was typical, then expectations, like Emotionality, might turn out to be a subtle but very important factor in the transition experience and for much the same reason. Like Emotionality, expectations might subtly influence how a new parent perceives common transition challenges such as exhaustion, intrusive in-laws, or an unsatisfying sex life. I thought it likely, for example, that individuals who expected these and similar problems would not be disoriented when they encountered them, whereas those who did not expect them—either at all or every so often—would be disoriented. In time their confusion and upset would bleed over into their marriage, as it seemed to have done in my friend's case.

The pre-Project interviews I conducted with transition veterans a few years later strengthened my conviction that expectations were an important if as yet unappreciated transition factor. Most of the couples we spoke with had encountered their share of common transition bumps. Yet I found that the reaction to these bumps varied enormously. While some men and women seemed to have sailed over them effortlessly, others had become all but undone by them. Could the *X* factor in these different reactions be the nature of the individual's expectations, I wondered? That is, did expecting intrusive in-laws and three A.M. feedings make dealing with these problems easier, and not expecting them make dealing with them harder, more stressful?

The general research on expectations that I consulted suggested that the answer to both questions was a resounding yes. This work showed that how we perceive an experience is determined not just by its nature—how easy or difficult it is—but also by the expectations we bring to it. Simply put, if a bad experience is the emotional equivalent of being hit over the head by a lead pipe, then a bad experience that also violates our expectations is the emotional equivalent of being hit over the head by a lead pipe with spikes on it. The research also explained why violated expectations make a difficult situation feel even worse than it is. To a great extent, how hard or easy an event feels is determined by how many emotional and intellectual resources we mobilize to meet it. And how many resources we mobilize is, in turn, determined by our expectations. Sometimes consciously but usually unconsciously, as we approach a given event or experience we gear ourselves up psychologically. If our expectations turn out to be on target, usually we have enough resources on hand to cope with the experience—even if it is a difficult one—without losing hope or heart. If we overestimate the event's severity, we may have so many resources on hand that it ends up feeling a little easier than it actually is. Conversely, if we underestimate the situation's severity, the resulting lack of resources will often make even relatively trivial upsets and setbacks feel very painful.

As I read over the research on expectations, it occurred to me that it helped explain several transition paradoxes that had long puzzled researchers. Among them was why even individuals who have a relatively smooth passage to parenthood (such as my divorced friend) sometimes experience major declines in marital satisfaction. Expecting almost no problems, they mobilize almost no psychological resources to meet them, and the large stresses that even minor problems then create end up spilling over onto the marriage. Why do new parents respond so differently to similar transition experiences such as a cranky baby or an abdomen covered with stretch marks? They mobilize different levels of resources to cope with these problems. And why do couples who approach the transition full of doubts and ambivalences often do better than they or anyone else expected? Unconsciously these pessimists mobilize so many resources that often they can handle just about anything the transition throws at them.

What expectations are most important to new parents?

After we decided to make Expectations one of our transition domains, this was the next question we faced. Initially we thought two types of expectations would be important: How do prospective mothers and fathers think the baby will change the marriage and how do they think the housework and baby chores will be divided? But a little epiphany I had one day just before the Project began made me think that perhaps we were not casting our net wide enough. For reasons I am still not able to explain, driving home from work, I found myself thinking about my own, then very recent, transition experiences and how they had been lightened by my father's unexpected sensitivity and understanding.

I suppose subconsciously I had expected him to react to my passage to parenthood the same way he had to my choice of career—with a great deal of material support but not a lot of understanding. My dad's mind had been shaped by Depression-era limits and post-war opportunities, and to such a mind it was incomprehensible that a talented son would deliberately choose a low-paying profession such as academics. If I wanted a profession, he said, why not become a lawyer? And if I wanted to control my own destiny, why not follow in his footsteps and become an entrepreneur, go into business? Even when I was finishing my studies at Cornell, he was still struggling with these questions. Just before I was to receive my Ph.D., and while waiting to assume my position as assistant professor at Penn State, he called to say that a group of friends were thinking of opening a restaurant in Key West. Would his son the professor-to-be like to run it?

I'm still not sure why he responded to my becoming a father with such unexpected sympathy and understanding. Maybe having three sons of his own, he could empathize with this area of my life in a way that he could not with my career choice. Or maybe now that I had a family of my own, he was finally ready to believe that I was adult enough to make my own decisions. Whatever the case, after my son Daniel's birth this rough-and-tumble restaurateur with the gravelly voice and the gruff New York manner suddenly metamorphosed into the soul of sensitivity. He displayed an understanding, a tact, a wisdom I had not seen before—qualities I had not, in truth, dreamed were there before. These qualities not only brought us closer together, they made all the new bills, all the new work, and all my long nights walking the floor with Daniel that much easier to bear.

Certain that my experience with my father was not unique, the morning after my epiphany I suggested to my staff at the Project that maybe we also ought to examine our subjects' expectations about parental and in-law support. One of my graduate students said that if we were going to do that, maybe we also ought to look at how the subjects expected the baby to change the way they felt about themselves. By the time the morning was over, we had concluded that if we hoped to get a comprehensive picture of the Expectations variable, we would need to study six, not two, types of new-parent expectations. They were expectations about the following:

• *Overall Marriage.* Would the baby improve or undermine it? In order to tap into expectations in this area, we asked such questions as: During the transition, do you expect your spouse to become more or less sensitive to your feelings? more or less likely to offer expressions of love? to make sexual advances? to buy you gifts and presents?

• *Marital Conflict.* Expectations about this issue were explored via such questions as: Do you expect the baby to increase or decrease the amount of harmony in your marriage? Do you think you and your spouse will spend more or less time arguing about money, how often to go out, and who does the chores?

• *Personal Opinion.* How did the individual think the baby would change his or her feelings about self? This area was explored via such questions as: Do you think parenthood will make you feel more self-confident, competent, fulfilled, and happy?

• *Extended Family.* The questions we asked participants about this topic were pretty straightforward. Did they expect to get more or less material and emotional support from parents, in-laws, siblings, aunts, and uncles? Did they think these figures would be intrusive, or would they respect their desire for a degree of privacy?

• *Relations with Friends and Neighbors.* A great many couples approach the transition thinking the baby will become a magnet for new friends. In order to explore our participants' expectations on this point, we asked such questions as: Do you expect to make more new friends? to see more or less of your old friends?

• *Shared Caregiving.* How did our participants expect to divide all the new labor the baby created? To tap into the expectations in this area, we asked such questions as: Who do you think will get up with the child at night? be primarily responsible for his bathing and feeding? oversee his day-care arrangements? schedule his visits to the pediatrician?

At the start of the Project we formed two major hypotheses about the expectations in these categories. The first involved personal perceptions of the transition. We hypothesized that the more realistic a new parent was about what lay ahead vis-à-vis the marriage, family, friends, and so forth—that is, the more room he or she left for unexpected disappointments and surprises—the less upsetting an insensitive spouse, an intrusive in-law, or a cranky baby would be to that parent. Conversely the less room a new parent left for such unexpected disappointments, the more likely it was that the common transition bumps would get blown out of proportion and be transformed into major sources of unhappiness.

Our second hypothesis involved the marriage. We conjectured that men and women with overly optimistic expectations would be more vulnerable to declines in marital satisfaction because they would be more prone to three types of marriage-disrupting behavior. One was blame. Not feeling as blissfully happy as expected, the disappointed spouse would be inclined to point an accusing finger at a spouse and say, as my divorced friend had, "It's your fault." It also seemed likely to us that because they would perceive even minor transition problems as very stressful, overly optimistic parents would be more prone to disruptive acting out. They would yell, shout, and generally act in ways that were likely to be alienating or off-putting to a spouse. It seemed equally likely to us that the violation of overly optimistic expectations might create such a profound sense of disappointment that the individual would withdraw from the marriage and refuse to provide any more help to a spouse.

Project data bore out these hypotheses. Unrealistic expectations do indeed transform garden-variety transition problems into bigger sources of disappointment, and the unhappiness and stress these disappointments produce do end up spilling over into the marriage. On average, Project participants with unrealistic expectations exited the transition nearly twice as dissatisfied with their marriage as participants who had dared to dream small.

On the whole, how accurate are new-parent expectations about life with baby?

The answer to this question constituted our second major finding about the Expectations domain. And to a degree this finding violated one of our expectations. Because the larger culture, family, and friends tend to take a Norman Rockwell view of parenthood, we imagined the picture of the transition emanating from these sources would distort our participants' expectations. But we found that the transition veterans they met at Lamaze classes, at work, and at the obstetrician's office ended up acting as a counterweight.

Overall, our couples' expectations only turned out to be slightly inaccurate. However, a breakdown of our data on a category-by-category basis revealed some variation in this general "overall":

Most Accurate	Expectations about relations with family, friends, and neighbors
Slightly Inaccurate	Expectations about the way baby would change me (Personal Opinion)
Somewhat Inaccurate	Expectations about baby's effect on marriage and incidence of fighting
Most Inaccurate	Expectations about how child care would be shared

It is important to emphasize that inaccurate expectations do not always work against a new parent. Sometimes things turn out better than expected, and because that creates an excess of emotional and physical energy, the transition begins to seem a little easier than it is. Tina Carlson's experience provides a case in point. Lem being Lem, she expected a fairly significant division-of-labor contribution from him. What she did not expect is that he would in effect become a kind of guardian angel—someone who always managed to be there to rescue her in moments of distress. And like all positively violated expectations this one produced a significant dividend. For someone with her negative disposition, Tina had a much smoother passage through the first nine months of the transition than I would have predicted.

However, because things rarely work out quite as well as new parents hope, most violated expectations get violated negatively, not positively. At the start of the Project this fact inspired a question. Is there a set of factors that determine an individual's vulnerability to negatively violated expectations—that is, that determine whether he or she is very, moderately, or only a little upset by unexpected disappointments or setbacks? The answer to this question constituted our third major finding about Expectations. When we analyzed our data at the end of the study, we found that vulnerability is indeed governed by several factors, and the most important of them is gender. New mothers get much more upset than new fathers when the transition does not go as well as hoped. And their disappointment takes a much bigger bite out of their marital satisfaction. On average, negatively violated expectations produced a 10 percent decline in the marital satisfaction of Project husbands but a 25 percent decline in that of Project wives.

What makes new mothers more vulnerable to unexpected disappointments and dashed hopes?

We found that there are two major reasons. The first lies in their greater need for physical support. A wife who does not do as many household or baby chores as expected is an inconvenience to a husband. In order to pick up the slack, he may have to sacrifice some of his free time. But because he has plenty of time as well as lots of energy, his wife's failure to live up to his expectations is not a calamity. However, a husband who does not help as much as a wife expected is a calamity because every broken promise of his requires her to reach that much deeper into her already low reserves of physical energy and somehow pull out one more three A.M. feeding or one more evening of vacuuming and cleaning. The second reason for the woman's greater vulnerability is a greater need for emotional support. Because she is the parent whose body is stretched out of shape, who faces the pain and uncertainty of birth, who usually ends up isolated postpartum, and who worries most about the new child's health and development, a woman approaches the transition needing and expecting much more support from the marriage than her husband does. She expects it to be a source of understanding, encouragement, affirmation, compassion, and companionship. And according to a recent Columbia University study, when a marriage fails to provide the support she had hoped for, a new mother's disappointment and upset are especially sharp.

Like our Project staff, Dr. Debra Kalmuss and her colleagues also found that violated expectations upset new mothers more than fathers. But the Columbia team also looked at which violated expectations upset mothers most. They found that violated expectations about the relationship and the degree of emotional support it provides were most distressing. According to Dr. Kalmuss and her colleagues, in order of descending importance the unexpected disappointments that prove especially unsettling to a woman are those involving:

1. Relationship and emotional support
2. Physical well-being
3. Maternal competence
4. Maternal satisfaction
5. Shared child care
6. Support from family and friends

(Items 2–4: These three items were equivalent to our Personal Opinion category)

Personality, or perhaps more accurately psychological needs, also seems to influence a new parent's vulnerability to negatively violated expectations. Over the course of the Project we did notice that different kinds of violated expectations appear to bother different kinds of people. For example, not altogether surprisingly, violations involving child care were especially upsetting to our mothers who worked and who were, by ideological conviction, Egalitarian. In part their greater vulnerability can be explained in terms of simple need. As working mothers they required more spousal assistance and help than stay-at-home moms. But it also arose from their ideological convictions because broken child-care promises often served to remind these women that, maritally speaking, they continued to ride at the back of the bus.

A thumbnail sketch of individuals who tend to be very upset by violated expectations about the marriage (it does not improve as much as they thought it would) or about conflict (it does not decline as much as they anticipated it would) would show that they enter the transition concerned about the marital relationship, see the baby as a kind of marital cure-all, and, like my divorced friend, expect this medicine to work quickly, effortlessly, and painlessly. Also like my divorced friend, these individuals often end up disillusioned, because while a baby can do many wonderful things, it can't turn an unhappy marriage into a happy one.

Violated expectations about Personal Opinion are upsetting to another group of individuals who see the baby as the answer to a problem. In their case the problem lies not in the marriage but within themselves. They do not feel as fulfilled, competent, or purposeful as they would like, and they imagine that the child will be able to do for them what they cannot do for themselves.

The experiences of a Project mother called Jeannie Cahill provides a case in point. After dropping out of graduate school in the mid-1970s, Jeannie drifted aimlessly. While husband Kevin moved steadily up the academic ladder, first at the University of Minnesota, then at Penn

State, she moved from job to job, career to career. She worked as a public relations official, a computer programmer, a consumer affairs consultant, and an editor at a small publishing house.

When I met the Cahills in the summer of 1984, Jeannie had just made a new career choice. She was going to be a stay-at-home mother to her soon-to-be-born child. At the intake interview she described this choice as the fulfillment of a lifelong dream. But as I listened to her talk that afternoon, I began to think that parenthood was just one more stop in her search for meaning and purpose. I also began to think that her upset would be very sharp if it did not turn out to be as fulfilling as she expected—or, more accurately, hoped—it to be.

During the Project there were a number of times when I dearly wished events would prove me wrong, and meeting Jeannie provided one of those times. But unfortunately events did not prove me wrong. It took her about six months to realize that her new son was not going to be able to fill the hole in her life. After that she became depressed, and as her depression grew, she began to drink. I can only hope that somehow that search for herself took her to Alcoholics Anonymous, as we lost contact with the Cahills after several missed appointments.

I had some firsthand experience with another violated expectation that upsets many new parents. During my last year at Cornell my daily walk to the main campus took me past a small baby park that lay midway between the university and the house I shared with two other graduate students. While it was an unremarkable place in most respects, the park did have—to me—one interesting feature. Next to the sandbox there was a small, cozy arbor of trees where mothers and fathers would gather on warm fall and spring afternoons, coffee cups in hand, to talk and watch the kids. I always felt an odd mixture of envy and anticipation passing the park on such afternoons. To my rootless, lonely graduate-school self, the young men and women gathered under those trees seemed to belong to a big, happy extended family, and some days, oh, how I longed to be a part of it.

Several years later, when the Project began, I learned that the hopes and dreams of friendship that park inspired in me are fairly common. A number of men and women approach the transition with fairly significant social expectations—that is, they expect the child to provide them with access to a new network of friends. I also learned that, like me, many new parents feel rootless or lonely or both. For career or other reasons they moved around a great deal before the baby's birth. Now that they are finally settling in, they hope that the baby will be able to provide them with new acquaintances. Or, alternatively, they see the baby as a way of providing them with couple friends to replace the individual friends they lost when they got married. In time, my own social expectations about parenthood were tempered by the realization that while a child can create opportunities to meet people, in the baby park or elsewhere, the normal rules of friendship still apply. But sometimes, out of loneliness or a sense of disengagement, new mothers and fathers set themselves up for disappointment by continuing to imagine what I half imagined as I stood by the fence of that Ithaca baby park—that just being a new parent will automatically make a friend out of every other new parent you meet.

What about men and women who are especially vulnerable to violated expectations about family and in-laws?

We found that they tend to fall into two groups. The first consists of mothers and fathers who also see the baby as a remedy. However, in their case what he is supposed to remedy is not a marriage or a weak sense of self but a fragile, strained, or unhappy relationship with a parent or in-law. My experience with my dad illustrates that on occasion this expectation can be realized. But because of the intractability of human nature, in all-too-many instances it is not. An overly critical or domineering parent or an intrusive in-law is unlikely to undergo a change of heart at the birth of a grandchild. And because violated expectations tend to make difficult problems feel even more difficult, the new parent who hopes for such a conversion often ends up perceiving the parent or in-law as an even bigger pain than he or she really is.

A thumbnail sketch of parents in the second group would show that they are young (sometimes barely into their twenties), inexperienced, and financially pressed. And therein lies the source of their vulnerability. These very young parents often require the emotional, psychological, and physical assistance of mothers, fathers, and in-laws in a way that older, more mature, and financially secure parents do not.

In addition to gender and psychological need, we found that one other factor also influences how much sting a negatively violated expectation carries: how far outside the realm of ordinary experience it is. The transition holds unpleasant surprises for everyone, but there is a certain group of surprises—a birth defect, a serious illness, the loss of a job, the death of a close relative, an affair—that are so off the charts in terms of both their unexpectedness and their severity that they can end up destabilizing an individual and a marriage.

An example of this phenomenon was the event that produced an unexpected twist in Lem and Tina Carlson's marital fortunes. It took the form of an announcement Frank Marshall made one May afternoon about five months after the Carlsons moved into their new house. By this point Lem did not think anything his father-in-law said or did could surprise him. But this announcement managed to exceed —by a considerable margin—even his wildest imaginings. At the Carlsons' follow-up interview Lem recalled that as soon as he pulled his VW bus into the driveway that afternoon, he began to feel vaguely uneasy. There were not any lights on in the living room, and usually at this hour his in-laws, avid game-show watchers, were in front of the TV set watching *Jeopardy*. Lem also recalled that his unease began to turn into something like alarm when he found Tina and her parents sitting at the Ping-Pong table in the downstairs playroom. Some atavistic impulse told him that the pile of legal documents they were examining held a very unpleasant surprise for him, and he was not disappointed.

The documents were deeds of ownership. Frank Marshall and his wife, Helen, had recently purchased a burial plot at the Cresthaven Cemetery near Lewiston, a small farming community midway between Harrisburg and State College. "Do you know Cresthaven, Lem?" Frank Marshall asked as he showed his son-in-law the deeds.

Lem shook his head.

"It's quite beautiful. It's surrounded by old sycamore trees, and there's a wonderful little lake at the far end. My parents, grandparents, and great-grandparents are all buried there."

Lem began to calculate: There were four Marshalls and four graves, therefore . . .

Frank Marshall got to the end of his thought before his son-in-law. "The plot is a family plot," he said. "But I did make inquiries, and there's an individual gravesite three hundred yards away. I could purchase it for you if you'd like. It has a lovely lake view."

At the follow-up interview Lem burst into laughter as he described the disappointed look on his father-in-law's face when he declined this offer. But at the time nothing about it struck him as funny. Sitting in the playroom that May afternoon, Lem said he felt as if he had been slapped in the face. And the sting hurt tremendously. The presumption, the arrogance! How dare Tina's father intrude into his marriage like that! He and Tina lived as husband and wife, and when the time came, they would be buried as husband and wife. Lem was sure Tina felt the same way. But when he turned to her for support, he got his second unpleasant surprise of the afternoon. She gave no sign of protesting her father's plans. She sat in her chair, silent and dutiful.

Later that evening Tina did try to make amends for her acquiescence. "I'm sorry. I know my father can be a blockhead sometimes," she said as she and Lem were getting ready for bed.

"A big blockhead."

Tina frowned. "C'mon, that won't help. I'll talk to him and Mom. I promise."

"When?"

"Soon."

But Tina made no effort to confront her father that weekend. On Sunday when it was time for the Marshalls to leave, there was again a fervent hug in the living room, a second in the driveway, and another stream of tears as their black Oldsmobile disappeared behind the tree line at the end of the Carlsons' street.

As I noted earlier, one way negatively violated expectations commonly affect a marriage is by producing withdrawal. One partner becomes so upset by an unpleasant surprise that he retreats into himself, leaving the other to fend for herself. And that is more or less what happened in the Carlsons' case. Seven years later Lem still was not sure what had stunned him more that afternoon: the level of his father-in-law's presumption and intrusiveness or Tina's failure to support him and their marriage and family. But after it his attitude toward her changed. If "us" wasn't first with her, it wouldn't be first with him either.

After that decision Tina's family life changed. All the little acts of spousal assistance, all the little grace notes that had so facilitated her adjustment to the transition, gradually stopped. Lem remained close to Will, but now if Tina wanted to go to an aerobics class, she had to find a sitter to cover for her. And now if she wanted to talk—about herself or anything else—she had better pick a time that did not conflict with her husband's favorite TV programs. At the follow-up interview, the subject of Lem's withdrawal was mentioned and discussed.

Lem continued to maintain that he was justified. Given what had happened, he said, his response was mild. "Another man would have told Tina to make up her mind. Who is she married to, me or her parents?" But Tina still felt Lem had behaved insensitively, selfishly. "I was so young; I was only twenty-three and I had so much to cope with. Lem could have been, he should have been, more patient and understanding. He behaved like a vindictive little boy."

For a while we had thought the Carlsons would end up in our Improver group. But the combination of unpleasant surprises that grew out of that scene in the playroom undermined the upward trend in their marital satisfaction. Shortly after Will's first birthday their marital-satisfaction scores began to dip, not seriously enough to place them in our Decliner group but enough to suggest a lost opportunity. The transition would not irreparably damage the Carlsons' marriage. But the baby would not, as we once thought it might, bring them closer together either. Lem and Tina appeared headed toward our middle group of No Changers.

12

At the Finish Line

June 25, 1987. My log that day shows I had a ten A.M. graduate seminar, a noon meeting at the dean's office, and a three P.M. appointment at the Project's videotape laboratory. Next to the last entry is the notation "Three-Year Follow-up Visit," and beneath it the names of Calvin, Jennifer, and Allison Renselear. Looking at the entry now, some particulars of that June afternoon come back to me. I remember it was almost tropically hot and humid. I remember hearing Jennifer's clear, bell-like voice reading *The Cat in the Hat* to Ali as I walked into the lab's reception area. And I remember how surprised I was to see a slight swelling under Jennifer's summer dress when she stood up to greet me.

I also remember one other detail about that steamy June afternoon. Earlier in the week we had begun analyzing a new batch of study data, and on my way over to meet the Renselears I stopped at my office to examine the results. Reading them over as I walked to the video lab, I realized I was looking at confirmation of the Project's two main hypotheses. The data on the computer printout confirmed our belief that six elements in a couple's personality and relationship—what we called our six study domains—had an important influence on determining how successful that couple was in bridging the chasms and divides of the His and Hers transition. The data also bore out our hypothesis that changes in marital quality have an important influence on what kind of parent an individual becomes.

I haven't said much about parenting in this book. But it was a major focus of our study. Indeed, as I noted earlier, the Project was inspired by an observation I made about parenting while studying the father-child relationship. The data on the printout sheets confirmed and extended this observation. It showed that the happier a man or woman feels about a marriage, the more sensitive and nurturing his parenting; the unhappier he is, the more insensitive and intrusive he becomes.

In a sense the purpose of the three-year follow-up visits was to examine how these two hypotheses played themselves out in the arena of an individual marriage. Via questionnaires we explored how the six study domains manifested themselves in a couple's marriage, and, via a series of videotaped parent-child interactions, how the couple's marital satisfaction shaped their parenting. What we are going to do in this chapter is use the medium of the follow-up interview to take a final look at our three Project couples.

Typically the trajectory of a couple's marital satisfaction did not change much between the end of the child's first year (our last direct contact with Project participants) and the end of his third year (the date of the follow-up interview).* And this was true for the Renselears, the Akerses, and the Carlsons. But as we review the results of their interviews, I think it will be apparent why, given the strengths and weaknesses each couple brought to the transition's starting gate,

* Why the long interregnum? We originally hypothesized that most of the changes that affect a marriage and parenting skills occur within the baby's first year, which is why we focused most of our attention on this period. But we realized we would not be able to tell how lasting the changes we observed were unless we let some time elapse and then returned for a final assessment. The child's third birthday was selected as the most appropriate time for that final look because by that point, we reasoned, any changes that were still apparent were now a relatively permanent feature of the marriage.

the Akerses ended up in our Improvers group, the Renselears as Decliners, and the Carlsons in the middle as No Changers.

THE RENSELEARS

Except for a certain subdued quality, Jennifer Renselear hadn't changed much. She was still the long-stemmed, attractive young woman I remembered from our last meeting two years earlier. But Cal, who arrived a few minutes later, looked almost middle-aged now. He had the beginnings of a paunch, and when he bent down to kiss Ali, I noticed a bald spot winking at me from the top of his head.

I was surprised to see both Renselears today. The three-year follow-up visit was an individual assessment. We brought one spouse and child into our lab, then, a month later, the other spouse and child.

When I mentioned my surprise to Jennifer, she said, "We couldn't decide who should go first, so we thought we'd both come and decide here. I hope that isn't an inconvenience?" She seemed a little embarrassed.

"No, not at all," I said, trying to put her at ease. "It's good to see the two of you. How have you been?"

"Except for this," Jennifer replied, patting the slight swelling under her dress, "about the same. We're still at the house on Willow Creek and Cal's still at Crayton Data, aren't you, Cal?"

Cal nodded and gave me a tight-lipped grin. He seemed tense. I wondered if Jennifer had made him come. As soon as the three of us were seated in a small room adjacent to the video studio, I opened the Renselears' Project file and took out the notes I made the previous evening when I reviewed it. There were two pages of them and, taken together, they told a fairly simple story.

Cal and Jennifer had entered the transition with some notable advantages. They were free of the money problems that beset so many new parents. And being a little older, they had the added advantage of maturity and perspective. The Renselears' strengths extended to several of our study domains. Work and division-of-labor differences are a leading source of new-parent tensions. But Cal's and Jennifer's shared Gender Ideology prevented these from becoming big issues in their marriage. And their reasonably positive dispositions (Emotionality) and Expectations meant that neither was especially prone to the pessimism that can sour an individual on a partner, a marriage, and even a baby.

Given these strengths, why did the Renselears' marriage go into such a precipitous decline during the transition?

Actually the chief challenge facing Cal and Jennifer at its start was a fairly common one. Like a great many women Jennifer hoped a baby would finally make Cal step all the way into the marriage. And like a great many men Cal was reluctant to surrender his independence and take that final big step in. How successful a couple is integrating their two individual selves into a larger "us" is mediated by three components of Self: security, autonomy, and affiliation. Secure men usually find it easier to step all the way into a relationship and begin pulling their weight because their self-confidence frees them from dependence on autonomous activities, such as work and sports, that less secure men need to boost their self-esteem. And secure women find it easier to facilitate this stepping in because their self-confidence makes them less prone to the clinging, dependent behavior that can drive a man away.

Reviewing my notes, I saw that at their intake interview I felt the Renselears' insecurities might make the Self domain a problem for them. But what I had not foreseen at the time was that Jennifer's insecurities would make her so needy, and Cal's would make him so emotionally withholding that every time they tried to function as "us," they ended up flying apart instead of coming together. Exhibit A was the way Jennifer's dependency drove Cal away during the hematoma episode, and Exhibit B was the way his emotional withholding drove her away during the abortion episode.

At the start of the Project we imagined that some of our domains might prove more important than others. That is, we imagined some would be essential to the marital happiness of all new parents. But by the time of the Renselears' exit interview, we had discovered that because couples vary, the domains important to their marital satisfaction also vary. Every husband and wife have a few key ones. And if Self was one key domain for the Renselears, a second was Conflict Management.

My notes showed that at the intake interview I also thought this domain might give them trouble. Cal's childhood experiences led me to believe he might fear confrontations, and I suspected that Jennifer would be unwilling to challenge his avoidance. This prediction also proved accurate, which meant that unlike some of our other couples, the Renselears were unable to offset weakness on one key domain with strength on another. Not that fighting would have made Cal's withholding and Jennifer's neediness go away. But at least the frustrations these problems produced would have been ventilated. And frustrations that are ventilated and effectively dealt with are much less likely to push a couple apart than ones that sit and stew as the Renselears' did.

When I looked up from my notes, Jennifer was staring at me.

"What do you want us to do?"

"Oh, I'm sorry," I said. "In a few minutes I'm going to ask one of you to fill out a Marital Quality Questionnaire and then go into our video lab and help Ali with a teaching task. But why don't we chat for a few minutes first? It's been a long time. Tell me what you and Cal have been up to since our last talk."

"That would have been right before the Boston trip, wouldn't it?"

"I think we met about a month later," I said.

Jennifer looked uncomfortable again.

"I'm sure you noticed we weren't very happy then."

I nodded.

"Well," she said, "Ali and I spent some time at my parents', then when we came back to Pennsylvania, Cal and I talked about a separation. But we decided to try therapy first. Cal wasn't crazy about the idea. But I think it helped us. I think we're in much better shape than we were. Don't you?" She looked over at Cal.

"Much better," he agreed.

However, six weeks later, when we had both Renselears' Marital Quality Questionnaires in hand, we found that things really hadn't changed much between them. They were still unhappy and for pretty much the same reason. They still hadn't successfully integrated their individual selves into a larger "us." This result didn't surprise me, since the more Cal and Jennifer talked that tropical June afternoon, the clearer it became to me that the new pregnancy represented their latest attempt to resolve this problem. Somewhere in the back of her mind Jennifer was hoping that this child would do what Ali had not done—finally bring Cal all the way into the marriage. And Cal seemed to be hoping that if he surrendered and gave Jennifer what she wanted this time, she would be so preoccupied caring for two children that she would stop making demands and leave him alone.

I was not optimistic for them. In the short run this new baby might bring a measure of harmony. But in the long run I was pretty sure they would find themselves at odds again, because no matter what Cal gave, Jennifer's insecurities would make her feel it wasn't enough. And no matter how reasonable Jennifer's demands for support, Cal's insecurities would make him feel they were unreasonable. And if that isn't a recipe for chronic marital unhappiness, I don't know what is.

How did the Renselears' marital satisfaction influence their parenting?

After Cal and Jennifer decided that, today, Cal would do the interview, I gave him a copy of our Marital Quality Questionnaire. A few minutes later the two of us were next door in the video lab, where I explained that we were going to videotape him helping Ali complete two increasingly difficult versions of a clown puzzle.

"The easy version is on the table," I said. "It has five of its eight pieces already in place. The harder version is on the shelf next to you. It only has three pieces in place."

"I'm supposed to help Ali put in the missing pieces?" Cal asked.

I told him yes.

"How?"

"However you want. Start when you see that begin to blink," I said, pointing to a red light over a wall mirror at the other side of the studio. It means we've begun taping."

Cal asked if the mirror was one-way.

"I'll be on the other side."

He frowned.

"Don't worry, you'll do fine," I said. "Just relax and be yourself."

While Ali worked on the first version of the puzzle, Cal remained relatively disengaged. She did not seem to need his help, so he let his attention wander, first to a plastic Bobo doll on the other side of the room, then to a model of the space shuttle *Columbia* on the shelf. When he reached over and picked it up, Ali glanced up from the puzzle. She looked unhappy. Children like to display their competence to a parent, and she had noticed that Cal was too preoccupied to admire her skill as a puzzle solver.

Like most of our Project three-year-olds Ali had a much harder time with the second version of the puzzle. And this provoked a very different response from Cal. Now, instead of being disengaged, he became directive and intrusive. An example was his reaction when Ali tried to hammer a puzzle piece into place. "Hey, what are you doing?" he said, taking the piece from her. "Look, it's round. If you have a round piece, you try to find a round place to put it." Cal stopped and examined the board. "Ah, here!" he exclaimed. "Here's a round spot, look." He placed the piece in it. "I got a perfect fit. Now, that's what I call using your bean."

When Ali tried to hammer another puzzle piece into place, Cal's reaction was sharper. "Hey, what did I just tell you? Here, give me that." This time he did not so much take as grab the puzzle piece out of Ali's hand. "You're not using your bean, sweetie. This piece is shaped like a triangle." He ran his finger along its edge to illustrate the point. "You're trying to put it in a square. Here, here's where it goes." Cal put the piece in its proper place. "See, your dad's not as dumb as he looks."

Outside of humor the main parenting traits Cal displayed in these interactions were disengagement and intrusiveness, and both have been associated with developmental difficulties. Disengagement, for example, has been shown to undermine a child's self-confidence because it makes her feel her thoughts do not merit Daddy's interest and attention. Intrusiveness has been found to undermine her sense of mastery because every time Daddy solves a problem for her, it makes her feel like "I can't do it on my own." Why these two parenting traits are common among men in Decliner marriages is linked to a fundamental male-female difference we found during the Project. While a woman will strive to be a good, involved parent no matter what, in many cases a man will not.

I suspect this difference arises, in part, from the very different biological investments a man and a woman typically make in a baby. Because hers is huge, a woman will do everything she can to nurture her offspring. But because his is frequently small, a man's nurturing efforts are usually contingent on his feelings about his wife. If he is happy with her, he will be present often enough to develop the two foundations of good parenting: a close tie to and a great knowledge of his child. But if he is unhappy with his wife, he will spend so much time outside the family that neither of those foundations will develop. Hence, when circumstances throw him together with his child, he will behave a lot like Cal did in these videotaped interactions. He will respond with indifference and disengagement to his youngster's triumphs because lacking a close emotional bond, those triumphs will not have any special resonance for him. And his attempts to help her will be intrusive and heavy-handed because he lacks the intimate knowledge of her that a parent needs to facilitate a child's ability to learn.

The interactive task we assigned Jennifer, a month later, when she returned to our studio with Ali took a different form, but like Cal's it involved helping her daughter master a series of progressively difficult tasks. As I escorted Jennifer to a brightly colored Formica table on the far side of the studio, I explained that on the shelf next to the table she would find a picture of seven red, green, and blue blocks stacked according to a certain color pattern. Next to it were two partially assembled versions of the pattern, one with five blocks already stacked in place, the other with two. "Start with this version," I said, putting the five-block stack on the table. "It's easier."

Jennifer nodded, then leaned over and gave Ali a big hug. "Wait until everyone sees what a smart little girl you are." Ali glowed. Then Jennifer took the picture from the shelf and held it up. Ali studied it for a moment, then placed a red block on top of the stack. Jennifer was ecstatic. "Oh, look, you got it right! What a smart girl. I'm so proud of you, baby." Ali's next choice, also correct, earned an even more fulsome broadside of maternal praise. Jennifer had become a one-woman cheerleading squad.

While Ali worked on the second, harder version of the block task, the stream of maternal praise continued unabated. But during this portion of the interaction there was a new and important development. Putting a block in place, Ali accidentally pushed the stack toward the edge of the table. She was about to push it back, but Jennifer intervened and did it for her. "Whoops," she said, patting Ali on the arm, "you almost had a little accident, but there, Mommy's fixed it."

On the face of it Jennifer's behavior in this interaction appears to be a perfect illustration of a point I made a moment ago. Because of her large biological and psychological investment in a child, a woman will typically strive to be a sensitive parent. But even an impulse as deeply rooted as maternity is not entirely impervious to the influence of marital satisfaction. And in the case of Decliner wives, frequently this influence tends to take the form of the oversupportiveness Jennifer displayed in her interaction with Ali.

Exhibit A was her fulsome, nonstop praise and encouragement. Exhibit B was her rescue of Ali's stack instead of letting Ali rescue it herself. In moderation both of these behaviors are laudable. Encouragement and praise build confidence, and saving a child from her mistakes can facilitate her ability to succeed. But in excess these traits hurt more than they help because they inhibit the child's ability to begin separating from mother. In order to establish an individual identity, a youngster needs to begin standing apart, and this is much easier to do if she is allowed to do what Jennifer, in her desire to be supportive, would not allow Ali to do: make and correct her own mistakes and work alone (that is, without a cheerleading squad constantly shouting "Hurray" in the background).

We believe one reason why unhappily married women like Jennifer lean toward oversupportiveness is that unconsciously they look to the parent-child relationship for the emotional nurturance the husband-wife relationship does not provide. Under the best of circumstances the close biological bond between mother and child makes maintaining a sense of distance difficult for many women; when this bond is also called on to fill emotional needs left unfulfilled by the marriage, often all hopes of maintaining any kind of distance evaporate and a very intense form of maternal preoccupation develops. All of the child's little setbacks and defeats are magnified tenfold because on some level the woman feels those setbacks and defeats are happening to her—and to the smallest, most vulnerable part of her at that. In the videotaped interaction Jennifer was not rescuing Ali so much as herself, because if those blocks had gone tumbling off the table, on some level it would have upset her more than Ali. Unfortunately, in her desire to avoid this upset she did what overly supportive mothers unwittingly often do: She deprived her youngster of an experience (making and correcting a mistake) that would have facilitated her move toward a separate identity of her own.

In addition, there may be another reason why unhappy wives are prone to oversupportiveness. They may be engaging in a form of compensation. Because their husbands tend to alternate between disengagement and intrusiveness with the child, such women may feel they have to provide enough love, support, and understanding for two parents.

For what are, I think, obvious reasons, we maintained a certain clinical detachment toward our subjects. But saying good-bye to Jennifer after her follow-up interview, I found I had a little trouble remaining the cool, detached scientist. Despite all their travails, she and Cal were two good, well-intentioned people, and they had so much going for them. Yet despite their best efforts they had been unable to overcome their differences.

That afternoon it all seemed very sad to me.

THE AKERSES

I also remember a few details about the day of Sue Akers's three-year follow-up visit because it happened to occur on my thirty-fifth birthday, July 7, 1987. I remember that around noon some friends came by to take me to Vesuvio's for lunch and that when I got back to my office at one-thirty, I found a gift from my secretary, a hanging plant, sitting on my desk. I also remember that as the two of us were attaching it to a metal hook in my window, I saw a stroller with a toddler inside suddenly materialize from under the elm tree outside my window. When I saw who was pushing it, I smiled. "Sue and Ian Akers are here," I told my secretary. "We'll have to leave the plant for now."

It had been nearly three years since I looked at the notes I had made at the Akers intake interview. But reviewing them that morning, I saw that, like the Renselears, Ron and Sue had also entered the transition with some notable advantages. Indeed my notes showed that after the intake interview, I scored them positive on five of our six study domains: Expectations, Emotionality, Self, Communication, and Conflict Management. My one concern had been about Gender Ideology. Sue was clearly a Personality-Based Egalitarian, but that night I had not been able to identify Ron's ideology. And my notes showed that I thought Sue's large demands for help and assistance might prove a problem if he did not share her Egalitarianism.

Why were the Akerses, unlike the Renselears, able to take advantage of their strengths?

Ron's and Sue's transition experiences provide a good example of how a couple's key domains often work in conjunction. In addition to Gender Ideology and Communication, the other key domain for them was Self, and what made it a key was Sue's ambitions. When she opened the video store a few months after Ian's birth, Ron felt she was putting her own hopes and dreams ahead of their new family and marriage. And this had a notable effect on his marital satisfaction. Between the intake interview and the three-month postpartum observation his score on all four of the indexes we used to measure marital satisfaction dropped markedly. Thus at the end of the transition's first trimester, the Akerses' marriage was almost as troubled as the Renselears' and for pretty much the same reason: One partner appeared to be putting "me" ahead of "us."

However, what makes subjects Improvers is not that they are immune to transition stresses and difficulties but rather that when they encounter a problem, instead of flying apart, they join hands to face it. And the Akerses' file showed that their ability to come together was facilitated by three factors. One was that, unlike Cal Renselear, Sue possessed the security to regulate her autonomy impulse. While success was important to her, it was not the life-and-death matter it often is to less secure individuals. Hence she found it relatively easy to pull back and begin tailoring her ambitions to her family and marriage. The second factor was the one I had been worried about at the Akerses' intake interview: Ron's Gender Ideology. It turned out that he shared Sue's Egalitarianism, and that not only prevented division of labor from becoming an issue between them, it also had another important benefit. For all his unhappiness about the video store, Ron never viewed it as a threat. As long as Sue was willing to give him a part of herself, he wanted success for her as badly as she did. The third factor that allowed the Akerses to pull together was in many ways the most important. If Project data tell any one big story about marriage and the transition, it is that a couple's reactions to its divisions and polarizations are largely determined by their prebaby relationship. If it has been satisfying and nurturing, if it has produced a meaningful communication system, then, like the Akerses, the husband and wife will fight tooth and nail to overcome their differences, because they do not want to lose something they both consider very valuable. But if their relationship has been unsatisfying, if it has been a superficial form of companionship, then often, like Cal and Jennifer Renselear, they will surrender to their differences and divisions because neither partner feels anything of great value has been lost.

"Jay."

I was standing by the windowsill holding the hanging plant in my hand when my secretary walked into my office.

"Mrs. Akers is due at the video lab now."

Behind her I could see Sue and Ian sitting patiently on a couch in the reception area. Ian, I noticed, was beginning to look a lot like his mother.

"You're taking them over, aren't you?"

"I am indeed," I said.

Ten minutes later Sue and I were sitting in the small room adjacent to the video studio where I had met with the Renselears a week earlier.

"How have you and Ron been?" I asked as we waited for a Project worker to bring us a copy of the Marital Quality Questionnaire.

"Well, the big news is we want to have another child."

"Congratulations."

Sue shifted uneasily in her chair.

"Congratulations are a little premature, Jay. We've been trying since March, and so far nothing's happened."

"Everything's all right, isn't it?" I asked.

Sue stopped shifting and put her hands on her lap. She looked prim and proper. "According to my obstetrician I'm as healthy as a horse. But five months is a long time. Ron thinks what I'm really worried about is having another miscarriage. God, I don't think I could go through that again . . . all those doctors and tests."

When I asked how Ron felt about the delay, Sue brightened.

"What a pair! We're like Jiminy Cricket and Pinocchio. Every time I think I'm about to be swallowed by the whale, he tells me, 'Lift up your heart, everything will turn out all right, you'll see.' I don't want to sound drippy. But honestly, I don't know what I'd do without him."

The Marital Quality Questionnaire, which Sue filled out a few minutes later, and Ron's the following month, indicated that, like most of our Improver couples, the Akerses' marriage continued to grow deeper, richer, more nurturing. This is not to say it was without problems. At his follow-up visit Ron made it clear that he was less than happy with Sue's plan to pursue a new business venture. "What is it with my wife? Every time she gets an itch to have a baby, she gets an itch to open another business."

"Some people thrive on challenge," I said.

"Boy, Sue sure does," Ron replied with a laugh.

I asked him if he was worried about becoming overextended.

"I need another business like I need another hole in the head. But somehow Sue always seems to manage, doesn't she?"

"Yes," I said, "she does."

How did the Akerses' Improver status influence their parenting?

I wasn't surprised that during her interaction with Ian, Sue proved to be a fairly demanding teacher. An example was her response when Ian complained that the second version of the clown puzzle was "too hard." Sue listened to this complaint with sympathy but made it clear that she expected the puzzle to be done. A few minutes later, when Ian announced that he wanted to stop after correctly putting three of the puzzle's five pieces in place, Sue again was sympathetic but insistent. Instead of acquiescing she suggested a compromise. "I'll tell you what, pumpkin," she said, "I'll put the next piece in place if you do the last one."

On the face of it, Sue's behavior in this interaction appears to stand the correlation between high marital satisfaction and good parenting on its head; which is to say, in it she appears not only less sensitive than Ron did when we taped him and Ian a few weeks later but also less than Jennifer Renselear. But in fact Sue's apparent pushiness was fostering a quality that Jennifer's solicitousness subtly undermined: self-reliance. Still, don't all the parenting books warn about the danger of being too pushy and demanding with a child? Yes, and rightly so.

However, in this interaction Sue was not demanding that Ian succeed at a task beyond his developmental competence, which is what an overdemanding parent does. Though difficult, the five-piece clown puzzle is within an intelligent three-year-old's capabilities. And because Sue recognized that and was resolute in encouraging Ian to finish the puzzle by himself, she was teaching him what he could accomplish on his own when he really put his mind to it.

The parent who wants to instill this valuable life lesson in a boy or girl must have a fairly high pain threshold because it involves temporarily stepping back and watching someone you love wriggle in misery and discomfort for a while. Why Sue could maintain this distance during her teaching task while Jennifer could not is in part a reflection of each woman's marital satisfaction. Unlike Jennifer and other unhappily married mothers, who invest all their emotional energy in the child, happily married women such as Sue divide theirs between husband and child. And this division makes it much easier for a woman to distance herself from a child's immediate distress and see what an overidentifying mother often can't see: Though painful to watch, the child's struggles with a problem are a normal and necessary part of his development into an independent, self-reliant individual.

The videotape we made of Ron and Ian a month later provides two good examples of how high marital satisfaction enhances a man's parenting. The first example occurred during the easier version of the block task. Placing a block on top of the stack, Ian accidentally pushed the stack toward the edge of the table. Ron's reaction to this near-calamity was instructive. When Ali Renselear had a similar brush with disaster, Jennifer not only rescued her by pushing the stack back to the middle of the table, she called attention to her help. She in effect told Ali, "Mommy's rescuing you." Ron's help was more subtle. When Ian attempted to put another block on the almost-over-the-edge stack, Ron, almost unnoticeably, put his hand on the stack to steady it, but he said nothing about this gesture. Thus, unlike Ali, Ian finished this task thinking he had succeeded on his own.

A little later Ron facilitated his son's success in another equally subtle way. Like a lot of our toddlers Ian found the five-block version of the matching task hard. He would put a block in place only to discover that it did not match the picture in Ron's hand or, what seemed to frustrate him even more, he would put a block on the stack and it would fall off. The second time this happened, Ian got up, walked over to the shelf, and began examining the model of the space shuttle *Columbia* that had fascinated Cal Renselear. This was an attempt to self-regulate. Ian needed a moment away from the task to dissipate his frustration, and Ron's response showed that he recognized this. Instead of criticizing Ian for leaving the table or calling him right back to the task right away, as a lot of our fathers did in this situation, Ron began discussing the *Columbia* model with Ian. When he sensed that his son was calm, he then quietly summoned him back to the table. On his next try Ian successfully completed the stacking blocks.

Developmental psychologists call what Ron did in both of these instances facilitating the child's success. And it is a building block of two important qualities—mastery and competence—because the more ways a parent knows how to foster independent success, the more such successes a child will have; and the more the child feels he can succeed on his own, the better he will feel about himself. How high marital satisfaction fosters such a sensitive, responsive style is a complex process, but it can be boiled down to a point I made a moment ago. Men appear much less likely than women to distinguish between their feelings about their child and their feelings about the marriage. If a man is dissatisfied with the latter, he will usually stay away from his family, even if it means sacrificing the opportunity to get to know and form a close bond with his youngster. Conversely if a man is happy in his marriage, he will spend so much time with his family that he will become very attached to and knowledgeable about his child. The understanding and caring Ron displayed for Ian in these two interactions were very real, but these qualities all grew from the same soil: his desire to be with Sue and in his family.

THE CARLSONS

My log shows that Tina Carlson's three-year follow-up visit was scheduled to take place on March 25, 1988, but was changed to April 18 at her request. I remember the morning she called to make the change. It was one of those dreary, wet March days when winter feels as if it will never end. I also remember the reason why Tina wanted to reschedule. By some miracle her father had gotten tickets for *Cats*, then the hottest show on Broadway, for the twenty-fifth. "I know I should have a more serious reason," she said half apologetically. "But Lem and I really want to go up to New York. We're getting a little stir-crazy, do you mind?"

I told her I didn't mind at all, and we rescheduled her visit for April 18. I was a bit surprised by the young woman who walked into my office that morning. The slim, slightly coquettish Tina of the intake interview now looked like one of the dozens of mothers I saw at the supermarket on Saturday mornings. With her short hair, crisp shirtwaist dress, and sensible shoes, Tina could have just stepped out of an Ivory Snow ad. Lem, who said he had tagged along for moral support, also looked quite different. He had acquired a mustache, a beard, and, like Cal Renselear, the beginnings of a bald spot. At twenty-eight he was starting to look professorial.

When I asked him how he'd liked *Cats*, he frowned.

"It was lousy."

"Mr. Intellectual," Tina said, rolling her eyes. "It was wonderful."

Lem began to reply but was interrupted by my secretary, who suddenly appeared in the doorway. Could one of the Carlsons go down to our playroom with her? Will had fallen and was crying.

"Is he hurt?" Tina asked, alarmed.

"No, just a little frightened," my secretary said.

"I'll go."

"I'll go too," Lem said, running after Tina.

I used this unexpected interruption to take a final look at my notes. There were some interesting parallels between the Carlsons' Project experiences and the Akerses'. At the intake interview, for example, Lem and Tina also scored positive on five of our six domains: Expectations, Gender Ideology, Communication, Self, and Conflict Management. And as with Ron and Sue, one domain loomed especially large for them. Lem clearly had the kind of positive Emotionality that would allow him to take the transition's stresses in stride. However, at the intake interview Tina struck me as being prone to negativity and pessimism, and I had not been sure how well she would stand up to the transition's stresses, especially if Lem did not put his sunniness at her disposal.

In a surprisingly large number of cases our initial assessment of Project couples proved accurate. That is, the domains we scored positively at the intake interview usually ended up working for a couple, those we scored negatively, against them. But the Carlsons, or more particularly Lem, proved an exception to this fairly general rule. Typically couples like Lem and Tina who have unexpected pregnancies enter the transition with so many doubts and anxieties that almost nothing can turn out worse than they expect. So the night of the intake interview I had scored both Carlsons positive on Expectations. I thought, like Tina, Lem's initial trepidations would protect him against the effects of negatively violated expectations. I still do not think this classification was entirely wrong; which is to say, I'm still pretty sure that if Lem had not encountered an off-the-chart negative violation, his expectations would have proved transition-worthy. But of course in Frank Marshall he came up against the wall in its most implacable form.

There is one other interesting parallel between the Akerses and the Carlsons. In both cases the curve of their marital satisfaction was V-shaped. But in Ron's and Sue's case the V was upright. Between the intake interview and the three-month observation, their marital happiness had declined; then after Sue stepped back into the marriage, it began moving upward again. In the Carlsons' case the V was inverted. Thanks largely to the protective effect of Lem's sunny temperament, at the end of the transition's first trimester he and Tina were actually happier than they had been at its start. But the $25,000 loan from Tina's parents changed this trajectory. Stunned by the strings that were attached to this money—that is, stunned by his father-in-law's increased and insufferable intrusiveness and Tina's willingness to permit it—Lem began to pull away from her, and his withdrawal impacted on the Carlsons' other key domain, Emotionality. Without the benefit of Lem's positive temperament Tina began to fall prey to her own negativity and pessimism. As this happened, suddenly Will, her work, and life in the transition began to seem much harder than they had been. In our files the Carlsons are classified as No Changers, but by Will's first birthday their marital satisfaction was actually a bit lower than it had been at the intake interview.

Looking up from my notes I saw a red-eyed Will standing in the doorway. He was holding the hand of his mother, who was whispering something in her husband's ear. Behind them my secretary was gesturing frantically. It was time to go; the Carlsons were due at the videotape studio.

Our walk to the lab was instructive. When I asked Tina for an update on the Carlsons' lives, she essentially gave me an update on the Carlsons' and the Marshalls' lives. Somewhere in the back of her mind the two seemed to have become inextricably linked. She told me about the cabin in the Poconos the two couples shared and the vacation they had taken in New Mexico the previous summer. She also told me how attached Will was to his grandparents and how much time he spent with them. She told me about her mother's diabetes and her father's heart condition, and how much she and Lem worried about them.

"What about you?" I said, turning to Lem, who was walking a few steps behind us with Will.

"I'm still teaching," he replied, "and I'm halfway through a master's in European History."

"You're taking courses here?"

Lem nodded. "I want to get my doctorate next. Someday I'd like to do what you do."

Lem also said that lately he had become active in a group called the Friends of Nicaragua. "It's a humanitarian aid organization primarily," he explained. "But we do some political things. Last Sunday I was in Washington for a march against the Contras."

"Dad thinks Lem's become a communist," Tina observed dryly.

"Your father thinks everyone to the left of Genghis Khan is a communist," Lem shot back.

By the time we arrived at the video lab, it was apparent that the gulf that had opened up between the Carlsons during the transition remained. Tina still seemed deeply involved with her parents, while Lem appeared to be devoting more of his time and energy to his own ambitions and interests. Like Cal Renselear but in a less extreme form, he was keeping one foot outside the marriage. The results of Tina's and, a month later, Lem's Marital Quality Questionnaires confirmed my suspicions about their relationship. Lem's and Tina's scores had not changed much since our last contact with them. Largely because the Marshalls remained a source of divisiveness, they were still mildly polarized. Like a lot of couples, they had settled into a marriage that was tolerable enough to keep the general peace, but that left each feeling a little lonely, empty, and alienated.

How did the Carlsons' marital satisfaction influence their parenting?

Tina's behavior during the teaching task provides a good example of how mixed feelings about a marriage often produce mixed skills as a parent. An example was a mother-child exchange that occurred midway through the second version of the block task. Will was having trouble deciding what color block to stack next, blue or green. He looked at the picture in Tina's hand, picked up a blue block, checked the picture again, then changed his mind. He put the blue block down, picked up a green one, and put it on top of the stack.

Crash!

A startled Tina asked why he knocked the green block off the stack.

"It's wrong, Mommy."

Tina checked the picture in her hand.

"No it's not, honey. You got it right. Look," she said, pointing to the picture. "The green block was supposed to go next. Poor baby, you're a little frustrated. Come here."

Tina reached over and lifted Will into her arms. "Blocks are hard, aren't they?"

Will nodded silently.

"But Mommy knows you can do this. You do things that are much harder at home. Now, I want you to take a deep breath like this." Tina inhaled and exhaled; Will followed suit.

"Feel better, now?"

Another silent nod.

"Good. Why don't you get down from Mommy's lap and finish."

A moment later a now thoroughly calmed Will was putting the last block in place.

The last part of this mother-child exchange was a tribute to Tina's skills as a comforter. She had taken a very frustrated little boy and in less than a minute calmed him and refocused him on a task. But Tina's comforting would not have been necessary if she had noticed Will's earlier confusion about which block to choose and then intervened (by, say, hinting that his choice of the green block was correct) to ease it before Will got so frustrated that he began knocking blocks about. This ability to spot a child's big difficulties but not the little ones that lead to those big difficulties is often characteristic of parents in marriages like the Carlsons', and it is a reflection of what the relationship does and does not give them.

A key element in a parent's ability to accurately read and respond to a child's need is focus. In an interaction a mother or father must be able to hold in check parental preoccupations and focus attention on the child. How successful a parent is at this kind of setting aside depends on the nature of his or her preoccupations. Big ones tend to absorb so much parental energy that much of what the child says or does can go by unnoticed, while little ones usually leave a mother or father free to notice the subtle little things that happen. Parents like Tina tend to fall somewhere in the middle of this sensitivity spectrum, and their halfway sensitivity is often a reflection of the halfway-satisfying nature of their marriages. While their unhappiness and dissatisfaction often produce preoccupations big enough to interfere with the ability to pick up on the little things the child does, because their marriages are not that bad, they can usually muster enough focus and attention to notice his big needs and difficulties. Hence, like Tina, such parents tend to be more skilled at rescuing than observing. In the end their children usually get the help they need, but they have to undergo a difficulty large enough to catch Mommy's or Daddy's eye before they get it.

A month later, watching Lem help Will with the clown puzzle, I was reminded of Ron Akers. Both men were very understanding and sensitive and each knew his child well enough to know how to work with him when a difficulty arose. In Lem's case a good example of this knowledge was the way he gently nudged Will into the clown puzzle. Almost as soon as father and son sat down, Will began to prattle on about this and that. Often, a three-year-old who launches into a stream-of-consciousness monologue when confronted with a task is stalling—he does not want to do it, because it looks either too hard or too boring. Engaging a child who is in this frame of mind is a formidable task, but Lem knew his son well enough to know what to do.

"Do you remember when we went to the circus?" he asked.

Will looked up and nodded.

"You know, I think the clown in this puzzle sort of looks like Dilly. Remember him? He was the big fat clown with the baseball bat."

Will smiled.

"But you know," Lem continued, "I can't really tell because this clown has some pieces missing from his face. Why don't you put them in and we'll see if he looks like Dilly?"

Will's smile was now in the 1,000-watt range. Suddenly the clown puzzle seemed like a terrific idea.

On the face of it Lem's behavior in this interaction also appears to turn the correlation between marital satisfaction and parenting on its head. And in this case the inversion is not illusory, as it was in Sue Akers's case. Lem's behavior showed him to be a skilled facilitator of his son's success (and hence his son's self-confidence). Yet the results of the Marital Quality Questionnaire also showed his feelings about his marriage to be, at best, mixed. How can that be? At first we were a bit puzzled by this paradox, which we encountered several times during the Project. But as we thought about it, a fairly simple explanation emerged. Just as a phenomenon as complex as marital satisfaction is not determined by any one single domain but by a host of them working in unison, similarly a phenomenon as complex as parenting is also the by-product of a host of factors. And while marital satisfaction is among the most important of them, its effects can sometimes be offset by the effects of another equally important factor. In the language of this book, for example, you could say that Lem's parenting skills were a reflection of his positive Emotionality, which often helps foster good parenting because it leads a parent to expect good things from his child just as it leads him to expect good things from life in general. Or more simply you could say that Lem's sensitivity was a reflection of his love for his son, which was so great that it swept away the obstacles that might hamper other mothers and fathers.

Epilogue

By the time the Project ended in the fall of 1988, we had published numerous articles about our findings. Over the next few years we would publish many more, completing what was, in many ways, a startlingly new portrait of the transition to parenthood. Our work, for example, did away with the myth that marital decline is inevitable among new parents. We found that there are not one but at least three common marital trajectories during the transition: Improvement, Decline, and No Change. We also answered a question that had long puzzled and upset new mothers and fathers: Why do so many marriages feel different after the baby's arrival? It turns out that the "faceless something" that produces this unpleasant sense of differentness has a very concrete source. It arises from a couple's handling of the six transition domains—Self, Gender Ideology, Emotionality, Conflict Management, Communication, and Expectations. Quite simply, husbands and wives who know how to make most of these domains work see their marriage improve, while those who don't see theirs decline.

When John Kelly and I began this book, the greatest challenge facing us was how to make these findings, which were expressed largely in complex statistical analyses reported in scientific journals, relevant and accessible to new mothers and fathers. Our solution to this problem was what led to my final round of interviews with the Akerses, the Carlsons, and the Renselears. John and I decided that the best way to illustrate the Project's discoveries would be via the experiences of a group of study couples. And after an extensive review of Project files we decided that Cal's and Jennifer's, Sue's and Ron's, and Lem's and Tina's stories best exemplified the ways marriages change during the transition and the role the domains play in determining the course of that change.

One unexpected consequence of the interviews we conducted with them in July and August 1991 is that I got an opportunity to answer a question I'd asked myself more than once since the Project's end: How lasting were the effects of the marital changes we'd observed? Our data showed that, for some couples, marital satisfaction continued to change between the end of the first-year postpartum and the end of the third—but what happens after that? Were Improvers still Improvers and Decliners still Decliners a decade later, or by that time had the marital effects of the transition dissipated?

I arrived at the Renselears' with some thoughts about this question already in mind. About a year earlier I'd run into Cal one afternoon at a bank on College Avenue. He'd been appropriately convivial when I asked about Jennifer, but he didn't try to pretend that they'd resolved all their difficulties. "We still have our problems," he said. "But things aren't too bad. Like everyone else, we have our good days and our bad." Evidently I'd scheduled the interview with Cal on one of their bad days. At the beginning, when I spoke with both of them, they sat at opposite ends of the couch and rarely exchanged glances or words. Almost all of their comments and remarks were directed to me.

While it was evident from separate interviews with each of them that neither had much faith in their marriage anymore, the Renselears seemed to have responded to its deterioration in different ways. The once-bubbly Jennifer had become reserved and distant. I had the feeling that this change was at least in part an attempt to maintain self-control. Jennifer had no doubt about who was responsible for undermining her marriage, but if she gave vent to her feelings about that, well, who knows what would happen then? As the interview with her progressed, however, her self-control did begin to slip a bit. At one point she commented on how heavy Cal had gotten and at another she made an invidious comparison between him and an old friend of theirs whose career had progressed more rapidly.

If Jennifer appeared filled with suppressed rage, Cal seemed resigned and fatalistic. He responded to her sly digs the way you might to an annoying but harmless fly, with a swat of the hand. I had the feeling he'd heard it all—and much worse—a dozen times before and was now inured to anything Jennifer might say or do. In his own mind I suspect Cal saw himself as "doing time." I surmised that he would stay in the marriage until he felt Ali and the Renselears' younger child, Jonathan, were old enough to handle a divorce, then leave. In the meantime he'd do what he could to make the best of a bad situation. He would spend as much time as possible at work, lean on his friends and colleagues for companionship, and stay as far away from Jennifer and her sharp tongue as decency would allow. After the interview I felt the same way I had after the Renselears' three-year follow-up. Here were two people who had started with so much and now were so alienated, they could barely look each other in the eye. It seemed very sad.

Ron and Sue Akers had moved since leaving the Project, and due to a miscommunication between Sue and me, it took me the better part of a rainy July evening to find their new home in Lemont. On the phone Sue had said to take Route 45 to the Lemont Road, drive just to the entrance of the Nittany Expressway, and turn right across a small stream. But when I got across the bridge, it was unclear which way to proceed, since three right turn options were available. A woman in one of the houses nearby said she had never heard of Lancaster Avenue, and neither had the attendant at the gas station I pulled into a few minutes later.

"Jay, I said to go past the entrance to the expressway."

I was sure Sue had said to turn right there, but since it was raining and the pay phone I was calling from was outdoors, I decided I wouldn't argue with her. At that moment I wanted to be dry a lot more than I wanted to be right.

"I must have gotten confused," I said. "I guess I wasn't paying attention."

"Oh, come on. All you men have trouble with directions."

I laughed.

"Do you want to know how to get here?" she asked.

"Please."

Twenty-five minutes later I pulled up in front of the Akerses' new home, a handsome gray-and-white neo-Victorian in an expensive section of Lemont. Obviously the Akerses were still prospering. At the door, Sue greeted me with a hug, then ushered me into a spacious, well-lit living room, where I found Ron sitting on the couch with a copy of *Field & Stream* in his lap. If the atmosphere at my follow-up visit at the Renselears' had been bleak to the point of funereal, that at the Akerses' was warm and relaxed. Ron and Sue touched often and laughed easily. Which is to say, they behaved like two people who were still very much in love. No marriage is perfect, however. And over the past three years the Akerses had encountered their share of dissapointments, as I learned in separate interviews with each of them.

At the three-year follow-up they had been trying to have a baby. But when I asked Sue about their new child, she suddenly stiffened. There was no new child, she said. Six months after our last meeting she had been told she couldn't have any more children. She said this in a way that made it clear she had no wish to discuss the diagnosis or the dreams that had died with it. The subject was still too painful for her.

When a sleepy Ian wandered into the living room a moment later, her mood brightened considerably. "Isn't he adorable?" she gushed, "and so smart." Despite this shower of maternal praise, I noticed that Ian gravitated toward his father. After getting a hug and kiss from Sue, he climbed into Ron's lap and fell asleep. Ian's behavior confirmed a suspicion I'd begun to form earlier in the evening. While Ron was getting a lot of Sue, he still wasn't getting as much of her as he wanted, and so, in compensation, like Jennifer Renselear, he had formed an especially close bond with his child. In his case, though, the bonding seemed to be a force for good for the entire family. Ian got more of his father than most children do, Ron felt filled up emotionally, and Sue got more freedom than she otherwise might have to pursue her entrepreneurial ambitions. It wasn't the kind of happy ending you read about in the marriage manuals, but it was a happy ending nonetheless.

I don't know why, maybe because I'd always seen him through Lem's eyes, but I imagined Frank Marshall to be at least ten feet tall. So, at my visit to the Carlson's for the follow-up interviews, I was surprised when Lem identified the small, white-haired, bantam rooster of a man in the photo on the living-room mantel as "Tina's dad." "She took this about a month before the heart attack," Lem said, handing me the photo. Close up, Frank Marshall reminded me a bit of Popeye. He had a bony-wiry body, a protruding jaw, a pugnacious squint, and sticking out of his Bermuda shorts, the most perfect set of bowlegs I'd ever seen.

I asked Lem how Tina was adjusting to her father's death.

"They were very close."

"I know," I said.

Lem smiled. "Of course you do—I complained enough about it. It's been hard, but there's so much to do, she doesn't have much time to think." Just then Tina walked into the kitchen. She'd been upstairs feeding the Carlsons' new baby, Samantha.

"Jay, how are you?"

When I offered my condolences, Tina thanked me, then asked if Lem had told me the big news. I had the feeling, as I'd had with Sue Akers in a similar situation, that Tina still found her father's death too painful to talk about.

"That you have three kids now. Yes. Congratulations."

Here, Tina said pointing toward the kitchen table, "Sit down. Coffee?"

It'd been nearly four years since the Project's end, so I'd forgotten how hard it can be to have a conversation with a young child—or, in the Carlsons' case, two young children (ages seven and four)—in the house. Every time I asked a question, I seemed to be interrupted by a cry. However, by the time I finished up interviews with both Carlsons, it was clear to me that the Carlsons' marriage, like the Akerses' and the Renselears', hadn't changed much since they'd left the Project.

Lem and Tina were still muddling through. Very large, very young families don't leave a couple much time for themselves. So I wasn't surprised that the Carlsons were a little uncomfortable discussing their relationship. Still, after completing both interviews, I had the feeling that their awkwardness was rooted in something more than just a lack of together time. Despite what Lem had said earlier, Tina still seemed deeply affected by her father's death. I noticed when I spoke with both of them together that whenever she talked about him, she used the present tense—as if emotionally she still hadn't come to terms with his passing. And I also noticed that while her references to him were infrequent, each one made Lem jump a little. Even in death Frank Marshall remained a source of contention. To his daughter he was still the gold standard against which all other men were judged, and to his son-in-law, a fearsome and seemingly indomitable rival.

I don't want to paint too bleak a picture of the Carlsons. Indeed, by the time I'd finished my discussions with each, I found myself feeling rather optimistic about their future. There was still a lot of affection and mutual regard in their marriage. Tina spoke with great feeling about Lem's supportiveness in the months after her father's death, and Lem of what a good and skilled mother Tina had become. I thought the next few years would be very chaotic for the Carlsons—how could they not be with three young children to raise? But after that, I felt, Lem and Tina had a chance of settling into a very satisfying marriage.

Bibliography

Acitelli, Linda K. (1992). Husbands' and wives' marital satisfaction. University of Michigan News and Information Services.

Antonuccii, T., and Mikus, K. (1990). The power of parenthood: Personality and attitudinal changes during the transition to parenthood. In G. Michaels and W. Goldberg (eds.), *The transition to parenthood: Current theory and research.* New York: Cambridge University Press.

Bassoff, E. (1984). Relationships of sex-role characteristics and psychological adjustment in new mothers. *Journal of Marriage and the Family,* 44, pp. 449–54.

Belsky, J. (1979). The interrelation of parental and spousal behavior during infancy in traditional nuclear families: An exploratory analysis. *Journal of Marriage and the Family,* 41, pp. 62–68.

———. (1981). Early human experience: A family perspective. *Developmental Psychology,* 17, pp. 3–23.

———. (1985). Exploring individual differences in marital change across the transition to parenthood: The role of violated expectations. *Journal of Marriage and the Family,* 47, pp. 1037–46.

———. (1990). Children and marriage. In F. Fincham and T. Bradbury (eds.), *The psychology of marriage: Basic issues and applications* (Chap. 6, pp. 172–200). New York: Guilford Press.

Belsky, J., and Isabella, R. (1985). Marital and parent-child relationships in family of origin and marital change following the birth of a baby: A retrospective analysis. *Child Development,* 56, pp. 342–49.

———. (1988). Maternal, infant, and social-contextual determinants of infant-mother attachment. In J. Belsky and T. Nezworski (eds.). *Clinical implications of attachment* (pp. 41–94). Hillsdale, N.J: Lawrence Erlbaum Associates.

Belsky, J.; Lang, M.; and Huston, T. (1986). Sex typing and division of labor as determinants of marital change across the transition to parenthood. *Journal of Personality and Social Psychology,* 50, pp. 517–22.

Belsky, J.; Lang, M.; and Rovine, M. (1985). Stability and change in marriage across the transition to parenthood: A second study. *Journal of Marriage and the Family,* 47, pp. 855–66.

Belsky, J.; Lerner, R.; and Spanier, G. (1984). *The child in the family.* Reading, Mass.: Addison-Wesley.

Belsky, J., and Pensky, E. (1988). Developmental history, personality, and family relationships: Toward an emergent family system. In R. Hinde and J. Stevenson-Hinde (eds.), *Relationships within families: Mutual influences* (pp. 193–217). Oxford, Eng.: Oxford University Press.

———. (1988). Marital change across the transition to parenthood. *Marriage and Family Review,* 12, pp. 133–56.

Belsky, J.; Pensky, E.; and Youngblade, L. (1990). Childrearing history, marital quality, and maternal affect: Intergenerational transmission in a low-risk sample. *Development and Psychopathology,* 1, pp. 291–304.

Belsky, J.; Perry-Jenkins, M.; and Crouter, A. (1985). Work-family interface and marital change across the transition to parenthood. *Journal of Family Issues,* 6, pp. 205–220.

Belsky, J., and Rovine, M. (1984). Social network contact, family support, and the transition to parenthood. *Journal of Marriage and the Family,* 46, pp. 455–62.

———. (1990). Patterns of marital change across the transition to parenthood: Pregnancy to three years postpartum. *Journal of Marriage and the Family,* 52, pp. 5–19.

Belsky, J.; Rovine, M.; and Fish, M. (1989). The developing family system. In M. Gunnar and E. Thelen (eds.), *Minnesota Symposia of Child Psychology,* Vol. 22, *Systems and development* (Chap. 4, pp. 119–66). Hillsdale, N.J.: Lawrence Erlbaum Associates.

Belsky, J.; Spanier, G.; and Rovine, M. (1983). Stability and change in marriage across the transition to parenthood. *Journal of Marriage and the Family,* 45, pp. 567–77.

Belsky, J., and Volling, B. (1987). Mothering, fathering, and marital interaction in the family triad: Exploring family systems processes. In P. Berman and F. Pedersen (eds.), *Men's transition to parenthood: Longitudinal studies of early family experience* (pp. 37–63). Hillsdale, N.J.: Lawrence Erlbaum Associates.

Belsky, J.; Ward, M.; and Rovine, M. (1986). Prenatal expectations, postnatal experiences, and the transition to parenthood. In R. Ashmore and D. Brodzinsky (eds.), *Thinking about the family* (pp. 139–45). Hillsdale, N.J.: Lawrence Erlbaum Associates.

Belsky, J.; et al. (1991). Patterns of marital change and parent-child interaction. *Journal of Marriage and the Family,* 53, pp. 487–98.

Berman, P., and Pedersen, F. (1987). Research on men's transitions to parenthood: An integrative discussion. In P. Berman and F. Pedersen (eds.), *Men's transition to parenthood.* Hillsdale, N.J.: Lawrence Erlbaum Associates.

Berman, P., and Pedersen, F. (eds.). (1987). *Men's transition to parent-*

hood: Longitudinal studies of early family experience. Hillsdale, N.J.: Lawrence Erlbaum Associates.

Bernard, J. (1972). *The future of marriage.* New York: World.

Campbell, S.; et al. (1992). Course and correlates of postpartum depression during the transition to parenthood. *Development and Psychopathology,* 4, pp. 29–47.

Cohen, S. E. (1982) Maternal employment and mother-child. In J. Belsky, ed., *In the beginning,* (pp. 233–45). New York: Columbia University Press.

Cowan, C., and Cowan, P. (1985). Transitions to parenthood: His, hers, and theirs. *Journal of Family Issues,* 6, pp. 451–82.

———. (1988). Who does what when partners become parents. *Marriage and Family Review,* 12, pp. 105–131.

———. (1992). *When partners become parents.* New York: Basic Books.

Cox, M. (1985). Progress and continued challenges in understanding the transition to parenthood. *Journal of Family Issues,* 6, pp. 395–408.

Cox, M., et al. (1985). Intergenerational influences on the parent-infant relationship in the transition to parenthood. *Journal of Family Issues,* 6, pp. 543–64.

Cronenwett, L. (1985). Parental network structure and perceived support after birth of first child. *Nursing Research,* 34, pp. 347–52.

Cutrona, C. (1984). Social support and stress in the transition to parenthood. *Journal of Abnormal Psychology,* 93, pp. 378–90.

DeVries, R. (1988). Normal parents: Institutions and the transition to parenthood. *Marriage and Family Review,* 12, pp. 287–312.

Duncan, S., and Markman, H. (1990). Intervention programs for the transition to parenthood. In G. Michaels and W. Goldberg (eds.), *Transition to parenthood: Current theory and research.* New York: Cambridge University Press.

Elliott, S.; Watson, J.; and Brough, D. (1985). Transition to parenthood by British couples. *Journal of Reproductive and Infant Psychology,* 3, pp. 28–39.

Elliott, S., et al. (1983). Mood changes during pregnancy and after the birth of a child. *British Journal of Clinical Psychology,* 22, pp. 295–308.

Entwisle, D. (1984). Becoming a parent. In L. L'Abate (ed.), *Handbook of family psychology.* Homewood, Ill.: Dow-Jones-Irwin.

Entwisle, D., and Doering, S. (1981). *The first birth.* Baltimore: The Johns Hopkins University Press.

Fedele, N., et al. (1988). Psychological issues in adjustment to first parenthood. In G. Michaels and W. Goldberg (eds.), *Transition to parenthood: Current theory and research.* New York: Cambridge University Press.

Feldman, S., and Aschenbrenner, B. (1983). Impact of parenthood on various aspects of masculinity and femininity. *Developmental Psychology,* 19, pp. 278–89.

Feldman, S., and Nash, S. (1984). The transition from expectancy to parenthood. *Sex Roles,* 11, pp. 61–78.

Fischer, L. (1988). The influence of kin on the transition to parenthood. *Marriage and Family Review,* 12, pp. 201–220.

Fish, M.; Belsky, J.; and Youngblade, L. (1991). Developmental antecedents and measurement of intergenerational boundary violation in a nonclinic sample. *Journal of Family Psychology,* 4, pp. 278–97.

Glass, J. (1983). Pre-birth attitudes and adjustment to parenthood: When preparing for the worst helps. *Family Relations,* 32, pp. 377–86.

Glenn, N., and McLanahan, S. (1982). Children and marital happiness: A further specification of the relationship. *Journal of Marriage and the Family,* 65, pp. 63–71.

Goldberg, W., and Michaels, G. (1988). The transition to parenthood: Synthesis and future directions. In G. Michaels and W. Goldberg (eds.), *Transition to parenthood: Current theory and research.* New York: Cambridge University Press.

Goldberg, W.; Michaels, G.; and Lamb, M. (1985). Husbands' and wives' adjustment to pregnancy and parenthood. *Journal of Family Issues,* 6, pp. 483–503.

Gottlieb, B., and Pancer, S. (1988). Social networks and the transition to parenthood. In G. Michaels and W. Goldberg (eds.), *Transition to parenthood: Current theory and research.* New York: Cambridge University Press.

Gottman, J., and Krokoff, L. (1989). Marital interaction and satisfaction: A longitudinal view. *Journal of Consulting and Clinical Psychology,* 57, pp. 47–52.

Grossman, F. (1987). Separate and together: Men's autonomy and affiliation in the transition to parenthood. In P. Berman and F. Pedersen (eds.), *Men's transition to parenthood.* Hillsdale, N.J.: Lawrence Erlbaum Associates.

———. (1988). Strain in the transition to parenthood. *Marriage and Family Review,* 12, pp. 85–104.

Grossman, F.; Eichler, L.; and Winickoff, S. (1980). Pregnancy, birth, and parenthood. San Francisco: Jossey-Bass.

Hackel, L., and Ruble, D. (1992). *Changes in the marital relationships after the first baby is born: Predicting the impact of expectancy disconfirmation.* Unpublished manuscript. New York University.

Harriman, L. (1983). Personal and marital changes accompanying parenthood. *Family Relations,* 32, pp. 387–94.

Hawkins, A., and Belsky, J. (1989). The role of father involvement in personality change in men across the transition to parenthood. *Family Relations,* 38, pp. 378–84.

Isabella, R., and Belsky, J. (1985). Marital change during the transition to parenthood and security of infant-parent attachment. *Journal of Family Issues,* 6, pp. 505–22.

Johnson, D.; Amoloza, T.; and Booth, A. (1992). Stability and developmental change in marital quality. *Journal of Marriage and the Family,* 54, pp. 582–94.

Kalmuss, D.; Davidson, A.; and Cushman, L. (1992). Parenting expectations, experiences, and adjustment to parenthood: A test of the violated expectations framework. *Journal of Marriage and the Family,* 54, pp. 516–26.

Kirckpatrick, S. (1978). Adjustment to parenthood: A structural model. *Genetic Psychology Monographs,* 98, pp. 51–82.

Lane, A.; Wilcoxon, A.; and Cecil, J. (1988). Family-of-origin experiences and the transition to parenthood. *Family Therapy,* 15, pp. 23–29.

LaRossa, R. (1986). *Becoming a parent.* Beverly Hills, Calif.: Sage.

LaRossa, R., and LaRossa, M. (1981). *Transition to parenthood: How infants change families.* Beverly Hills, Calif.: Sage.

Leifer, M. (1977). Psychological changes accompanying pregnancy and motherhood. *Genetic Psychology Monographs,* 95, pp. 55–96.

MacDermid, S.; Huston, T.; and McHale, S. (1990). Changes in marriage associated with the transition to parenthood: Individual differences as a function of sex-role attitudes and changes in the division of household labor. *Journal of Marriage and the Family,* 52, pp. 475–86.

Markman, H. (1984). The longitudinal study of couples' interactions: Implications for understanding and predicting the development of marital distress. In K. Hahlweg and N. Jacobson (eds.), *Marital Interaction.* New York: Guilford Press.

McKim, M. (1987). Transition to what? New parents' problems in the first year. *Family Relations,* 36, pp. 22–25.

McLaughlin, S., and Micklin, M. (1983). The timing of the first birth and changes in personal efficacy. *Journal of Marriage and the Family,* 43, pp. 47–55.

Michaels, G., and Goldberg, W. (eds.). (1990). The transition to parenthood: Current theory and research. New York: Cambridge University Press.

Miller, B., and Sollie, D. (1980). Normal stresses during the transition to parenthood. *Family Relations,* 29, pp. 459–65.

Miller, W., and Newman, L. (ed.). (1978). *The first child and family formation.* Chapel Hill, N.C.: Carolina Population Center.

Moran, G., et al. (1992). *The division of household duties and its relation to marital adjustment and parental stress.* Paper presented at the Eighth International Conference on Infant Studies, Miami, Fla.

Moss, P., et al. (1986). Marital relations during the transition to parenthood. *Journal of Reproductive and Infant Psychology,* 4, pp. 57–67.

Myers-Walls, J. (1984). Balancing multiple role responsibilities during the transition to parenthood. *Family Relations,* 33, pp. 267–71.

Newman, P., and Newman, B. (1988). Parenthood and adult development. *Marriage and Family Review,* 12, pp. 313–38.

Osofsky, J., and Osofsky, H. (1982). Psychological and developmental perspectives on expectant and new parenthood. In R. Parke, et al. (eds.), *Review of child development research: Perspectives on the family, an interdisciplinary approach.* Chicago: University of Chicago Press.

Palkovitz, R. (1988). Trials and triumphs in the transition to parenthood. *Marriage and Family Review,* 12, pp. 1–6.

Palkovitz, R., and Copes, M. (1988). Changes in attitudes, beliefs, and expectations associated with the transition to parenthood. *Marriage and Family Review,* 12, pp. 183–97.

Parenting Magazine (1990). That's my baby, pp. 87–90.

Pedersen, F., et al. (1990). *Change in positive marital sentiment during the transition to parenthood.* Poster presented at the conference on Human Development, Richmond, Va.

Pistrang, N. (1984). Women's work involvement and experience of new motherhood. *Journal of Marriage and the Family,* 44, pp. 433–47.

Power, T., and Parke, R. (1984). Social network factors and the transition to parenthood. *Sex Roles,* 10, pp. 949–72.

Roosa, M. (1988). The effect of age in the transition to parenthood: Are delayed childbearers a unique group. *Family Relations,* 37, pp. 322–27.

Roosa, M., and Fitzgerald, M. (1986). *Sex role orientation, home/employment orientation, division of labor, and marital adjustment across the transition to parenthood.* Paper presented at the annual meeting of the National Council of Family Relations, Dearborn, Mich.

Ruble, D., et al. (1988). Changes in the marital relationship during the transition to first-time motherhood: Effects of violated expectations concerning division of household labor. *Journal of Personality and Social Psychology,* 55, pp. 78–87.

Russell, C. (1974). Transition to parenthood: Problems and gratifications. *Journal of Marriage and the Family,* pp. 294–302.

Ryder, R. (1973). Longitudinal data relating marriage satisfaction and having a child. *Journal of Marriage and the Family,* pp. 604–606.

Sirignano, S., and Lachman, M. (1985). Personality change during the transition to parenthood. *Developmental Psychology,* 21, pp. 558–67.

Snowden, L., et al. (1988). Marital satisfaction in pregnancy: Stability and change. *Journal of Marriage and the Family,* 50, pp. 325–33.

Steffensmeier, R. (1982). A role model of the transition to parenthood. *Journal of Marriage and the Family,* 43, pp. 319–34.

Stewart, R. (1990). *The second child.* Beverly Hills, Calif.: Sage.

Suitor, J. (1991). Marital quality and satisfaction with the division of household labor across the family life cycle. *Journal of Marriage and the Family,* 53, pp. 221–30.

Ventura, J. (1987). The stresses of parenthood reexamined. *Family Relations,* 36, pp. 26–29.

Volling, B., and Belsky, J. (1991). Multiple determinants of father's involvement during infancy in dual-earner and single-earner families. *Journal of Marriage and the Family,* 53, pp. 461–74.

Waldron, H., and Routh, D. (1981). The effect of the first child on the marital relationship. *Journal of Marriage and the Family,* 37, pp. 785–88.

Wallace, P., and Gotlib, I. (1990). Marital adjustment during the transition to parenthood: Stability and predictors of change. *Journal of Marriage and the Family,* 52, pp. 21–29.

Wandersman, L.; Wandersman, A.; and Kahn, S. (1980). Social support in the transition to parenthood. *Journal of Community Psychology,* 8, pp. 332–42.

White, L., and Booth, A. (1985). The transition to parenthood and marital quality. *Journal of Family Issues,* 6, pp. 435–50.

Worthington, E., and Buston, B. (1986). The marriage relationship during the transition to parenthood. *Journal of Family Issues,* 7, pp. 443–73.

Wright, P.; Henggeler, S.; and Craig, L. (1986). Problems in paradise? A longitudinal examination of the transition to parenthood. *Journal of Applied Developmental Psychology,* 7, pp. 277–91.

Index

A

B

C

F

G

H

I

K

L

M

N

O

P